Searle and Foucault on Truth

This book compares John Searle's and Michel Foucault's radically opposed views on truth in order to demonstrate the need for invigorating cross-fertilization between the analytic and Continental philosophical traditions. By pressing beyond familiar clichés about analytic philosophy and postmodernism, C. G. Prado shows that a surprising convergence of Searle's and Foucault's views on truth emerges. The analytic impression of Foucault is of a radical relativist whose views on truth entail linguistic idealism or denial of the objective world. Searle himself has contributed to this impression through his aggressive critique of postmodern thinkers, especially Derrida. Prado's book lays this misperception to rest. He shows analytic philosophers that Foucault's ideas about truth are defensible and merit serious attention, and he also demonstrates to Continental philosophers that Searle's ideas about truth cannot be ignored. Further, he shows that Foucault not only is as much a realist as John Searle but also is much closer than many imagine to Donald Davidson, a model analytic thinker.

C. G. Prado is Professor Emeritus in the Philosophy Department at Queen's University in Kingston, Ontario. A recipient of grants and fellowships from the Social Sciences and Humanities Research Council, the Canada Council, and Queen's University, he is the author and editor of many articles and books, including *A House Divided: Comparing Analytic and Continental Philosophy* and *Starting with Foucault: An Introduction to Genealogy*.

Searle and Foucault on Truth

C. G. PRADO

Queen's University

CAMBRIDGE
UNIVERSITY PRESS

CAMBRIDGE UNIVERSITY PRESS
Cambridge, New York, Melbourne, Madrid, Cape Town, Singapore, São Paulo

Cambridge University Press
40 West 20th Street, New York, NY 10011-4211, USA

www.cambridge.org
Information on this title: www.cambridge.org/9780521855235

First published 2006

Printed in the United States of America

A catalog record for this publication is available from the British Library.

Library of Congress Cataloging in Publication Data
Prado, C. G.
Searle and Foucault on truth / C. G. Prado.
p.   cm.
Includes bibliographical references and index.
ISBN 0-521-85523-3 – ISBN 0-521-67133-7 (pbk.)
1. Searle, John R.   2. Foucault, Michel.   3. Truth.   I. Title.
B1649.S264P73   2006
121'.092'2–dc22   2005006332

ISBN-13   978-0-521-85523-5 hardback
ISBN-10   0-521-85523-3 hardback

ISBN-13   978-0-521-67133-0 paperback
ISBN-10   0-521-67133-7 paperback

Once more, for Catherine

Contents

Acknowledgments

My thanks to John Searle and Wallace Matson for their e-mail responses to my questions, some of which I quote in this book. I had the privilege of having both for undergraduate and graduate professors, and now I must add their help with this project to the intellectual debt I owe them.

My thanks also to the late Terence Moore, my first contact at Cambridge University Press, and to Beatrice Rehl, who made it all work.

Searle and Foucault on Truth

1

Polar Opposites

Pilate saith unto him, What is truth?
The Bible (*Oxford Dictionary of Quotations*, 1980, #44, 72)

This book is a study in contrast. Its main focus is the contrast between two radically opposed conceptions of truth as held and expounded by two prominent and influential philosophers. Consideration of this substantive contrast also involves consideration of two other contrasts: one of these can be described as ideological and has to do with philosophical canons and traditions; the other can be described as constitutive in that it has to do with what is thought to be the nature of philosophy.

The object of the contrastive exercise is to better understand how contemporary thought about truth can be as divided and sectarian as it is and still be about *truth*, about the same thing. My aim is to show that the two radically opposed conceptions of truth that I consider here, which arguably represent the two extremes of contemporary views, are tied together by the role that *realism* plays in both. My hope is to demonstrate that the indifference and dismissive attitudes so widely held by adherents of each tradition-bound conception of truth toward the other are misconceived and counterproductive. In particular, I will attempt to show that the most central basis for the split between the two camps, the issue of realism, has been seriously misconstrued. This comparative study, then, is intended to contribute to a *rapprochement* between the two camps. In this, I am pursuing efforts begun in *Starting with Foucault: An Introduction to Genealogy* and continued in *A House Divided: Comparing Analytic and Continental Philosophy* (Prado 1995, 2000, 2003a, 2003b).

1

The first difficulty I face is that the scope of the opposition between the contrasted conceptions of truth makes description of the contrast difficult because it seems that the conceptions are of truth in name only, given how much they differ. More particularly, it is difficult to describe the two conceptions while avoiding terminology that introduces the canonical and methodological baggage both carry.

The basic difference between the two conceptions is that in the first conception, the truth of sentences, and I shall speak of sentences rather than of propositions or statements, bears a relation to states of affairs, while in the second conception, truth is detached from states of affairs. This means that consideration of the opposed conceptions of truth immediately embroils us in the issue of realism, as well as raising well-known questions about just how true sentences relate to extralinguistic states of affairs. For want of better, in what follows I will refer to the first conception of truth, which many will immediately think of as the correspondence theory, as the *relational* conception, in order to avoid troublesome connotations. The second conception can best be described as the *discursive-currency* or, more briefly, the *currency* conception, for reasons that soon will emerge.

The baggage problem is immediately illustrated by the fact that, as just noted, as soon as I mention that the first conception relates true sentences to states of affairs, readers inevitably will think of the correspondence theory, with all its attendant difficulties. But the first conception of truth at issue here does not necessarily involve "correspondence," at least not in the most familiar theoretical sense. As we will see below, correspondence can be given an innocuous, though not altogether trouble-free, sense. In any case, the essence of the first conception is that the truth of sentences consists "in a relation to reality, i.e., . . . truth is a relational property involving a characteristic relation (to be specified) to some portion of reality (to be specified)" (Marian 2002). What matters most in drawing the contrast between the relational and discursive-currency or currency conceptions is not some specific theoretical understanding of the relation of true sentences to reality, but that in the first case truth is dependent on extralinguistic states of affairs, while in the second case truth is wholly linguistic.

The description of the first conception of truth as relational is intended to capture not so much *how* sentences relate to reality, but rather how they are *assessed*. As John Searle puts it, sentences "are assessed as true when . . . the way they represent things as being is the way that things really are" (Searle 1995, 219). This need not imply anything about correspondence in the theoretical sense. Crucial to the contrast I am exploring, however, is that whether sentences are true in saying how things are depends on them being "*made* true by how things are in the world" (Searle 1995, 219; my emphasis). Description of a conception of truth as "relational," then, captures not only that truth depends on reality, it also captures that true sentences derive their truth from reality in the sense that how things are somehow determines their truth, regardless of how this determination is "to be specified."

The discursive-currency, or currency, conception is the presently dominant form of relativism that makes truth wholly internal to discourse or language, thus separating truth from extralinguistic reality. The currency view reconceives truth as a property attributed to expressions sanctioned by contextual and historical linguistic-practice criteria. The currency conception is usually termed *constructivism* but, like *correspondence*, this term also has too many counterproductive connotations. One of those connotations is of the greatest importance here because it is part of what defines the contrast I am drawing. Whereas the relational conception is correctly seen as entailing realism, the discursive-currency conception is commonly but problematically seen as entailing irrealism in a way I describe later. *Linguistic idealism* is the term perhaps most often used to describe the metaphysical position assumed to be entailed by the currency conception of truth.

It is central to my project to deny that the currency conception of truth entails linguistic idealism or irrealism of some other sort. I do not deny that the currency conception is compatible with linguistic idealism, but most of what follows has to do with demonstrating that the relational and discursive-currency conceptions of truth, as held by the two philosophers I compare, are both realist in nature and commitment, contrary to commonly held views.

The two philosophers I compare as paradigm exponents of the relational and discursive-currency conceptions are John Searle and Michel Foucault, and they are as opposed in tradition, method, and style as they are on truth. Searle is perhaps the most committed and outspoken contemporary exponent of the conception of truth as accurate depiction of what is the case. Foucault is arguably the most significant and systematic exponent of the conception of truth as a socially constructed attribute of sanctioned discursive elements. For Searle, truth is sentences getting it right in the sense of saying precisely how things stand in extralinguistic reality. For Foucault, truth is wholly discursive and, as discursive, neither succeeds nor fails in depicting what is the case in extralinguistic reality.

As suggested above, what will emerge as the crux of the difference between Searle's relational conception and Foucault's discursive-
currency conception of truth is the role each assigns or fails to assign to
realism. Searle's relational view is grounded on and entailed by the most
robust direct realism, while Foucault's discursive-currency looks to many
as if it entails denial of extralinguistic reality. Establishing that Foucault
is not an irrealist is central to showing that his and Searle's views on truth
both merit serious consideration and are not incommensurable in defining paradigmatic realist and irrealist understandings of truth. Once it is
seen that Foucault is as much a realist as Searle, their accounts of truth can
be better understood in light of each other's strengths and weaknesses.

One complication with my contrastive/comparative project is that I
need to do two things that are at odds with one another. The first is to
offer enough exposition of Searle's and Foucault's positions to support
my claims about their conceptions of truth and their views on realism,
and this involves discussing material needed to situate their views on truth
and realism, but that does not bear directly on truth and realism. The
second thing is to not try the patience of readers familiar with one of
my protagonists and the tradition he represents, but unfamiliar with and
likely uninterested in or dismissive of the other protagonist and the tradition he represents. The tension between these two needs will prompt
some to see my project as hopeless, but the acid test is whether the exposition I do offer supports my conclusions. I therefore ask readers to bear
with me as I say what I need to say about both Searle and Foucault.

I also ask readers to keep in mind that my interest in Searle and Foucault is limited to comparing their views on truth and realism, always
allowing for the need to consider other aspects of their work relevant to
those views. My aim is *rapprochement,* not amalgamation or assimilation.
It is not my intent to discern hidden philosophical agreement on truth
or other matters between Searle and Foucault; even in showing them
both to be realists, I will stress the difference in *how* each is a realist. Nor
is it my intent to explore the contrasts I described as between canons
and traditions, on the one hand, and between views of what constitutes
philosophy on the other. I consider these contrasts only to the point
that doing so is necessary to better situate Searle's and Foucault's views.
Given that self-imposed limit, though I draw fairly heavily on the work of
Donald Davidson and of Richard Rorty, I will not discuss other philosophers in Searle's and Foucault's respective philosophical camps, beyond
drawing one or another helpful parallel and using the odd expedient
quotation.

Three Contrasts

Drawing and considering the contrast between Searle's relational and Foucault's discursive-currency conceptions is complicated by more than the difficulties of characterizing and articulating the relational and currency conceptions of truth. As noted, the contrast cannot be considered without reference to two other intersecting contrasts between canons and traditions, and between conceptions of the nature of philosophy. The first of these, which I will call the *canonical* contrast, is between supposedly incommensurable philosophical traditions, the so-called analytic and Continental traditions. My choice of Searle and Foucault as protagonists is partly determined by the fact that they are not only model exponents of the relational and discursive-currency conceptions of truth, but also model representatives of the analytic and Continental traditions.

The second intersecting contrast, which I will call the *priority* contrast, is one between divergent conceptions of philosophy that run deeper than the canonical-tradition distinction, which is based on textual and methodological differences. The priority contrast is between conception of philosophy as ahistorical and of it as historical. Specifically, the priority contrast is between conception of epistemology as either prior to or as consequent on broadly scientific developments. Here again, my choice of Searle and Foucault is due to their being model representatives of the ahistoricist and historicist positions.

The canonical and priority contrasts intersect because the priority contrast cuts across the canonical one; both analytic and Continental philosophers can be, and are, either ahistoricists or historicists, though it appears that somewhat more ahistoricists fall into the analytic rather than the Continental camp. Searle's views on truth, language, and consciousness put him in the ahistoricist subset of analytic philosophers. This is of importance for my project primarily in that, as a consequence, fewer Continental philosophers, who largely are historicists, read Searle than otherwise might. Foucault, a poststructuralist and postmodern, is firmly in the historicist subset of Continental philosophers, so fewer analytic philosophers, who largely are ahistoricists, read Foucault than otherwise might. Counterproductive, ideologically based neglect of each of my protagonists by philosophers on the other side of the canonical divide is what first prompted this project.

The canonical is the most general and familiar of the three contrasts and is largely a function of academic bias or ignorance; and while it is the one most often discussed, it is currently being eroded by various cooperative initiatives (Prado 2003a). The less familiar but more significant contrast is the priority one between conceptions of philosophy as autonomous and timeless, as application of rationality unaffected by history or science, and of philosophy as shaped by historical and scientific developments, changing values, and varying objectives. On the ahistoricist understanding, philosophy is the "queen of the sciences," broadly understood, and the arbiter of reason. This is the conception that Rorty has spent most of his career attempting to debunk, one that Searle staunchly defends, and one for which Foucault has no time at all. On the historicist understanding, philosophy is, as Rorty puts it, one more voice in the conversation of humankind (Rorty 1979a, 264). Moreover, it is not only politics that makes for strange bedfellows. With respect to the canonical and priority contrasts, our two protagonists are aligned with some likely and some not-so-likely predecessors and contemporaries. Searle is aligned with Gottlob Frege, Rudolf Carnap, and Saul Kripke, as one might expect, but also with Edmund Husserl, and Jürgen Habermas. Foucault is aligned with Friedrich Nietzsche, Martin Heidegger, and Hans-Georg Gadamer, again as one would expect, but also with the later Wittgenstein, and Donald Davidson.

The contrast that most concerns me is the one between radically opposed conceptions of truth as a property of sentences that accurately depict how things are and of truth as a property of sentences that are current in a given discourse. Instantiation of these conceptions in the work of Searle and Foucault is enhanced by how Searle's is perhaps the most aggressively pursued exposition and defense of truth as relational, and by Foucault's being arguably the most cogent instance of postmodern relativization of truth to discourse. Unfortunately, the stimulating opposition between the two is distorted by the attitudes supporting and surrounding the canonical divide, especially as drawn between analytic and postmodern thought. Though the canonical split is not as fundamental as the priority split between philosophy conceived as ahistorical and as historical, it is nonetheless a division that has had tremendous influence. Stanley Cavell claims that the "[a]ntagonism and mutual misrepresentation between so-called analytical and Continental philosophy have helped shape . . . every significant development in Western intellectual life since the 1960s – structuralism, poststructuralism, postmodernism, gender studies, etc." (Critchley 2001, back cover).

The main negative influence the canonical divide has on Searle's and Foucault's views on truth is that antagonism and mutual misrepresentation ensure that most of Searle's and Foucault's respective peers simply do not consider that both are doing philosophy. Searle's peers dismiss Foucault's work as tendentious ideological history, and think his discursive-currency account of truth a modish relativism that is manifestly untenable because it entails irrealism and, likely, irrationalism. Foucault's peers dismiss Searle's work as so many tiresome and unproductive technicalities, and consider his defense of a relational account of truth as tedious rehearsal of a bankrupt representationalist doctrine. A particular exchange in a debate between Searle and Rorty, who often serves as a North American surrogate postmodern, captures this unproductive partisanship. Referring to analytic philosophers' reaction to postmodernism, Searle remarks, "most of this stuff just passes them by. They wonder, why should I waste my time attacking it?" Rorty responds that while it is true that analytic philosophers scorn postmodernism, "analytic philosophy is not taken very seriously anywhere except by analytic philosophers" (Rorty and Searle 1999, 58).

The unhappy result of this mutual disdain is that consideration of the issue of truth fails to incorporate the different insights to be found in the work of philosophers on opposite sides of the canonical and priority divides and, in particular, of Searle and Foucault. This is most unfortunate because Searle's views contain important ideas about what Bernard Williams describes as the commitment to truthfulness, and Foucault's views contain important ideas about what Williams describes as our suspicion regarding truth. Again, Searle's lapses illustrate that the commitment to truthfulness needs a wider and more flexible understanding of truth than is offered by relational views, while Foucault's excesses illustrate that suspicion about truth has been overdone. To proceed, then, we need to focus on the central question.

Pilate's Question

What is truth? Pilate's question was not intended as a genuine question. How it was intended is better reflected in Francis Bacon's rendition of the biblical passage quoted above: "What is truth? said jesting Pilate; and would not stay for an answer" (*Oxford Dictionary of Quotations* 1980, #28, 27). Bacon better captures the mocking nature of Pilate's question, but his rendition still falls short of how the question most likely was intended, and that is as rhetorical in the sense of expressing powerlessness to resolve an intractable impasse over competing accounts or descriptions. As such, the question does not call for an answer, but neither is it as dismissive as usually thought. The point is that Pilate's question was more a recognition of powerlessness than anything else, and this should not surprise us. Until quite recently, it was only in philosophy seminars and writings that Pilate's question called for an answer. But that has changed. Pilate's question recently acquired urgency as a genuine question, and did so well beyond the borders of academic philosophy. Thomas Nagel remarks that the question of truth now "runs through practically every area of inquiry" and has "invaded the general culture" (Nagel 1997, 3).

The source of the new urgency is the historically recent but widespread support of more and less sophisticated versions of relativism in areas running from the humanities and social sciences through politics and the law to the media and individuals' arguments about abortion, terrorism, or a president's morality. What led to the espousal of relativism is that, over the past several decades, relativism took hold in the humanities and social science disciplines. It affected how research was conducted in those disciplines and, more significantly, how their respective subject matters were taught to the people who themselves now dominate not only the humanities and social sciences but also politics and the media (cf. Rorty and Searle 1999).

Relativism's sway outside philosophy has resulted in an odd development within philosophy that has contributed to Pilate's question becoming urgent. Too many philosophers, whose responsibility it is to sort out the issue of truth, have responded to the spread of relativism with dismissive invective rather than engaged analysis and rebuttal. At the heart of this reaction is a misguided construal of relativism as not a serious philosophical position because it is supposedly self-defeating – a judgment facetiously glossed by saying that relativism inconsistently claims it is objectively true that everything is relative.

This dubious response to relativism appears legitimate to its exponents because they erroneously believe that all forms of relativism are what Michael Krausz calls "extreme relativism" or the view that "all claims involving truth . . . are on a par" (Krausz 1989, 1). Construing relativism as holding that "every belief . . . is as good as every other" is a mistake if only because, as Rorty remarks, "[n]o one holds this view . . . [e]xcept for the occasional cooperative freshman" (Rorty 1982, 166). I think Rorty is right; however, that does not change the fact that philosophers' misconstrual of relativism has meant that nonphilosophers, especially students, end up being exposed to relativism on every side, while being offered only facile and unpersuasive treatment of relativism by those most able to explain and critique it.

The dismissive reaction to relativism is prompted by the idea that relativism is not just about truth; it also reconceives the standards for intellectual inquiry as contextual and historical. The importance of this is that, as we will see with Foucault, rationality itself is historicized along with truth, and this is something that many philosophers cannot accept. Hilary Putnam offers a typical repudiation of historization of rationality, saying that chronologically varying historical standards "cannot define what reason is" because they inescapably "presuppose reason . . . for their interpretation" (Putnam 1987, 227). For Putnam and many others, reason is prior to and independent of its applications; rationality is "a regulative idea" that governs all inquiry and is independent of the activities and institutions it governs. Rationality enables us "to criticize the conduct of all activities and institutions" because it is ahistorical, universal, and wholly independent of our practices (Putnam 1987, 228).

Some see Putnam's response as question-begging because it presupposes what is at issue: the ahistorical nature of rationality as regulative. Others see philosophers holding truth and rationality to be ahistorical as simply defending a self-attributed status as adjudicators of reason. For their part, Putnam and like-minded others are simply at a loss to understand how intellectual inquiry could be conducted on the assumption that rational standards and methods are historical and contextual. This impasse is characteristic of the divisions marked by the priority contrast.

The problem with a too-ready dismissal of relativism is that truth simply is not as straightforward as ahistoricist objectivists think. The idea that truth is a depiction of how things are has proven difficult to unpack and generates conundrums about verification and the relation between true sentences and what they describe. There are also problems about just what it is that is true: sentences or propositions. Basically, the trouble is that truth is a property of beliefs and sentences (or propositions), and beliefs and sentences are intentional, and hence are about their intentional objects. But we seem never to have been able to say, clearly and unproblematically, just what sort of relation there is between those intentional objects, considered as true, and the nonintentional states of affairs most are about. The major stumbling block is that extralinguistic reality does not come packaged in convenient "facts" or naturally delineated states of affairs to which we can relate particular beliefs and sentences. We have not been able to establish an acceptable account of how what is deemed "a fact" is a *relatum* to a true belief or sentence. Referring to this inability, Williams notes that "[t]here is no account of facts that at once is general enough for the purpose and does more than trivially reiterate the content of the sentences for which it is supposed to be illuminating the truth conditions" (Williams 2002, 65).

Both objectivists and relativists have valid points to make in their ongoing debate, but while philosophical debate about truth has been going on since at least Plato and Protagoras, and we seem no closer to a satisfactory account of it, things actually have changed. What has changed is that concern with truth is no longer only of philosophical interest. There is now a new and profound ambivalence regarding truth's possibility, and it goes well beyond philosophy. Williams captures this ambivalence in his contention that two opposed ideas are "very prominent in modern thought and culture." The first of these ideas, though ancient, gained special force in the late seventeenth century and is "an intense commitment to truthfulness," what Williams also describes as "a readiness against being fooled, an eagerness to see through appearances to the real structures and motives that lie behind them." The second idea, though its roots are in early Greek skepticism, has only recently acquired significant predominance; it is "an equally pervasive suspicion about truth itself," namely, the nagging question of "whether [truth] can be more than relative or subjective" (Williams 2002, 1).

The first idea, the commitment to truthfulness, is what Nietzsche called "the will to truth." This is an impetus to discover precisely what is the case, but it entails two realist assumptions: an ontological assumption that things must be just one way, and an epistemological assumption that the way things are is accessible and, just as important, statable. Despite this impetus, we are haunted by the realization that discovering and/or saying how things are is always problematic because it is always revisable and so, perhaps, ultimately unachievable. This second idea has many incarnations, all denying the ontological and epistemological assumptions entailed by the will to truth. Some versions of this second idea focus on epistemology, and hold that we lack access to how things are or lack the capacity to accurately determine and say how things are; others focus on ontology, and hold to some degree that things are not objectively any way at all or just are as we believe and say they are.

The root of suspicion about truth's objectivity, accessibility, and statability basically is recognition that awareness is always aspectual, a function of perspective. We are always aware of the world, and ourselves, from some point of view. Physical position, inescapable interpretive elements, values, preconceptions, presuppositions, assumptions, expectations, interests, objectives, fears, and even moods condition our awareness. The moment this point is acknowledged, its corollary becomes relentless: perspectives differ from individual to individual, from group to group, from culture to culture, and for the same individuals or groups or cultures at different times. Truth, then, looks unattainable and relativism inescapable.

To understand the significance of recognition of the aspectual or perspectival nature of awareness, we need to go back to John Locke and Immanuel Kant. Much of our present uncertainty about truth is rooted in Kant's introduction of conceptualization into philosophizing about knowledge, but the decisive enabling event was Locke's introduction of a distinction between "nominal" and "real" truth (Locke 1975, 577; Allen 1993, 34–35).

Locke distinguishes between nominal truth as agreement of words with ideas, and real truth as agreement of ideas with the objective realities they purportedly represent. This is a first step toward recognition of conceptualization's role in determining awareness. It is a step that initiates a distinction between how things appear to us and how things are independently of us and, in so doing, opens a gap between ideas and their objects that does not exist between words and ideas. Kant then introduces full-blown conceptualization, and how things are then becomes how things are *in themselves*. As a consequence, access to how things are becomes problematic, because it is necessarily filtered through conceptualization.

Contrary to his best intentions, his own epistemological objectives, and his account of the role of the categories of the understanding, Kant inadvertently introduced the inescapable possibility of variance in conceptualization of the noumenal world. This means that, even where we do not adopt the Kantian phenomenal/noumenal distinction, or what Donald Davidson calls the "scheme/content" distinction, we nonetheless must face the fact that the aspectual nature of awareness allows that there can be intractable perspectival conflict. The only question is whether such conflict is resolvable or not in principle; that is, the only issue is whether we have to acknowledge incommensurability or conceptual relativism, or can argue that perspectival conflict, though practically intractable, ultimately is resolvable and does not entail conceptual incommensurability.

There is no getting around how Kant permanently changed debate about truth by altering our understanding of perception from one of direct apprehension to one of perception as a complexly interactive process. Once the role of conceptualization is appreciated, the ground of description is forever changed. It ceases to be the world itself and is realized to be a *product* of physical, cognitive, and neurophysiological factors. With this change, the distinction between what we think is the case and what the case is becomes blurred, and we face the inexorable thought that, in the end, it may be *we* who shape everything we think we know, not the world or anything else independent of us. Nagel puts the point succinctly, saying that we realize that "the first person, singular or plural" may well be "hiding at the bottom of everything we say or think" (Nagel 1997, 3).

Even if it is possible that we are at the bottom of everything we say or think, "What is truth?" becomes pressing and complex. The question seems to morph into "Whose truth?" and "Which truth?"

Minimal Perspectivism

Recognition of the inherently aspectual nature of awareness, and so of the perspectival nature of claims and judgments, does not require adoption of relativism. Searle's position illustrates this, as I show later. To refer to acknowledgment of the aspectual nature of awareness, then, without implying anything about relativism, I will use the phrase *minimal perspectivism*. Minimal perspectivism is simply recognition that awareness is aspectual or perspectival, and that our claims, descriptions, and judgments are therefore also aspectual or perspectival. But such recognition does not necessarily lead to abandonment of the possibility of objective knowledge. How this is so can be clarified by considering Alexander Nehamas's explication of Nietzschean perspectivism as denial that "there could ever be a complete ... interpretation of anything, a view that accounts for 'all' the facts" (Nehamas 1985, 64; cf. Nietzsche 1968, 267, and Williams 2002, 10).

Minimal perspectivism also is denial that there could ever be a complete interpretation of anything, in the sense of one that rationalizes all divergent perspectives on the object of interpretation. But whereas Nietzschean perspectivism holds that it is *in principle* impossible to rationalize diverse perspectives, minimal perspectivism holds only that it may prove impossible to do so *in practice*. Knowledge, then, is in principle possible, but its achievement – that is, identification of some beliefs *as* knowledge – may require considerable time and effort, as in the case of establishing a complex scientific hypothesis, and may elude us in the end.

Minimal perspectivism attributes perspectival conflict to enculturation, education, and social and personal history; that is, it attributes that conflict to the vast range of acquired beliefs, values, objectives, and interests that shape our cultural and individual perspectives, and often makes them incompatible. Minimal perspectivism may lead to one or another form of relativism, but it is not itself inherently relativistic in the way that Nietzschean perspectivism is relativistic. Minimal perspectivism does not endorse Nietzsche's radically relativistic – and problematically intelligible – claim that there are "only interpretations" (Nietzsche 1968, 267). My point here is that minimal perspectivism is not "conceptual relativism" and does not entail incommensurability. Essentially, minimal perspectivism is a psychological rather than epistemological or metaphysical position. It attributes perspectival conflict to divergence of individuals' judgments and perceptions, not to incommensurable conceptualizations of noumenal content.

The relevance of minimal perspectivism to what follows has to do both with Searle's treatment of conceptual relativism and with Foucault's discursive-currency view of truth, especially his emphasis on how personal history shapes awareness. Specifically, minimal perspectivism shows that acknowledgment of the aspectual nature of awareness and of perspectival conflict, even practically intractable conflict, does not commit one to any form of relativism entailing irrealism through abandonment of the possibility of objective knowledge or attainment of truth. The key point is that an inability to resolve perspectival conflict by recourse to how things are does not, by itself, impugn that things are as they may be. It is possible to be suspicious of truth's attainability and statability by acknowledging perspectival diversity and still not commit oneself to one or another irrealist ontological or epistemological position.

The importance of this is that, because of their intolerance of relativism and irrealism, some philosophers engage in facile dismissal of real questions about truth's attainability and statability. Though Davidson's argument against the coherency of conceptual relativism and incommensurability is well known, some philosophers take a tendentious shortcut by simply precluding conceptual incommensurability (Davidson 1973/1974). I consider Searle's version of this preclusion later, not to defend incommensurability, but to bring out the inescapability of minimal perspectivism. What needs to be noted here is that the preclusion improperly assumes against proponents of conceptual relativism that there cannot be genuine perspectival incommensurability because perspectival conflict is always resolvable by recourse to independent reality.

The way this too-ready preclusion of conceptual relativism works is by relying on a combination of assumptions. One of these is ontological, and is the main corollary of realism, namely, that given an objective world, things just are one way or another in that world. A second assumption is epistemological, and is that how things are in the determinate objective world is accessible to us. However, to these sound assumptions is added a more problematic third assumption to the effect that, since the world is just one way, and we can know how it is, perspectival conflict can only be apparent. This dubious assumption amounts to accepting that perspectival conflict is due only to confusion about operant measuring systems or some similar sort of error. The preclusion, then, is questionable in a compound way. First, it assumes that where there is perspectival conflict, one or the other party is wrong, and that resolving the conflict is a matter of establishing who is right. The trouble here, as I clarify in the next paragraph, is that perspectival conflict does not always turn on someone being right and someone being wrong. Second, the preclusion further assumes that we always have recourse to how things are in order to determine who is right and who is wrong to resolve perspectival conflicts, but conceptual relativism precisely denies that we have such recourse.

To clarify perspectival conflict of the sort minimal perspectivism acknowledges, consider a common example that illustrates the intractability of practical perspectival conflicts and also shows that such conflicts do not always involve one party being right and another wrong, nor admit of resolution by recourse to "the facts." John Wisdom describes a man and woman in the process of ending their marriage of some years. One party, looking back and focusing on the good times, judges the marriage to have been a happy one; the other, looking back and focusing on the bad times, draws the opposite conclusion. In this case, and others like it, there can be no recourse to matters of fact to resolve the conflict because matters of fact are not at issue. The two parties do not disagree about the individual events that comprised their married life; what they disagree about is how to "weigh the cumulative effect" of those events. The intractable perspectival conflict results from how each party sees "those features . . . which severally co-operate in favour of the conclusion" that each draws (Wisdom 1955, 195). The two individuals are differently construing the import of events that are not at issue other than in how they contribute to a holistic impression. Neither party is right or wrong, nor can there be recourse to anything that would show one's judgment right and the other's wrong.

Recognition of the reality of intractable interpretive judgments like the foregoing makes us realize that considered factors adding up differently for different individuals is not limited to judgments about human relationships but extends to all forms of judgments. Nor can we exempt scientific judgments by appealing to the supposedly cumulative self-correcting nature of scientific methodology. History will not allow that move for a rather ironic reason. Williams again offers a concise statement of the reason, telling us that the desire for truth *itself* "drives a process of criticism which weakens the assurance that there is any secure or unqualifiedly stateable truth." In other words, our drive to discern truth fosters suspicion about truth because of the nature of the very process of inquiry. In testing and assessing judgments, we realize how "[a]ccounts which have been offered as telling the truth . . . often turn out to be biased, ideological, or self-serving" (Williams 2002, 1). As we delve ever more deeply into whatever we are investigating, the nature of the investigative process prompts us to systematically doubt the objectivity of whatever presents itself as the truth at each stage of the process. In effect, in inquiry we continuously apply Cartesian doubt to our judgments because we have been wrong before. But, unlike Descartes, we have no recourse to self-evidency to resolve doubts, so doubt remains ever present and we grow suspicious about truth's attainability.

Williams is right about how we grow suspicious of truth in the very process of trying to find it, but in presenting this source of our suspicion, he misconstrues a kind of institutionalized perspectival diversity that Rorty calls "redescription." Williams sees the diversity as a *consequence* of suspicion about truth, rather than as contributing to that suspicion, and deals with the diversity only indirectly in his critique of Rorty and others he calls "deniers" of truth. Rorty's take on redescription is very different. He contends that "toward the end of the nineteenth century . . . [i]t became possible to juggle several descriptions of the same event without asking which one was right." Rorty's point is that it became possible to see what previously were taken as mutually exclusive descriptions as each being contextually valid. It supposedly became possible to see two or more competing descriptions as "redescriptions," to see each "as a tool rather than a claim to have discovered essence" (Rorty 1989, 39). According to Rorty, then, competing descriptions came to be assessed relative to their roles in particular contexts and hence as not necessarily mutually exclusive. Rorty sees redescription as a positive development, as a maturing of the Cartesian worldview; Williams sees it as a negative development, as a diminishment of the value of truth.

Williams's construal of redescription as a consequence of suspicion about truth, rather than a contributing factor, indicates that he sees redescription as relativistic, and is one reason he considers Rorty a denier of truth. Regrettably, Rorty's standard response to charges of relativism is less than compelling, being only that to attribute relativism is to continue to apply misconceived Cartesian epistemic categories. In short, Rorty does not grant the notion of relativism application outside the traditional epistemology he eschews. This is not the place to consider Rorty's position, but we need to be clearer about relativism before proceeding to consider Searle's rejection of it and Foucault's version of it.

Clarifying the Relativist Challenge

Relativism, according to what I consider the most succinct and viable definition, is the view that "cognitive, moral, or aesthetic claims involving . . . truth . . . are relative to the contexts in which they appear" (Krausz 1989, 1). What is most significant at this point is that relativism, as defined, properly is more a consequence of, than itself the central antiobjectivist thesis about, truth. This is because that central thesis – construal of truth as wholly linguistic and as having to do only with relations among sentences and not between sentences and things and events – is prior to discursive contextualization of truth. In other words, it is the detachment of truth from extralinguistic reality that enables discursive contextualization of truth, and it is precisely the detachment of truth from extralinguistic reality that many philosophers most object to because they see that detachment as being or entailing irrealism.

While it may appear paradoxical to some readers, relativism presupposes that truth, as a property of sentences, is not a function of a relation between those sentences and their objects in the world, but is instead a function of relations among sentences. This crucial idea, oddly enough, is most clearly articulated not by Foucault or one of his postmodern peers, but by Wilfrid Sellars. In a statement to which I will return, Sellars asserts that attributions of truth have to do with relations among propositions and "do not assert relations between linguistic and extra-linguistic items" (Sellars 1968, 82).

As indicated, it is the taking of truth as wholly linguistic, the detaching of it from states of affairs, that prompts perception of consequent relativist views as entailing irrealism and therefore makes relativism so unpopular in philosophy – an unpopularity in sharp contrast to relativism's ascendancy in other disciplines in the humanities and social sciences. Many philosophers see the internalization of truth to discourse as absurd implicit or explicit denial of extralinguistic reality. Their thinking is that if it is claimed that truth is not about the world, the implication must be either the epistemological one that we have no access to anything beyond language or, worse still, the ontological one that there is nothing beyond language.

The trouble is that, as also indicated, however right it may be, the idea that truth "is a relational property involving a characteristic relation . . . to some portion of reality" has proven difficult to unpack (Marian 2002). Most notably, versions of the correspondence theory of truth invariably bog down when it comes to saying just what the correspondence relation consists of, and how it is that we establish that the putative relation holds. We are unable to independently identify what true sentences correspond *to*, so we cannot give content to the claimed relation between them and their objects.

We seem, then, unable to improve on Aristotle's observation, in *Metaphysics*, that "to say of what is that it is, and of what is not that it is not, is true" (Aristotle 1941, 1011b). Williams agrees with this elemental explication of truth, citing Davidson in doing so. He also goes further, again in agreement with Davidson, and contends that "we should resist any demand for a definition of truth . . . because truth belongs to a ramifying set of connected notions, such as meaning, reference, belief, and so on, and we are better employed in exploring the relations between these notions than in trying to treat one . . . as the basis of the others" (Williams 2002, 63). But these remarks take us a long way from the Cartesian idea that truth is simple and, in so doing, threaten to take us down the slope to the very discursive contextualization of truth that so many want to avoid.

The rightness of Aristotle's formulation seems undeniable. The scholastic formulation of the basic idea also is compelling, explaining truth, as it does, as "adequacy" of the intellect to the things themselves. The precise formulation, attributed to Avicenna, is "veritas est adaequatio intellectus ad rem," where "adequacy" is understood as representative aptness or faithfulness (Allen 1993, 186n1). In both cases, what is central is that truth is an accurate cognitive or verbal depiction or representation of how things stand, and this exactly captures our deepest intuitions about truth. The snag is saying precisely how sentences are true by bearing some relation to what they represent or depict. Nor does it seem sufficient to rest content with "disquotation," saying that to attribute truth to a sentence simply is to assert that sentence; that is, that to say "'p' is true" is to drop the quotes around p and assert that p. The inadequacy is manifest in the Tarskian formula, which, though admittedly making only a semantic point about what it means to attribute truth to a sentence, nonetheless tacitly juxtaposes sentences and states of affairs. The formula "'p' is true if and only if p" does relate "p," on the one hand, and p on the other. This is also true of Aristotle's remark. To say that truth is to say of what is that it is juxtaposes what is said to what is, so it seems we cannot escape the quandary of relating "p" to p but being incapable of identifying p without using "p" or some entailed proposition "p_1" through "p_n."

Persistent difficulties with formulations of truth as a replicatory or depictive relation between sentences and bits or the whole of extralinguistic reality has played a major role in prompting alternatives to the correspondence theory of truth. However, it is a telling comment on the history of philosophical debate about truth that alternatives to correspondence have not fared much better. The coherence theory resolves the relational issue by relating sentences or propositions to other sentences or propositions, but it leaves us wondering how mere coherence with other sentences could comprise the significance of any given sentence's truth. The pragmatic account of truth, which is not a theory but a rejection of theorizing about truth, also makes truth intralinguistic by equating being true with sentences' utility. But the pragmatic account is plagued by the inescapable idea that the real reason some propositions are "true" is that they are useful because they are true. Things are only a little better with respect to the so-called deflationary accounts; as indicated, the widely accepted disquotational account too often looks like an evasion. Like Tarski's formula, the disquotational account really does not address our concern about just how true sentences "hook up" to the world. Similar points can be made against more arcane accounts like the identity theory, which denies correspondence as a relation and rather unconvincingly maintains that a true proposition is identical with what makes it true (Zalta 2002). But it is not my intent to review these alternatives; my concern is less with an alternative to the relational conception of truth than with the need to acknowledge its complexity.

To sum up before proceeding, there is a new urgency to Pilate's question. Concern with understanding truth has spilled over the boundaries of academic philosophy. This has happened because we have newly realized that while we feel, on the one hand, impelled to discover the truth, we have, on the other, reason to be suspicious of what we find in that endeavor. This situation may be described as a result of widespread but largely tacit adoption of minimal perspectivism. However, resolution of the tension is impeded by the fact that, while the idea that truth is saying how things are is compelling, we seem unable to offer a convincing account of how what we actually say represents how things are. More specifically, though the relational account of truth is intuitively compelling, we cannot seem to properly explicate it theoretically. We feel driven, then, to adopt something like the discursive-currency conception, which obviates the problem of relating sentences to how things are.

The trouble is that the solution seems too radical. It seems to sacrifice precisely what is most compelling about the relational view: that truth is about how things are. For their part, Searle and Foucault have little patience with this uncertainty. The former uncompromisingly pairs up true sentences and objective reality; the latter equally uncompromisingly divorces truth from the extralinguistic world.

Clarifying the Context

Searle's and Foucault's views on truth occur in a complex context defined by numerous philosophical, cultural, ideological, and methodological factors. Chief among these are the oppositions marked by the canonical and priority contrasts. Before turning to Searle's and Foucault's positions, we need to say more about these contrasts and what they involve.

The canonical division is, as suggested, at once the least significant and the most prominent and influential. The division between analytic and Continental philosophers mainly results from how historical developments consigned thinkers with varied backgrounds and associations to supposedly irreconcilable philosophical traditions. These developments range from the impact of single individuals, most notably Rudolf Carnap, to broad influences, such as the effects of the Second World War on European intellectuals. The consequences of these developments are varied and complex, but their result is readily apparent in how Searle's and Foucault's positions on truth usually are not seen as contrary positions within philosophy, but rather as positions that help to define incommensurable conceptions of philosophy, or, for many, that define philosophy and pseudophilosophy.

The division drawn between analytic philosophy, of the sort that defines and is partly defined by Searle's objectives and methodology, and Continental philosophy, of the sort that grounds Foucault's postmodernism, is an entrenched one, regardless of how problematic it may be in fact. Whatever its origins, this division was deepened in the second half of the twentieth century with the development, mostly in France, of postmodernism and deconstruction – movements that took ideas rooted in Hegel's work, and developed by Nietzsche and Heidegger, to disturbing relativistic extremes. The result is that the bulk of North American, British, Australian, and Scandinavian philosophers, on the one hand, and French and most German philosophers, on the other, tend to see themselves not as members of different philosophical traditions engaged in divergent debates (and much less as members of a single, internally diverse philosophical community) but as members of distinct intellectual communities lacking common ground for professional engagement.

The labels *analytic, Continental, European,* and *postmodern* tend to conjure up rather simplistic stereotypes, but what concerns us here is that these labels obscure important similarities, parallels, complementarities, and, especially, opportunities. Still, these labels do undeniably mark significant differences. The best brief account I have seen of the nature of these differences is Giovanna Borradori's "The Atlantic Wall," the introduction to *The American Philosopher* (Borradori 1994). What emerges in her account is that most North American analytic philosophers are thinkers whose canon ironically was shaped more by British and German philosophers, notably Frege, Russell, Moore, and Wittgenstein, than by their own predecessors, such as Peirce, Lovejoy, and Royce. However, what matters most to how the canonical division was produced and is seen is that these transatlantic influences, rooted in logical positivism and the backlash against British Idealism, established an enduring logico-linguistic focus for North American philosophy. Most significant is that a key aspect of this focus is a special concern with epistemology, especially epistemology centered on issues in the philosophy of science. A central tradition-shaping consequence, then, was that a high order of technical expertise and a specialized vocabulary became and remain characteristic of analytic philosophy. This means that analytic philosophy's debates are not readily accessible to nonexperts. Isolation from the public, seen by most as necessary and worthwhile professionalism, is what prompts Rorty's claim that analytic philosophy is not taken seriously except by analytic philosophers (Rorty and Searle 1999, 58). This claim, while largely true, unfortunately is not seen negatively by analytic philosophers, whose professionalism is supported by their esoteric vocabulary and debates (a staunchly analytic colleague once commented to me that a philosophy paper's importance was in inverse proportion to the size of its audience).

As important as any other factor in the drawing of the canonical contrast was that the main British and European-positivist contributors to the North American analytic canon were united by nothing if not by their rejection of the metaphysical speculation so integral to the work of their own predecessors, most notably F. H. Bradley and Heidegger. Intolerance for metaphysics found ready acceptance on the part of North American and British philosophers, and what appeared to be the hardheaded philosophical approaches of Bertrand Russell, G. E. Moore, and John Dewey were enthusiastically emulated. North American philosophers, in particular, developed what I once heard called "physics envy," or what Rorty describes as professional philosophy's "self-image as a quasi-science" (Rorty and Prado 2003, 228). The persistent aspiration to scientific status, the entrenched antimetaphysical penchant, and a related inclination to typecast Continental philosophers as metaphysicians are evident in how, "[i]n America, the definition of analytic philosophy has always been posed in opposition to European thought" (Borradori 1994, 7).

The core of this opposition manifests itself in the methodologies favored by the two sides: analysis versus synthesis. Analytic philosophers typically try to solve fairly delineated philosophical problems by "reducing them to their . . . parts and to the relations in which these parts stand." Continental philosophers typically address large questions in a synthetic or integrative way, and consider particular philosophical issues to be "parts of larger unities," issues properly understood and dealt with only as elements of those unities (Matson 2000, 473). In line with this difference, Searle describes his own method as trying "to find the constitutive elements of consciousness, intentionality, speech acts, and social institutions by taking them apart and seeing how they work" (Searle 1999, 160). For his part, Foucault tells us that European philosophy "from Hegel to Sartre has essentially been a totalizing enterprise" (Foucault 1989, 38).

But methodology is only one aspect of the canonical divide, and in considering other aspects, we begin to see the importance of the priority or historical/ahistorical contrast in how philosophy is conceived. Philosophers who conceive of philosophy as ahistorical – and the majority are in the analytic camp – take what is best described as conceptual clarity as their main objective. "The project of analytic style philosophy, whether the analytic frame be that of ordinary language or logic, is clarity" (Babich 2003, 70). However, the clarity sought is not merely avoidance of ambiguity, equivocation, linguistic inelegance, or poeticism; the whole point, as is abundantly clear in Searle's writings, is that saying it clearly is taken as *getting it right*. In other words, conceptual clarity and truth are deemed to be of a piece. The underlying idea is what prompted use in the mid-twentieth century of the label *conceptual analysis* to capture the essence of analytic philosophy. The pivotal idea was that philosophy's main task is the careful mapping of concepts that are deemed to be universal and ahistorical. Roderick Chisholm's efforts to produce definitive criteria for intentionality, for instance, are a case in point; another is P. F. Strawson's attempt to revitalize metaphysical thought as "descriptive metaphysics" in *Individuals* (Chisholm 1957; Strawson 1963). In the next chapter we will see how Searle follows suit. That he does so is most evident in how he articulates the concept of collective intentionality without recourse to psychology or neurology or any other science, and goes on to make the conceptual claim that collective intentionality is irreducible as well as the plainly empirical claim that intentionality also is biologically primitive. Searle relies on what I am calling the ahistorical conception of philosophy to insist that any and all developments in cognitive science must respect and be bounded by the inherent and irreducible nature of intentional consciousness.

The quest for clarity is what drives analytic philosophers to consider most of the work of French, Italian, and many German philosophers as flawed by the interpretive latitude that characterizes their treatment of broad humanistic and political issues. For example, Russell offers a typically dismissive assessment of Nietzsche as having been "a literary rather than academic philosopher." In Russell's eyes, Nietzsche's philosophical failure was that, despite his vast influence, he "invented no new technical theories in ontology or epistemology" (Russell 1945, 760). What others see as depth and breadth of thought and interest, Russell and those of like mind see as lack of rigor and woolliness unredeemed by technical prowess. Analytic philosophers also consider Continental thought to be tainted by political partiality because of European intellectuals' efforts to come to terms with the implications of two world wars fought mainly on their own soil. These efforts, again, are seen as relinquishment of clarity for the messiness of the historical. Still another, often neglected aspect is that many analytic philosophers consider Continental thought, especially contemporary French thought and in particular deconstruction, to be nihilistic and irrationalist. Some think that, at bottom, it is nihilism that divides the analytic and Continental camps. Simon Critchley remarks, "it is the concept of nihilism that best permits one to distinguish analytic and Continental philosophy" (Critchley 2001, 22).

Searle's conception of philosophy is as autonomous and concerned with discerning ahistorical truth. The quest for conceptual clarity, then, is the essence, if not the whole, of philosophy, for discernment of conceptual truth can be achieved only through conceptual clarity. The task is to discern how things stand, both in the conceptual and the physical realms, and this involves clearly understanding how conceptual truths relate to what is the case in the physical realm. An example of this, to which I return later, is how Searle considers intentionality an irreducible, ineliminable property of some physical things, namely, those physical things, like ourselves, that are conscious. To the extent that philosophy achieves clarity on the concept of intentionality, then, it captures something undeniable about the physical world and unchangeable by history or science.

Therefore, no reductivist causal account of consciousness or of its defining property, intentionality, or aboutness can succeed. No developments in cognitive science have altered or ever could alter the concept of intentionality. There is an order of being, independent of us, to which what we believe and say must conform, and that order of being includes certain special properties of some physical things, specifically, the property of intentional consciousness. Insofar as cognitive science is committed to providing a causal or reductivist account of intentionality, therefore, it violates prior philosophically discerned truths and Searle rejects it as "founded on mistakes" (Guttenplan 1996, 546).

There is a most notable contrast to Searle's views within mainline analytic philosophy, namely, those of W. V. O. Quine, a philosopher who not only problematized the analytic/synthetic distinction, a cornerstone of ahistoricist analytic philosophizing, but who sought to "naturalize" epistemology. This "intracanonical" contrast is so fundamental that it raises the question of why the canonical divide has survived as long as it has. The answer is that, first, the divide does now seem to be collapsing or, more accurately, increasingly ignored. But second, the canonical division continues primarily as one having to do with preferred texts – one cannot read everything – and academic location, rather than with examined and accepted or rejected philosophical theses. Still, despite its problematic nature and perhaps moribund status, the canonical contrast needs to be pursued a little to better understand the perception, if not the substance, of the Searle/Foucault opposition.

Given the problematic nature of the canonical division, it is not surprising that the European perception of analytic philosophy is more difficult to describe than the analytic view of Continental philosophy. Primarily, the difficulty is rooted in the major differences among European philosophers, who may be existentialists, hermeneuts, phenomenologists, structuralists, poststructuralists, postmoderns, or deconstructivists. All of these vary in their assessment of and interest in analytic philosophy. Moreover, once we distinguish between historicist analysts and ahistoricist analysts, it emerges that it is mainly the latter group that constitutes the analytic half of the canonical contrast. Rorty is right regarding the lack of interest in analytic philosophy other than on the part of analytic philosophers, if he is thinking of the ahistoricist group within analytic philosophy. European philosophers may read Davidson, and they certainly read Rorty, but they are much less likely to immerse themselves in Searle's work.

Generally, the Continental view of analytic philosophy of both the historicist and ahistoricist sorts is that, on the whole, European philosophers see analytic philosophy as having long ceased to be a "socially engaged interdisciplinary enterprise," having become instead "a highly specialized occupation" (Borradori 1994, 4). Analytic philosophers are seen as having isolated their philosophizing from social and cultural issues in the process of professionalizing it. Rorty's criticism of analytic philosophy as overly professional, then, seems to accurately reflect the European view (Rorty 1982).

If we focus more closely on the contrast between ahistoricist analytic philosophy and postmodernism, it emerges that one of the main uses of the canonical distinction is exclusion. There is an intellectual imperative to engage with serious thinkers holding views opposed to one's own. We cannot rest content with consigning different conceptions of so fundamental a matter as truth, for example, to supposedly irreconcilable philosophical traditions. If we do so, we effectively adopt an unacknowledged and unexamined relativism, because the consigning entails acceptance that not only are there incompatible conceptions of how sentences are true, but that these incompatible conceptions of truth are contextually separable and separately viable. But engaging with those having very different views on fundamental questions is a difficult and demanding business. It is much easier to exclude their views as workable only from some peculiar perspective. This is, in effect, to employ a distinction between traditions to rule certain views confused and their adherents unwilling or incapable of understanding how and why they are so. These exclusionary efforts explain why there is so much facile mockery of each other by ahistoricist analytic and postmodern philosophers. The point of the mutual disdain is precisely to disallow that those on the other side of the divide are serious thinkers and merit philosophical engagement.

Our Protagonists

John Searle and Michel Foucault encountered one another in a way conditioned by the intellectual and cultural context just sketched. But despite each being a model of his respective philosophical tradition, they took each other seriously. Searle has been outspoken in his denunciation of postmodernism, and especially so in his intemperate treatment of Jacques Derrida (Searle 1983). However, he distinguishes Foucault from those with whom Foucault is usually grouped; in an e-mail to me, in 2002, he says of Foucault, whom he met in Berkeley, "I never thought he was a typical French fake." Searle also taught Foucault's *The Order of Things* in at least one course. For his part, Foucault read Searle's work and cited it. In "What Is an Author?" Foucault refers to "Searle's analyses" in discussing proper names (Rabinow 1984, 105). Again, in *Fearless Speech*, Foucault draws a comparison between himself and Searle with respect to his own use of the term *speech activity* and Searle's "*speech act*" (Foucault 2001, 13; Dreyfus and Rabinow 1983 has a discussion of Foucault's and Searle's positions on speech acts, 44–47, especially 46n1). Another point of contact is that both Foucault and Searle find it important to consider Velasquez's *Las Meninas* in some depth (Foucault 1973; Searle 1980). It is also notable – and surprising to many – that Searle and Foucault were in agreement regarding Derrida's work. Despite Foucault's erstwhile friendship with Derrida, his attitude toward Derridean deconstruction was as negative as Searle's. Edward Said comments that Foucault had a "genuine fear that . . . deconstruction was licensing an ahistorical laissez-faire attitude." Said adds that "there is an edge and a derisive scorn to [Foucault's] words about Derrida," qualities certainly present in Searle's treatment of Derrida (Arac 1991, 7).

Despite whatever philosophical contact and agreement they may have shared, Searle and Foucault are radically opposed on truth, and because they are, many analytic philosophers assume them to be equally opposed on realism. As I have indicated, this is a misperception because Searle and Foucault are, in fact, both realists, regardless of common perception of Foucault as a linguistic idealist or other sort of irrealist. There is, of course, no comparable misperception regarding Searle's realism, or what he calls "external realism" in contrast to positions such as Putnam's "internal realism" (Putnam 1987, 17). Searle unhesitantly avers that "[t]he world (or alternatively, reality or the universe) exists independently of our representations of it" (Searle 1995, 150). But Foucault, surprisingly to many, is equally emphatic in rejecting irrealism, insisting that positing diversity of discursive truth "does not mean that there is nothing there and that everything comes out of somebody's head" (Foucault 1988b, 17). This is explicit rejection of the currently fashionable postmodern linguistic idealism that collapses everything into language.

One contributing factor to misperception of Foucault as some sort of irrealist is that while Searle explicitly avows realism, Foucault rejects irrealism only in passing. The significance of this is that while there is a tight connection between Searle's realism and his relational conception of truth, there is little connection between Foucault's discursive-currency conception of truth and his realism. Whereas Searle's relational view follows from his realism, Foucault's relativization of truth to discourse, which divorces truth from how things are in the extralinguistic world, is indifferent to realism. This is to say that the erroneous attribution to Foucault of linguistic idealism is not just a mistake; his discursive-currency conception of truth at least is compatible with linguistic idealism, despite Foucault himself not being a linguistic idealist or other sort of irrealist. Unfortunately, Foucault addresses the issue of realism only when those who misinterpret his views charge that his relativization of truth to discourse entails irrealism.

The connection between Searle's realism and relational view of truth is that Searle holds what Williams describes as "a specifically realist idea of truth," a conception of truth determined by "an independent order of things to which our thought is answerable" (Williams 2002, 136). Searle unequivocally holds this view, maintaining that true sentences are "made true by how things are in the real world" (Searle 1995, xiii). I have called this the relational conception of truth, distinguishing it, as a broad conception, from the more specific correspondence theory, and it is what Barry Allen calls the "classical philosophy of truth." So conceived, truth is "mimetic fealty"; it is faithful replication of, or "adequacy" to, the wholly objective realm of "self-identical being" (Allen 1993, 9–28).

Illustrating the connection between truth and realism is Searle's belief that realism is a *condition of intelligibility*; his view is that each member of "a large class of utterances . . . requires for its intelligibility a publicly accessible reality" (Searle 1995, 190). Searle's realism, then, determines his conception of truth in the sense that his realism allows no alternative but to conceive of truth as true sentences accurately depicting how things are in publicly accessible reality.

The intelligibility-condition role of realism in Searle's thinking, however, is not that of an underlying propositional assumption, much less that of a reflected-upon philosophical tenet or precept. As I discuss later, in his philosophy of mind Searle introduces the notion of "the Background" (his capitalization), which he defines as "a set of nonrepresentational mental capacities that enable all representing to take place" (Searle 1987, 143). Realism is a fundamental Background factor for Searle; realism is an integral element of our thought and awareness. Realism is also an articulated philosophical position, but first and foremost it is a defining component of the nonintentional and nonrepresentational capacities that enable us to represent, manipulate, move about in, and talk and think about our environment and ourselves. Given his conception of realism as an inescapable precondition of representation, then, Searle considers conception of truth to be grounded in intuitive understanding of truth as accurate depiction of states of affairs (Searle 1995, xiii).

Against everything Searle holds regarding truth, Foucault holds the initially paradoxical view that truth has nothing to do with publicly accessible reality because truth is entirely intralinguistic. Unlike Searle, Foucault begins with truth – more accurately, with the *production* of truth – rather than with realism. That is, his starting point is not that the world is as it is, and that truth is getting it right; his starting point is that we are "subjected to the production of truth through power." He then sees his problem not as one of explaining the relation of true sentences to the world, but as one of determining "what type of power is susceptible of producing discourses of truth" (Foucault 1980b, 93).

I consider Foucault's somewhat elusive and often misinterpreted notion of power in Chapter 3, but it is necessary to mention here that Foucauldian power is not, as many think, covert manipulation, domination, or coercion. In Foucault's sense, power is dynamic, continuous change in networks of interrelated actions. The difficult but central point about Foucauldian power is that it bears on *actions*, not on agents. Most simply put, power is people consciously and unconsciously doing all manner of things, and what they do constraining or facilitating what others do. As will emerge, the production of truth is a complex enabling and limiting of discursive actions. Truth is produced by power in the sense that power relations determine what may and may not be uttered; in brief, power relations establish and sustain currency in discourse.

This idea of discursive currency is central to understanding Foucault's conception of truth. In *Knowledge and Civilization*, Allen makes the point in a more general way, but nonetheless captures what is crucial to Foucault's views: "*What is truth?* . . . Above all, truth is a value, a logical truth-value for statements. And it is an economic value, a matter of currency. For truth as for money, to be is to be exchanged, to circulate" (Allen 2004, 77). For Foucault, truth, being linguistic currency, is internal to discourse, so there is neither need nor possibility of articulating a theoretical account of true sentences' relation to how things are in the world outside language. The need is to understand how some sentences come to circulate as they do, to be regularly exchanged, and others fail to become or cease to be current.

The interpretive difficulty posed by Foucault's approach is that though his discursive-currency conception of truth is compatible with some forms of idealism, he does not consider this an issue because, in his view, questions do not arise about what true sentences relate to, since they do not relate to anything other than purely discursive standards that establish them as current or otherwise. Searle's objective reality simply does not enter the picture because confirmation, the establishing of some sentences as true or false, has to do with establishing the place of those sentences in discursive practices. It does not have to do with "squaring" them, as I will put it to avoid correspondist connotations, with how things are in the extralinguistic world. This essentially is Sellars's position, that attribution of truth to sentences does "not assert relations between linguistic and extra-linguistic items" (Sellars 1968, 82). Unfortunately, in Foucault's case, largely because of the views held by other postmoderns, detaching the truth of sentences from how things are in the world looks to many as not mere compatibility with idealism, but as the irrealist claim that things are not any way at all independent of what we say.

Below I argue that this alleged irrealism is based on little more than Foucault's indifference. Foucault's realism is *tacit*; he does not deny extralinguistic reality explicitly or by implication. His tacit realism is obscured because, contrary to analytic expectations, he affirms realism only in a few places and then in passing, as in the passage quoted above. Foucault sees no need to argue for realism, being of a mind with Rorty, who considers the philosophical issue of realism as no more than a Cartesian obsession and a discipline-defining conversational theme.

Returning to truth, the basic difference between Searle and Foucault can be put in the following way. Searle believes that there is a world of things and events untouched by how we represent them. Thus far there is no quarrel with Foucault, but Searle also believes that there can be objective knowledge about the world despite what he calls the "aspectual" nature of our awareness of the world, and that knowledge is instantiated in beliefs and sentences that are true in virtue of accurately portraying how the world is (Searle 1992, 131, 155). As we will see, Searle admits that the aspectual nature of awareness may raise problems, but he takes these as resolvable through clarification and especially confirmation of how things are. For Searle, extralinguistic reality plays the pivotal epistemic role because it is what makes beliefs and sentences true. This, then, is what most sharply separates Searle from Foucault, and, for that matter, from Davidson.

For his part, Foucault believes that truth is constructed by historical developments and discursive practices, and that knowledge is a historical, disciplinary, and discursive construct. Like Sellars and Davidson, and unlike Searle, Foucault rejects the idea that sentences are made true by how things are in the extralinguistic realm. Extralinguistic reality neither determines nor guarantees truth, the discursive currency of sentences. Peculiar as it may sound, truth is not about how things are beyond discourse; truth is about what goes on in discourse. For Foucault, then, questions about truth are questions about the histories of discourses and about present discursive practices; they are not questions about how sentences depict states of affairs. However, this is not denial of the world; it is assertion that extralinguistic reality plays no epistemic role in the determination of what is deemed to be true or to constitute knowledge; it is not the determinant of currency in discourse.

Given this preliminary discussion of Searle and Foucault on truth, and of the context in which they oppose one another, we now need to look more closely at their respective positions. In the next two chapters, I offer enough exposition and critical commentary of Searle's and Foucault's positions to substantiate my contrastive comparison. Because of the canonical division between analytic and Continental philosophy, some readers will not need the exposition of Searle and may find the exposition of Foucault too sparse, limited as it is mainly to those of his views that bear on the issue of truth. I apologize to those readers, and assume that they will understand both the necessity of saying enough about Searle to substantiate my claims and the impracticality of saying more than I do about Foucault. I encourage these same readers to read Gary Gutting's *The Cambridge Companion to Foucault* and the second edition of my own *Starting with Foucault: An Introduction to Genealogy*, which is expressly written for those with an analytic background and bent (Gutting 1994; Prado 2000). Of course, other readers will be familiar with Foucault's work but not with Searle's, and will be in the converse position. To them I extend the same apology, and assume the same understanding, with the principals reversed. I encourage these latter readers to read Searle's *Mind, Language and Society*, in which he offers a lucid summary of his views, and also Nick Fotion's *Searle* (Searle 1999; Fotion 2000).

2

Searle

Language, Mind, Society

Searle's work falls into three main areas: philosophy of language; philosophy of mind, including cognitive science; and social reality (Matson 2000, 586–96; Honderich 1995, 816; Guttenplan 1996, 544–50). But while a fairly distinct area, his work on social reality must be seen as a natural extension of his work on mind and, to a lesser extent, language. Searle himself summarizes his work in terms of the questions he addresses, saying that

the philosophical problems that most interest me have to do with how the various parts of the world relate to each other – how does it all hang together? . . . The theory of speech acts is in part an attempt to answer the question, How do we get from the physics of utterances to meaningful speech acts performed by speakers and writers? The theory of the mind . . . is in large part an attempt to answer the question, How does a mental reality, a world of consciousness, intentionality, and other mental phenomena, fit into a world consisting entirely of physical particles in fields of force? (Searle 1995, xi)

Searle's efforts regarding social reality are an attempt to answer the further question of how there can be "an objective world of money, property, marriage, governments, elections . . . in a world that consists entirely of physical particles" (Searle 1995, xi). His work in these areas is tightly interconnected, and his progress has been cumulative. His contributions in the philosophy of language and of mind are of a positive, innovative nature. Most notably, Searle introduces collective intentionality, "the Background," an account of institutional facts, "biological naturalism," and derivation of moral obligation from factual description. Searle's contributions in cognitive science are less innovative and center on his defense of the commonsense conception of consciousness against various reductive analyses, and on his critique of appeals to a permanent unconscious. Though he describes cognitive science as one of the most exciting areas of contemporary intellectual work, Searle laments that it was "founded on mistakes" (Guttenplan 1996, 546). As mentioned in the previous chapter, this contention is indicative of Searle's ahistoricist position within analytic philosophy. Philosophy, essentially conceived as conceptual analysis, is prior to and overrules empirical science. This conception is perhaps most evident in Searle's reliance on ingenious thought-experiments, like the famous "Chinese Room," to defend the irreducibility of consciousness.

Of course, Searle's work raises questions. As will emerge, those most relevant here have to do with collective intentionality, the Background, and his attempt to walk a fine line between dualism and reductive materialism. But the important thing to recognize about his work is that it is basically a kind of philosophical reverse engineering. That is, he begins with "end products" – language, the mind, social reality – and works to determine the details of their composition or structure by breaking them down analytically to learn and to say how they work and what elements are required for them to work as they do. His discussions of intentionality, collective intentionality, and the Background are Searle's attempts to map elements crucially operant in consciousness and action. He then uses the resulting descriptions to argue that the makeup of the mind, the nature of consciousness, cannot be adequately "blueprinted" by the various causal and reductive analyses offered by contemporary philosophers like Daniel Dennett and Patricia and Paul Churchland.

Searle first drew professional attention with his "How to Derive 'Ought' from 'Is,'" a paper in which he offered an argument purporting to derive normative judgments from factual descriptions (Searle 1964). The argument consists of five steps: (1) Jones utters the words, "I promise to pay you, Smith, five dollars"; (2) in uttering these words Jones promises to pay Smith five dollars; (3) Jones has placed himself/herself under an obligation to pay Smith five dollars; (4) Jones is thus under an obligation to pay Smith five dollars; (5) Jones therefore ought to pay Smith five dollars. If one accepts that steps one through four are factual, and since the fifth clearly is normative, the argument constitutes a derivation of an "ought," that Jones ought to pay Smith five dollars, from an "is," the fact that Jones placed himself under an obligation by uttering some version of the formula: "I, Jones, promise to pay you, Smith, five dollars."

What matters here is that Searle's argument was not an isolated clever move; the argument appeals to institutional facts, and both presages Searle's later work and indicates the integrated nature of his thought. Without institutional facts, there is no promising to repay a loan regardless of what may be said. This indicates that even in 1964, Searle was already embarked on making out a position that would not receive its most polished articulation until publication of *The Construction of Social Reality* in 1995. Wallace I. Matson notes that the importance of "How to Derive 'Ought' from 'Is'" actually "lay not so much in its Joshua-like breach of an ancient wall as in its focusing attention on the nature of the facts appealed to," facts that Searle would detail "thirty years later in his . . . comprehensive theory of institutional facts" (Matson 2000, 588).

Once Searle took center stage with his is/ought paper, his *Speech Acts* found an attentive and expectant audience (Searle 1969). The book and its sequel, *Expression and Meaning*, published a decade later, present Searle's philosophy of language (Searle 1979). Though obviously founded and expanding on John L. Austin's work (Austin 1962), Searle's analysis of the structure of language is innovative and more systematic than Austin's. Basically, Searle describes the rules operant in reference and predication with the intention of showing how it is that uttered sounds and inscribed marks have meaning for us.

Speech Acts and *Expression and Meaning* were soon followed by many articles and other books, the most notable of the latter being *Intentionality: An Essay in the Philosophy of Mind* in 1983, *The Rediscovery of the Mind* (1992), and *The Construction of Social Reality* (1995). But from the beginning, Searle's work was integrated in ways we find only in the writings of major thinkers. His overall objective is a comprehensive understanding of us as conscious material beings: matter that thinks and is capable of creating a social reality supervening on brute reality. Achieving this objective meant articulating a philosophy of language and a philosophy of mind. Only then could Searle tackle the question of the nature of social reality. He had to say what we are, as thinking beings, and how we employ language, before saying how we create social institutions.

One traditional area of philosophy to which Searle contributes less than he might is traditional epistemology. Fotion notes that Searle is impatient with how-do-we-know questions, seeing them as the unproductive legacy of Descartes (Fotion 2000, 236–40). The importance of this for my purposes is that Searle largely seems to identify epistemology with skepticism about the existence and accessibility of objective or "external" reality, seeing epistemology as a misconceived Cartesian indictment of the realism that is fundamental to his philosophizing about language, mind, and social reality. However, if we move beyond traditional conception of epistemology as concerned with what we can know beyond "immediate awareness," if we understand epistemology more broadly, and in light of the priority contrast between historical and ahistorical analytical philosophizing, then epistemology permeates most of Searle's work.

In Searle's view, we are capable of acquiring knowledge about mind-independent reality and some of the properties of its components, specifically, intentional consciousness, and we cannot learn that these properties reduce to certain causal sequences. Searle's claims about the mind, action, and social reality, then, are basically epistemological in being opposed to philosophical positions that countenance historically – and especially scientifically – grounded developmental change in concepts like those of intentionality and consciousness.

With respect to the philosophical positions he opposes, in *Mind, Language and Society* Searle offers a list of what he considers the major contemporary challenges to "the Enlightenment vision" of us as capable of acquiring knowledge of a reality wholly independent of our changeable representations and that determines the truth or falsity of what we believe and say about it. These challenges include the impact of relativity theory on fundamental assumptions about space and time, matter, and energy; set theoretical paradoxes' impugning of the rationality of mathematics; Freudian psychology's qualifications of rationality; Gödel's limitations on mathematics; quantum mechanics' infringement on determinacy; and Thomas Kuhn's and Paul Feyerabend's critiques of the objectivity and progressiveness of science. Searle includes two more strictly philosophical challenges, which are the interpretation of the later Wittgenstein as showing "that our discourse is a series of mutually untranslatable and incommensurable language games," and the postmodern claim that "there is no universally valid rationality [and] that different cultures have different rationalities" (Searle 1999, 4).

Searle adds, "I accept the Enlightenment vision. I think that the universe exists quite independently of our minds and that, within the limits set by our evolutionary endowments, we can come to comprehend its nature" (Searle 1999, 4). He expands this remark by posing a number of propositions that he holds true, and which he calls "default positions" because he rightly thinks that most people hold them true

whether or not they have ever reflected on them. The propositions
are:

> [1.] There is a real world that exists independently of us, independently of
> our experiences, our thoughts, our language.
> [2.] We have direct perceptual access to that world.
> [3.] Words in our language ... typically have reasonably clear meanings [and]
> can be used to refer to ... real objects in the world.
> [4.] Our statements are typically true or false depending on whether they
> correspond to how things are, that is, to the facts in the world.
> [5.] Causation is a real relation among objects and events in the world.
>
> (Searle 1999, 10)

To proceed, in the following sections I sketch the highlights of Searle's
work and positions on language, mind, and social reality, and then focus
more closely on his conception of truth. The section on mind is in proportion to the place of mind in Searle's philosophizing, and his observations
that "for a large number of philosophers, the philosophy of mind in now
first philosophy" and that a large number of philosophical topics "are best
approached by way of an understanding of mental phenomena" (Searle
1999, ix–x).

Language

Searle's philosophy of language is just that, a philosophy of language;
it is not linguistic philosophy employed to solve philosophical problems
"by attending to the ordinary use of ... language" (Searle 1969, 4). His
philosophy of language centers on recognition that "language is the fundamental human institution," and so is the ground of all other social
institutions (Searle 1999, 153). The focus in understanding language is
speech acts, which are the actions we perform with utterances. The aim
is to understand how we manage to give meaning to the noises we voice
and the signs we inscribe, and how we manage to convey that meaning
to others.

As Matson succinctly puts it, Searle's objective in philosophizing about
language is to set out "the rules whereby speakers are able to perform the
basic speech acts of referring and predicating" (Matson 2000, 588). However, Searle proceeds in a highly detailed manner that is difficult to sum-
marize, especially given the limits of this book. What I offer here, therefore, is less a summary than it is an impression of this aspect of Searle's
work. Readers desiring more should look at Fotion's book or, better,
read *Speech Acts*, given that Searle is his own best expositor (Searle 1969;

Fotion 2000, 11–95). The heart of Searle's interest in speech acts is best caught in the following passage:

> The reason for concentrating on . . . speech acts is simply this: all linguistic communication involves linguistic acts. The unit of linguistic communication is not, as has generally been supposed, the symbol . . . but rather the production or issuance of the symbol or word or sentence in the performance of the speech act. . . . [T]he production or issuance of a sentence token under certain conditions is a speech act, and speech acts . . . are the basic or minimal units of linguistic communication. (Searle 1969, 16)

The focus on communication, however, is qualified by the demands of Searle's philosophy of mind. Despite his emphasis on speech acts, Searle finds it necessary to draw "a clear distinction between representation and communication" because he understands meaning primarily in terms of representation rather than communication (Searle 1987, 165). Searle notes that someone intending to communicate something "both intends to represent some fact or state of affairs and intends to communicate this representation." So it follows that the "representing intention is not the same as [the] communication intention." He stresses that "[c]ommunicating is a matter of producing certain effects on one's hearers, but one can intend to represent something without caring at all about the effects on one's hearers." There are, then, "two aspects to meaning intentions, the intention to represent and the intention to communicate" (Searle 1987, 165–66).

Once representation and communication are distinguished, we need to understand what we do and how we do it when we communicate. Crucial to this understanding is appreciating that "speaking a language is engaging in a rule-governed form of behavior." In short, "talking is performing acts according to rules" (Searle 1969, 22). There is, though, a significant variety in the acts we perform in communicating. Particular speech acts have three different kinds of force, which Austin dubbed "locutionary," "illocutionary," and "perlocutionary" force. Uttering "The house is on fire" has locutionary or propositional force in that the sentence articulates the particular content that the house is on fire. Uttering "The house is on fire" has illocutionary force in that it warns the speaker's hearers that the house is on fire. This is the force the speaker most likely intends the utterance to have. And uttering "The house is on fire" has perlocutionary force in that, for example, it causes some to panic. This likely is not what the speaker intends, but it is a consequence of uttering "The house is on fire."

Aside from their types of force, speech acts vary in that we do many different things with them. We make promises and assertions; we express agreement and disagreement; we give descriptions; we issue warnings, commands, and requests; we ask questions; and so on. Particular speech acts may be quite different even though their reference and predication remain constant. Our utterances may have the same reference and predication but differ in that with one we assert something, with another we question something, and with still another we express a desire. For instance, in each of the following expressions, the referent is chocolate and the predicate is good-for-me, but the utterances are different and perform different tasks: "Chocolate is good for me"; "Is chocolate good for me?"; "Would that chocolate were good for me!" It may seem obvious that these are different speech acts despite sharing reference and predication, but recall that philosophers of language once misconstrued sameness of reference and predication, and insisted on treating assertion as the essential speech act.

In his groundbreaking work in the philosophy of language, Austin offered a taxonomy of speech acts that Searle enhances and extends (Austin 1962). Searle describes twelve ways that speech acts differ from one another. Utterances differ in their point or purpose and in whether their "direction of fit" is *word-to-world* or *world-to-word*. Utterances differ with respect to the psychological state expressed in the speech act and have different force. Utterers and hearers have one or another status, and utterances bear a fairly specific relation to utterers' and hearers' interests as well as to discursive contexts. And, of course, utterances differ in their propositional content. Another difference is whether a communicative act must be a speech act or not; for instance, promising must be a speech act, but conveying agreement or an auction bid may be done with a gesture. Then there is the relationship of utterances to institutions, in that some speech acts presuppose social institutions: only against a complex background does uttering "I do" or "I promise" count as marrying or undertaking an obligation. Utterances also differ regarding whether or not they require an illocutionary or performative verb. Making a promise or undertaking an obligation, for example, requires use of the verb "to promise" or some synonym. Finally, utterances differ in their manner or style of performance.

The details of Searle's taxonomy are not of immediate importance here. What is of greatest relevance to the comparison with Foucault on truth is how Searle's use of his taxonomical distinctions to categorize speech acts reflects his relational conception of truth and realism, especially in his notion of direction of fit, the second of the aforementioned speech-act differentia.

Searle distinguishes five broad sorts of speech acts: commissives (e.g., promises), directives (e.g., commands), assertives (e.g., descriptions and predications), expressives (e.g., "I don't like that!"), and declarations (e.g., "I hereby . . .") (Searle 1979, 16–17). These distinctions incorporate correspondism and realism because directives and assertives and, to some extent commissives, expressives, and declarations, have direction of fit.

Direction of fit has to do with how utterances have one or other of two sorts of "conditions of satisfaction," which is to say, they relate to how things are in one of two ways. Descriptions, for example, have *word-to-world* direction: "There are forty-two cars in the parking-lot" has a word-to-world fit in that the sentence asserts that a particular state of affairs obtains, so the sentence has to "fit" the world to be true – it must accurately depict how things are. On the other hand, commands, for instance, have *world-to-word* direction: "Shut the door" has a world-to-word direction of fit in that a state of affairs has to change to fulfill the condition of satisfaction of the command's propositional content – that the door be shut. When the command is obeyed and the door is shut, the command's propositional content is actualized; the world is made to "fit" that content. Searle's conception of truth, then, is clearly relational and realist in conception and application.

If Searle's speech-act taxonomy manifests his relational conception of truth and realism, his account of speech acts shows the tight integration of Searle's philosophy of language and his philosophy of mind. The complexity of the account of speech acts prompts the question of how people ever master and apply the numerous rules that govern the use of different sorts of speech acts, and how they manage to give utterances the properties Searle inventories. The connection to his philosophy of mind is clear in that the answer to this question is given in terms of Searle's notion of the aforementioned Background.

Basically, as children are reared in language-using communities, they internalize the rules governing speech acts as they are guided in learning to speak by their parents and emulate other elders and their peers. Children learn various linguistic practices by example and direction, and become experienced in piecemeal implementation of the rules implicit in those practices. As the rules are learned and children achieve competence in the use of language, the rules are assimilated into the Background as nonintentional capacities. Competent language users do not consciously apply the rules governing speech acts. They do not think, "Uttering an assertive requires that I..." or "I must now utter a commissive," or anything of the sort. In speaking and in writing, all but the very young exercise capacities that were internalized in the process of being guided in developing language-using ability. With practice, the rules become "second nature" in the same way other things we initially learn to do intentionally come to be done unreflectively. We learn to ride a bicycle or play tennis by consciously doing certain things, usually helped by someone else. If we manage to learn the necessary moves, we come to do them "without thinking"; in fact, beyond a certain point, if we think about the moves, we usually perform them less well. In Searle's view, this process is a matter of intentionally done actions becoming nonintentional capacities.

The assimilation of implicit rules in the acquisition of linguistic and practical expertise manifests the crucial dependency of Searle's philosophy of language on his philosophy of mind. Having detailed the rules of language, he has to explain how we apply those rules despite our not doing so intentionally nor most of us even being able to articulate those rules. Searle does so by contending that the rules become nonintentional Background capacities, and that means his philosophy of language presupposes his philosophy of mind. This is no surprise, as Searle explicitly acknowledges this relation, claiming that "the philosophy of language is a branch of the philosophy of mind." In this dependency of the philosophy of language on that of mind, we again see the fundamentality of Searle's relational conception of truth and realism. The dependency is not only the role of the Background in linguistic competence; the dependency has to do with how "[t]he capacity of speech acts to represent objects and states of affairs... is an extension of the more biologically fundamental capacities of the mind (or brain) to relate the organism to the world by way of such mental states as belief and desire, and especially through action and perception" (Searle 1987, vii).

Searle's speech-act theory, then, attempts to show how we move "from the physics of utterances to meaningful speech acts" by detailing the kinds of things we do with utterances and how the doing is governed by rules (Searle 1995, xi). Central here is that, for Searle, speech-act utterances are only derivatively intentional. They are meaningful only because they bear the mind's own intentionality or directedness. His philosophy of language essentially is an account of how minds endow utterances and inscriptions with intentionality. They do so by enacting rule-governed practices, the rules of which are internalized in the process of learning to use language. When internalized, the rules pass into nonintentional capacities of the Background, like being able to walk upright or to use the right fork.

We now need to better understand Searle's philosophy of mind and the place of intentionality and the Background in it. As we proceed, it is important to keep in mind that pivotal to the accounts of mind and of language is Searle's conception of the mind as an irreducible feature of certain organisms whose main function is to relate those organisms to the world by way of depictive – hence relational – mental states paradigmed by true beliefs.

Mind

The central element in Searle's philosophy of mind is irreducible intentionality, the defining "aboutness" or directedness of consciousness. Intentionality is what links Searle's work on language, mind, cognitive science, and social reality. Intentionality relates to his philosophy of language in that the intentionality of meaningful sentences derives from the mind's inherent intentionality. Intentionality is mind's essential property. Conception of intentionality as inherent to consciousness and as irreducible determines Searle's ontological stand against behaviorism and causal reductivist analyses of the mental. The irreducible nature of intentionality also determines Searle's opposition to cognitive science's functionalism and cognitivism, which equate mentality with programs running in the brain and ignore consciousness as a kind of by-product playing no explanatory role regarding behavior, and so only of subjective interest (Searle 1987, viii–ix). Additionally, intentionality determines Searle's opposition to the idea of an inaccessible unconscious. Lastly, collective intentionality is the linchpin of Searle's account of social institutions.

The irreducibility of intentionality, however, does not entail dualism for Searle as it does for some. Intentionality is not a property of a substantial mind, but of some matter that thinks. There is no Cartesian mental substance, rather some matter has intentional states: "mental phenomena are biologically based: they are both caused by the operations of the brain and realized in the structure of the brain" (Searle 1987, ix). What makes brains unique is that they have mental states that inherently "point to" or are about things, events, and other internal states. This reality cannot be reduced to behavior or causal input/output sequences. Moreover, as we saw in the case of language, this unique and irreducible mental feature of brains is transitive in that we are able to bestow intentionality on utterances, signs, and gestures, and thereby to make them meaningful to ourselves and others.

This last point raises the matter of Searle's heavy reliance on the Background. If intentionality is a defining characteristic of human beings, the Background is the foremost precondition of everything they do. As noted, the Background is a collection of nonintentional, nonrepresentational capacities that enable representation, communication, and the actions that we perform in communicating with one another, moving about the world, and dealing with our environment (Searle 1987, 143–45; 1992, 175–96; 1999, 107–9). Searle needs the Background to explain how it is that we use language and engage in other practices without consciously implementing rules, and usually without being able to formulate those rules.

The key idea in the notion of the Background is the transformation of intentional actions into nonintentional capacities, and the key function of the Background is essentially that of a repository of capacities that we take for granted and to which our attention is drawn only when the capacities fail, as in pathological cases. Everything that we have mastered and come to do without consciously thinking about it, from taking the next step as we climb stairs to knowing when we are being asked a question, is consigned to the Background. Anything we do without conscious, reflective attention is classified as the exercise of a nonintentional Background capacity, and exercising Background capacities is the fundamental precondition of doing anything consciously and reflectively.

Searle differentiates between "deep" Background, the nonrepresentational mental capacities common to all human beings, and "local" Background, the culture-specific nonrepresentational capacities we acquire. Knowing how to reach for something, for instance, is a shared deep Background capacity shared by all; knowing how to reach for it in a polite manner is a local Background capacity shared by members of a particular culture. Background capacities are at work in manipulating and navigating our physical environment and in grasping how things stand in that environment; they also are at work in engaging in social practices and understanding how things stand in our social environment.

The Background enables Searle to say how it is that we use language without applying or even consciously knowing the complex rules that govern speech acts. It also explains how so much of what we do as social beings in a social environment comes to be as automatic as what we do naturally as physical beings in a physical environment. But the notion of the Background raises a number of issues we need to note to better understand it.

The most pressing issue is that the Background's explanatory power, especially regarding our use of language, looks suspiciously opportune because it explains so much. One immediate question that arises is how the diverse nonintentional capacities that are somehow "in" the Background are stored and activated. The inclination is to think of Background capacities as dispositions, to obviate the need to postulate some sort of neural "database" functioning in some mysterious way. In fact, Background capacities raise many of the same problems dispositions raise, problems that began with Locke's and others' reliance on the elusive notion of a "power" (Locke 1975, 233–87).

At base, a disposition is a way of attributing a capacity without attributing present behavior to an organism or a thing. We can and do readily say that sugar dissolves in water even though no sugar is dissolving in water at the time; we can and do readily say that someone is aggressive when the person in question is sound asleep, or that someone speaks French while he or she is speaking English or not speaking at all. What is more problematic is whether in attributing dispositions we attribute existent behavior-causing states. In the case of sugar, we understand a good deal about sugar's chemical composition and why it dissolves in water; in the case of persons, the matter is less clear whether attribution of dispositions entails attribution of persistent though sometimes inactive nondispositional states. D. M. Armstrong argued against Gilbert Ryle's wholly behaviorist attribution of dispositions that having a disposition entails having a nondispositional state that on occasion causes the relevant behavior (Armstrong 1968, 85–88). Putnam comments that dispositions have been particularly problematic since the 1950s: "For some philosophers dispositions are simply part of 'the furniture of the universe'; for others, the use of a dispositional notion in a philosophical analysis is a sign of . . . willingness to 'explain the obscure by the still more obscure'" (Putnam 1987, 23).

Another way of eliciting the difficulties with dispositions is to ask what we are to say about the truth of counterfactual conditionals such as "If this cube of sugar were in water it would dissolve" (Putnam 1987, 9–12). Aside from what we might say about structural dispositions, like sugar's solubility, something like speaking Spanish is not a "strict" disposition that is enacted "no matter what" (Putnam 1987, 9). Someone capable of doing so may, in fact, never speak Spanish after learning it and retain the capacity to do so.

Whether or not we think of them as dispositions, Searle's Background capacities raise similar questions. As Putnam might put it, it seems that to assign an ability, such as using language without following rules, to the Background is to explain the obscure with the more obscure. For one thing, the capacities that Searle consigns to the Background are immensely diverse. Some Background capacities have to do with physical movement, others with interpretation, others with language use, still others with etiquette. How are these kinds of capacities differentiated in the Background? Or are all Background capacities of a kind? On Searle's own principles, Background capacities ultimately must be states or properties of the brain, so the variety of capacities is a serious one; it is not easy to imagine how brain states might be sufficiently differentiated to account for that variety. In fact, we cannot even be sure that asking questions about storage is acceptable; for instance, is doing so to wrongly reify the Background, making it a kind of neural storehouse? But if the Background is not ultimately a neural storehouse, then what is it? Is it, like intentionality, an irreducible property of some matter?

Clearly, we are capable of doing a great deal that does not require reflection or intentional thought, such as catching a ball tossed to us or getting a joke, but it does not seem helpful to be told that we have a host of innate and acquired nonintentional Background capacities. For one thing, that we learn how to do some things by first attending carefully to what we do and then slowly cease to attend to what we do when we become adept at doing it does not require introduction of a Background as a collection of capacities. Introducing a Background seems counterintuitive; our capacities vary so much that it seems wrongheaded to attempt to gather them as units of a collective. Consider that a fair number of our capacities, like riding a bicycle or playing tennis, are explained in terms of "muscle memory," and so the acquisition of nonintentional capacities, but other capacities, like being bilingual or getting jokes, seem to retain an intentional aspect, so it is difficult to understand how they could become nonintentional capacities. It is at least very difficult to draw a line between nonintentional capacities and their intentional actualization. Nonetheless, Searle is clear, "An Intentional state only determines its conditions of satisfaction – and thus only is the state that it is . . . against a Background of practices and preintentional assumptions that are [not] themselves Intentional states" (Searle 1987, 19).

The Background is not introduced to explain only or even primarily how we manage to implement the rules of language without even knowing them as rules; it is introduced as an integral and fundamental part of an account of mind and intentionality. Given the chronology of Searle's work, it is hard to imagine that his development of the idea of a collection of nonintentional capacities did not arise from his need to explain nonintentional implementation of linguistic rules. If this is so, it could be that the notion of the Background was expanded in a problematic and ultimately counterproductive manner as Searle developed his account of mind.

Just as the Background is central to Searle's philosophy of mind and to his account of language use, the notion of collective intentionality is central to his account of social institutions. However, collective intentionality is primarily an integral element of his philosophy of mind. Searle claims that "[m]any species... engage in cooperative behavior [and] share intentional states" (Searle 1995, 25). He seems to mean that we individually share intentional states quite literally, considering the care he takes to deny that he is arguing for some sort of collective consciousness. Collective intentionality is a rather puzzling notion, as I try to show later, but Searle is unequivocal about it, maintaining that, like intentionality, "[c]ollective intentionality is a biologically primitive phenomenon that cannot be reduced to... something else" (Searle 1995, 24). Nor can collective intentionality be understood as the mere coincidence of individuals' intentions. Individual intentions and collective intentions are different things: "In addition to singular intentionality there is also collective intentionality" (Searle 1995, 23).

Searle (1995, 41) considers collective intentionality fundamental to the creation and maintenance of social reality and to how it supervenes on brute physical reality: "The central span on the bridge from physics to society is collective intentionality." Collective intentionality enables social reality through the "collective imposition of function on entities that cannot perform those functions without that imposition." That is, social reality comes to be and is sustained in a world of physical states of affairs by "the imposition of a collectively recognized status to which a function is attached." What this amounts to is that we communally confer special status on various things like pieces of engraved paper and colored lights at street corners, which then count as components in various practices such as the use of currency and the control of traffic. For all of these practices to work, we must jointly intend and accept that a piece of engraved paper is a five-dollar bill exchangeable for goods and that we must stop at a red light at an intersection. However, Searle's view is that it is insufficient if each of us individually intends these things, and that just as team members have a collective intention to win the game, we have collective intentions about currency, traffic regulations, marriage, government, and everything else that makes society work.

Not only is collective intentionality not just coincidence of intentions, it is not just the sum of individuals' own intentional states and their beliefs about others' intentions. Collective intentionality is a defining trait of our and other species that enables sustainable and stable con-specific cooperative behavior. But Searle rejects the idea that collective intentionality is or entails some sort of "Hegelian world spirit, a collective consciousness, or something equally implausible" (Searle 1995, 25). He argues that in conceptualizing this basic condition of social reality, we are not limited to choosing "between reductionism, on the one hand, or a super mind floating over individual minds, on the other." So collective intentionality is neither just individuals' intentions and related beliefs, nor some Platonic consciousness in which we participate. Somewhat like the Background, then, the question arises as to just what we are talking about when we talk about collective intentionality as a feature of minds/brains.

Collective intentionality is what makes expressions like "we intend" and "we are doing so-and-so" literally true descriptions, rather than their being shorthand references to individuals' intentions and beliefs. Searle denies that "because all intentionality exists in the heads of individual human beings, the form of that intentionality can make reference only to the individuals in whose heads it exists" (Searle 1995, 25). Therefore, even though "all my mental life is inside my brain, and all your mental life is inside your brain," it does not follow "that all my mental life must be expressed in the form of a singular noun phrase referring to me" (Searle 1995, 25–26). Again like the Background, collective intentionality raises suspicions precisely because of how much it explains.

Collective intentionality is puzzling not only because of questions about its precise nature, but also because it appears redundant. In the case of the Background, Searle can be read as only giving an umbrella name and description to our ability to do all manner of things, from learning to manipulate things around us, to using language without consciously applying its rules. While he seems on the verge of reifying a too-diverse compilation of capacities, he does not quite do so. In the case of collective intentionality, though, Searle claims that we do not just share intentions with others, but actually have collective or communal intentions, and describes our doing so as a biologically primitive attribute we share with other species (Searle 1995, 23). We are very familiar with saying that we, as a group, intend this or that, and that they, as a group, intend this or that, but it is not at all clear that when we do so we are attributing something that is other than the individual intentions we each possess. Introduction of the Background prompts the thought, Yes, we do have many nonintentional capacities that are unreflectively exercised, and perhaps we need a unifying concept to describe that we do. But introduction of collective intentionality seems to prompt the thought, Of course we share intentions, but that doesn't mean we have both individual *and* collective ones.

We need to pursue this matter because of the claimed importance of collective intentionality to social reality, and because of how problems with collective intentionality reflect on Searle's relational conception of truth and realism as these apply to social reality. The key point is that Searle allows that "[t]he content of the individual intentionality...may vary from the content of the collective intentionality" (Searle 1995, 38). This is something that Searle must allow, but it raises questions about the relation between individual and collective intentions. Consider a simple example turning on only one collective intention: Jack and Jill are taking a walk. As a couple, they have the collective intention to do so, and it is that social-institution-supporting collective intention that makes it the case that Jack and Jill are engaging in the social practice of taking a walk together, as opposed to merely walking side by side as one might walk side by side with a stranger on the street. And note that speaking to one another does not suffice to make walking side by side into taking a walk together. One might speak to a stranger or even a friend that one is keeping pace with, and not be taking a walk with that person.

Along with the walk-enabling collective intention, Jill also has the individual intention to get to know Jack a little better, and along with the walk-enabling collective intention, Jack has the individual intention to ask Jill to dinner. However, after walking together for a time, something Jack says makes Jill realize that he is the person who offended a friend of hers. Jill's interest in Jack cools, and she suggests they head back. Consider, now, that at the point when Jill's attitude toward Jack changes and she suggests they head back, she ceases to have the collective intention to be taking a walk with Jack and is then merely walking alongside him as they return to their starting point. It must be possible for Jill to cease to have the collective intention, else it becomes wholly mysterious how persons have collective intentions along with their individual ones, as Searle insists they do. Jack, only vaguely aware of the change in Jill, still has his individual intention to invite Jill to dinner. The question is whether he can still have the collective intention to be taking a walk with Jill, since he has not changed his mind about doing so. The problem is that if Jack retains the collective intention, it collapses into an individual intention, since it cannot be a collective intention if only Jack has it. But if the collective intention does collapse in this way, it seems that the only thing that made it a *collective* intention was that Jack and Jill shared it. We are left wondering, then, just how collective intentions differ from coincident individual intentions, especially if the intentions coincide because of prior agreement.

Again, consider a variation of Searle's own example of football players executing a pass play. His point is that "I might be blocking the defensive end, but I am blocking only as part of our executing a pass play" (Searle 1995, 23). But while this is certainly correct, it cannot be so on the basis of so many individual intentions to execute a pass play. Searle holds that it is only given the collective intention to execute a pass play that an individual player can intend to block the defensive end, and succeed in blocking the defensive end, as opposed to merely getting in the way as a spectator might do. Imagine now that some players decide that the pass play is not going to work and abandon their individual intentions to execute it. Though the collective intention likely would survive one or two players ceasing to intend to execute the play, it is a peculiar but inescapable question how many players could change their individual intentions and the collective intention still survive. As in the case of Jack and Jill, it is difficult to see how collective intentions are had by persons over and above their having coincident individual intentions. It is even more difficult to see what is the case when someone no longer shares a collective intention because of a change of individual intentions, yet is still in some sense participating in the relevant activity. Consider also, as I do in the next section, that Searle might be driven to attribute collective intentions despite *none* of the participants in an activity having the relevant individual intentions.

The significance of the foregoing examples is that it is too unclear how attributions of collective intentionality are true, and, given Searle's position on truth, what it is that they correspond to when they are true. This is a serious matter; considered together, Searle's realist-derived relational conception of truth and his insistence on the irreducibility of collective intentions demand clarification as to what states of affairs make attribution of collective intentionality true.

Another aspect to note regarding how attributions of collective intentionality might be true is that they must be quite shallow to capture collective intentions that can supervene on and be compatible with diverse individual intentions. In Searle's own example, for instance, aside from the collective intention to execute a pass play, each player's individual intentions will differ in that one may intend to execute a pass play just to win the game, another may intend to execute a pass play to show teammates that he or she is a valuable player, and still another may intend to execute a pass play to gain the adulation of the fans. Attribution of collective intentionality, then, must always be couched in narrowly specific terms to avoid conflicts with individual intentions, and this suggests that the content of attributions of collective intentionality may be quite thin. This is one more reason to wonder how attributions of collective intentionality are true and what they are true of.

Searle's "biological naturalism" is as difficult to make out precisely as is his idea of collective intentionality (Searle 1999, 54). In his philosophy of mind, Searle is concerned to show it is the brain that thinks, has experiences, believes, anticipates, fears, and so on, and not a substantive mind that is something other than the brain. Searle rejects dualism, but at the same time he also rejects the reduction of consciousness to behavior or mere brain activity. For Searle, consciousness itself is inherently and irreducibly intentional brain activity. His objective is to articulate a philosophy of mind that "does not commit one to the view that there is some class of mental entities lying outside the physical world," but also a philosophy of mind that "does not deny the real existence . . . [of] mental phenomena" (Searle 1987, 263). As we have seen, this balancing act raises serious problems about what it is that true sentences about irreducibly mental collective intentions describe or correspond to in being true – or, in Searle's language, what objective states of affairs make those sentences true. For instance, these sentences are not true of so many causal processes in the brain. Searle's commitment to the objective reality of intentional mental states as irreducible properties of brains leads him to oppose cognitivism or the view that mental activity is like a program running on an organic computer. It is not scientifically accessible brain activity, then, of which attributions of intentional states are true.

In this connection, the best-known argument Searle presents against cognitivism is the famous – some would say infamous – Chinese room thought experiment alluded to earlier. The thought experiment has an individual ignorantly converting from a set of Chinese symbols to a set of English symbols purely by matching symbols from one set with symbols in the other set according to an equivalence table. The point of the thought experiment is to demonstrate that "syntax is not the same as, nor is it by itself sufficient for, semantics" (Searle 1992, 200). We cannot get meaning out of rule-governed syntactical manipulation of symbols. The person in the Chinese room receives expressions couched in one symbol set or language, and produces equivalent expressions in another symbol set or language by following conversion rules. But since *ex hypothesi* the person does not know one or even both of the languages, he or she effects the conversion without understanding the content of the input or output expressions. The person's matching activity is precisely like a translation program running on a computer. Despite successful translation, there is no understanding of the content of the expressions translated.

As with the Background and collective intentionality, Searle's biological naturalism raises worrying questions. One is that in order to walk a fine line between dualism and reductive materialism, he has to maintain the causal efficacy of phenomenal experience – that is, what we experience has to be part of what makes us do what we do; behavior cannot be the product only of brain events lacking subjective content. At present, experience is usually discussed in terms of the nature, presence, absence, and efficacy of "qualia," which are defined as "the ways it feels to see, hear and smell, the way it feels to have a pain: more generally, what it's like to have mental states." In short, qualia are "experiential properties of sensations, feelings, perceptions" (Guttenplan 1996, 514). Many, if not most, contemporary philosophers of mind see phenomenal properties as incidental to behavior-producing brain activity. But Searle cannot allow qualia or experience, our very subjectivity, to be an inefficacious by-product. The difficulty he faces is that there is nothing incoherent about individuals who speak and behave in perfectly normal ways and lack qualia or phenomenal experience – so-called philosophical "zombies." Since neither the presence nor the absence of qualia can be discerned by observing behavior or even measuring brain activity, Searle cannot exclude the logical possibility that some of us who speak and act normally actually lack phenomenal experience, and he acknowledges this point (Dennett 1991; Searle 1992, 42–43).

Searle devotes a good deal of effort to rebutting the view that phenomenal experience can be reduced to brain activity or considered inefficacious, particularly in the first five chapters of *The Rediscovery of the Mind* (Searle 1992, 1–126). Intentional consciousness, complete with what it feels like to be aware, is irreducible for Searle, and his biological naturalism is defined by his claim that consciousness so conceived is a biological process like digestion. For him, then, phenomenal experience cannot be merely a subjectively interesting but impotent side effect. But given concession of the possibility of zombies, questions about truth arise again.

Searle's claim that intentional, phenomenally qualified consciousness is a biological process like digestion, but not reducible to brain activity, leaves us wondering just what it is in the physical world that makes true attributions of intentional conscious states to brains. Nor is this to impose some dubious metaphysical or ontological requirement on Searle. By his own principles, attributions of intentional consciousness are true in virtue of objectively real properties, just as attributions of digestion are true in virtue of ongoing peristalsis, breakdown of complex carbohydrates, and so on. But attributions of intentional consciousness are not true of brain events per se, since reductivism is precluded. So what is the "fact" to which a true attribution corresponds? The snag is an ancient one: we can only access our own intentional states, so if we deem attribution of intentional states to others to be true, it must be on their say-so, because access to their brain activity does not yield direct evidence of intentional states.

The picture that emerges of Searle's philosophy of mind, and his philosophy of language, is that we are material beings who have irreducible intentional or mental states as an inherent and defining part of our nature. In addition, we are able to perform speech acts that are meaningful to ourselves and to others in virtue of our utterances and inscriptions being intentional in a derivative way. We represent things, events, and experiences to ourselves and are able to communicate those representations. Much of what we do requires enabling Background capacities, because we act and communicate without consciously applying rules that govern our activities.

Mind, then, is some matter – human brains and perhaps others – thinking, representing, intending, and communicating. The philosophy of language is part of the philosophy of mind because it explains how mind communicates the representations that make up our sentience. Though Searle's temporal analytic progression was from language to mind, the logical progression is from mind to language. Searle's philosophy of mind explains how some matter is intentionally conscious and, given that consciousness, his philosophy of language explains how mind's internal representations are externalized and conveyed to others as meaningful utterances. In this way, Searle's philosophy of mind is intended to explain how irreducible intentional consciousness is a material property, and his philosophy of language is intended to explain how meaning supervenes on physical reality. What emerges, though, is that, on the one hand, Searle's realism and relational conception of truth require that true beliefs and sentences about intentional states and communicative intentions are true in virtue of depicting objective states of affairs, but on the other hand, it remains unclear just what those states of affairs actually are, since they cannot be "mere" brain activity. This lack of clarity leaves us with tough questions regarding precisely what true beliefs and sentences about Background capacities and collective intentions correspond to or, in Searle's terms, precisely what makes them true.

Social Reality

Paralleling Searle's rejection of mental/physical dualism is his rejection of cultural/biological dualism. He argues that "[j]ust as mental states are higher-level features of our nervous system, and consequently there is no opposition between the mental and the physical . . . so there is no opposition between culture and biology; culture is the form that biology takes" (Searle 1995, 227). The cultural form biology takes is, in greatest part, our social institutions. These collectively are our social reality: a multilayered, complexly interrelated structure of practices and resulting institutions that constitute a reality for us as real as the physical environment.

The question Searle sets himself is how there is "an objective world of money, property, marriage, governments, elections . . . games . . . and law courts in a world that consists entirely of physical particles" (Searle 1995, xi). His answer is that we are capable of communally creating and sustaining institutional facts or the elements of social reality, and thereby of manufacturing a social environment. Using Searle's own terminology, Matson succinctly articulates how social reality is constructed: "[C]ollective intentionality sets up constitutive rules that assign status-functions to things that do not exercise those functions by virtue of their intrinsic features" (Matson 2000, 593). In other words, we fabricate an edifice of institutional facts on a foundation of brute physical facts by communally deciding that certain things will play certain roles in certain practices. Searle's formula for this is "X counts as Y in context C" (Searle 1995, 28). A thing, event, or action comes to count as something else with a certain status in a certain type of situation when we collectively intend that it do so.

A simple example of how the X-counts-as-Y-in-C formula works is the way a carved piece of wood (an X) counts as a knight (a Y) in a particular context (C), the game of chess. There is nothing about the piece of wood's own properties, like its weight or color, that enables it to capture a pawn or check a king. What happens is that we collectively develop and articulate the constitutive rules that define chess and the knight's role in chess, and assign a status function to a certain piece of wood that then is moved on a board in rule-bound ways with various rule-determined consequences. Moreover, application of the formula is recursive. For instance, the winning of a game of chess may be a new X that counts as a new Y (the winning of a tournament) in a new context C (a competition for the status of grand master). Just as the collectively intended rules define the game of chess and assign status functions to pieces of wood, collective intentions also define a chess-playing hierarchy and assign a status function to the winning of a certain number of games under certain conditions.

Social reality is a vast compilation of practices; it is a complex structure of institutional facts in which things like slips of engraved paper count as currency, recitations of formulaic expressions count as binding pronouncements, and inscriptions of names count as signing contracts. In being assigned their diverse status functions, slips of engraved paper, formulaic expressions, and inscription of names, enable us to buy breakfast, marry someone, or buy a car. For Searle, the key to all this is collective intentionality. He believes that collective intentionality explains how pieces of wood or paper, recitations, and inscriptions come to play the roles they play, how they continue to play those roles, and how the uses of those pieces, recitations, and inscriptions have the consequences that they have.

What is new and unique to Searle's account of social reality is that assigning functions and constitutive rules requires collective intentions. Individual intentions, attendant individual beliefs, and the momentum of an ongoing practice do not suffice to create and sustain institutional facts; the intentions that create and sustain institutional facts must be collective to produce the elements of social reality. A complication is that the collective intentions that produce social reality are very numerous and complexly interdependent. For example, the collective intention of executing a pass play depends on many other collective intentions obtaining at various levels. Executing a pass play is nested in the collective intentions to win a game, to win a series, and to win a cup. But there are many other enabling collective intentions, like an inflated pigskin counting as a football, chalk lines on the grass counting as the boundaries of legitimate play, two groups of people counting as competing teams, and so on. Still other collective intentions enable spectators to pay admission, referees to govern playing, and, more fundamentally, spectators and players to engage in an activity that is at once cooperative and competitive.

Social action clearly presupposes a vast network of intentions and institutions, but it is not immediately clear that it helps to add collective intentions to the mix. The trouble is that the sheer volume of what supposedly is collectively intended in the maintenance of and participation in social institutions precludes that the collective intentions that enable, say, buying breakfast or casting a vote could be conscious. At the same time, it is not evident how collective intentions might be unconscious or implicit and still be collective *intentions*. It is unclear, then, how sharing unconscious collective intentions differs from people simply engaging in practices to which they contribute only as participants rather than as enablers. Moreover, Searle claims that anything that is unconscious is in principle accessible to consciousness (Searle 1992, 151–73). Any one of us, then, ought to be able to reflect on, to bring to consciousness, the shared collective intention to have pieces of engraved paper count as currency or birth within certain boundaries count as being a citizen of a given country. Nor can we assimilate collective intentions to Background capacities, instead of making them unconscious, because Background capacities are precisely nonintentional capacities and collective intentions, like individual intentions, are irreducibly intentional.

It might be thought that not all members of a society need to have the relevant enabling collective intentions; perhaps most of us function only with our individual intentions and unknowingly avail ourselves of social institutions enabled by fewer than all or even most members of our society. However, this is only an apparent solution. Consider cases where there is collaborative activity unrecognized as such by the majority of participants. An example was the Manhattan Project. In Searle's view, it would seem that everyone contributing to the atomic-bomb project had the collective intention to produce an atomic bomb or, at least, some new sort of weapon. Yet, as Matson remarks, "most of the proles at Oak Ridge were as astonished as everybody else at the news of Hiroshima" (Matson 2001, personal correspondence). The reason was that, for security reasons, most participants in the Manhattan Project did not know what the project was all about or what others in the project were doing. The Manhattan Project was a dramatic instance of cooperative activity where the participants did not share a collective intention, and, as such, it seems to constitute a serious counterexample to Searle's claims.

Searle contends that a player blocks an opposing player only as part of the team executing a pass play, that is, given the collective intention to execute a pass play. Are we to accept that unknowing technicians at Oak Ridge worked out equations, say, as part of creating an atomic bomb – that is, with the collective intention of creating an atomic bomb – despite having no knowledge of the project's goal? If we cannot attribute a collective intention in cases like the Manhattan Project, or can attribute a collective intention to the group only in virtue of a few in charge of the project having the intention, precisely what is it we are attributing when we attribute collective intentionality?

A way out of this problem, and perhaps also the Jack and Jill one, is to say that collective intentionality is "layered," that it has different levels. That is, it may be argued that in some cases, like executing a pass play, the collective intention is manifest to observers and shared by all participants. In more complex cases, like the Manhattan Project, the collective intention is attributable to a group, but is fully attributable only to some members of that group, and is attributable to others only partially or derivatively. The latter might be supported by arguing that individuals employed by an institution share some very general collective intention to further the institution's work. The layering, then, might be explained in terms of other collective intentions that are operant and are not themselves attributable only partially or derivatively. However, the difficulty with this line of argument is that it makes collective intentionality considerably more complex and elusive, thus raising again the question of its explanatory value. Worse still, it seems to reduce Searle's claim that collective intentionality is an irreducible, biologically primitive phenomenon to the much less philosophically interesting claim that many animals – including human beings – have the capacity for conspecific behavior.

Perhaps the most worrying obstacle to plausibly conceiving of collective intentionality as a necessary condition of coactive activity is the complexity of cases that must be covered. Searle's pass play example is plausible enough when cast in terms of individual and collective intentions; we readily understand how the players' individual intentions work with the putative collective intention. But paying for breakfast with a five-dollar bill is a matter of a different order. Consider the X-counts-as-Y-in-C collective-intention formula as it applies to the use of currency. The trouble is that for most people, dollars or euros or yen just are money. We learn how to use money by the time we are six or seven years of age, so it seems that as adults we do not intend, collectively or individually, that pieces of engraved paper count as dollars or euros or yen. In most cultures, the initial intention that pieces of fancy paper count as money surely is, in Searle's terms, a Background capacity for all but the very young who have to learn to buy and sell things along with how to talk and dress themselves.

The crux of the matter is that children are not taught to use money in terms of forming intentions other than to buy or sell something or make bank deposits and withdrawals. They are taught to use money as if currency's exchange value were an intrinsic property of the bills used. It is as if we can no longer separate out Searle's formula's Xs and Ys. Whatever collective intentions there may have been about pieces of engraved paper counting as currency seem to be on a par with the rules of speech acts. That is, it looks as if what is learned about money itself is learned in a tacit manner in the process of learning how to buy, sell, save, borrow, and invest. Just as we learn to use assertives and expressives in practice, and acquire the rules that govern them tacitly, we learn to use currency in particular cases, assimilating the rules for its use into Background capacities. We do not learn that engraved paper *counts* as money; we learn that engraved paper *is* money. The relevant collective intentions, then, seem to be pushed back into the same logical space occupied by, say, the social contract. That is, the collective intention that engraved paper counts as currency perhaps might best be thought of as like the social contract, as a useful myth that we tell to convey the gist of an otherwise lengthy explanation of how an entrenched practice originally developed. We might more plausibly explain the use of currency in terms of some individual who thought to give someone something in lieu of the cumbersome goods he or she was bartering, promising to later provide the goods in exchange for the "marker," and others following suit.

The first move, the provision of a marker, requires an individual intention that the marker represent the bartered goods, but following suit does not seem to require a collective intention or, for that matter, individual intentions about whatever is used as currency. All that is needed is invention by one and uptake on the part of many. Uptake does not require collective or even individual intentions about the particular new practice's elements. It requires only emulation, and for that it suffices that the emulators have individual intentions to do what they see others doing. They do not need intentions about something counting as currency; they only need intentions about trading some things for other things in accord with what they see others doing.

We have a relevant historical example of how this happens, one recent enough to have been documented: the complex institution of the stock exchange grew out of couriers congregating at a pub or coffeehouse and exchanging certificates there, rather than carrying the certificates from one bank to another. Here we can clearly visualize the first step as a couple of couriers exchanging the certificates each was carrying to the other's bank. The second or uptake step is just as easy to imagine, namely, other couriers thinking the exchange a great time-saver and following suit. In this connection, it is worth noting that Rorty, Dennett, and

Richard Dawkins all use the notion of uptake to explain the development
of culture through the propagation of new ideas, and none of them needs
collective intentionality to do so (Dawkins 1976, 206; Dennett 1991, 201;
Rorty 1991b, 4).

Given the foregoing, it merits stressing that my aim in this chapter is
to characterize Searle's general position. Critical comments on the Background and collective intentionality are intended to enhance exposition
by indicating the sorts of questions these notions raise, thereby clarifying
the notions. The aim is not to attempt to rebut Searle's claims.

Searle's accounts of language and social reality turn on what we, as conscious, representing, and intending entities think, say, and do. Language
and social institutions are produced and employed by us as intentional
beings engaged in the business of dealing with the world and each other.
Our agency is extremely complex. For Searle, everything we say and
every action we perform presupposes multiple collective and individual
intentions and equally numerous Background capacities enabling conformity to rules and procedures few of us are able to consciously apply or
even to articulate. The main problem, then, seems to be that in order to
explain complex behavior, Searle postulates an even more complex set of
enabling conditions. We end up with many, many Background capacities
of very varied sorts, and with many, many collective intentions that not
only are also of very varied sorts, but that seem to be integrated with one
another in very complex and diverse ways.

The requirement that we have both a large number of nonintentional
capacities and numerous collective intentions relates to the issues of truth
and realism as follows: First, according to Searle, realism is a condition of
intelligibility that underlies every Background capacity and every collective and individual intention. Second, truth applies every bit as much to
the constructed social world as it does to the extant physical world; there
is a way that things are, both in physical and in social reality, and in order
to function as we do, we must accept that things are one or another way in
both spheres. Additionally, contrary to some traditional epistemological
views, we are capable of discerning and knowing how things stand in both
the physical and social spheres. We now need to turn to a more detailed
examination of Searle's views on truth.

Truth and the World

The main objective in the previous sections was to sketch the highlights
of Searle's philosophical position. In this section, we need to focus more

closely on his conception of truth. This is best done by articulating a question that arises regarding Searle's notions of the Background and collective intentionality, on the one hand, and his claims about truth, on the other. Though more needs to be said about Searle's views on truth, enough has been said about his commitment to a relational conception of truth for us to consider the question often referred to above, that is, of precisely how sentences about the Background and collective intentionality are made true.

In proceeding to discuss Searle on truth, care must be taken to appreciate the relational nature of Searle's conception of truth without understanding that conception as correspondism, as I was inclined to do at one time and others have done (Fotion 2000, 233–36; Prado 2003a, 185–212). Searle accepts disquotation, as do most philosophers, but rejects the correspondence theory of truth as "absurd" (Searle 1995, 207). In an e-mail to me, he expresses his view as follows: "correctly interpreted, the correspondence theory is trivially true, indeed it is an extension of disquotation." However, what Searle thinks absurd about the traditional correspondence theory, that is, the requirement that we be able to "isolate [a] proposition and then compare it to reality" as if we were comparing two things, is problematic (personal correspondence). In my view, this is too literal an understanding of correspondence; nonetheless, it is why Searle does not consider himself a correspondist and may, in fact, not be a correspondist theorist in any philosophically exploitable sense (Fotion 2000, 233–36).

What matters here is that Searle's conception of truth is, as described above, *relational*; it is so in the sense that the truth of sentences depends on extralinguistic states of affairs: "Statements are made true by how things are in the world that is independent of the statement[s]" (Searle 1995, 219). The significance of the relational nature of Searle's conception does not have to do with arguing that he is, after all, a correspondist; it has to do with the contrast with Foucault's conception of truth.

To proceed, at its baldest the question that arises with respect to the Background and collective intentionality is this: how are claims and statements about the Background and collective intentionality true? If statements are made true by how things are in the world, what do we check to establish that such sentences are, indeed, true?

The reason the question arises in a pressing way is that possession of Background capacities seems to be, as noted earlier, possession of certain dispositions, and it is not altogether clear how assertions about dispositions are true. Moreover, collective intentions in many cases seem to collapse into dispositions, so the same question applies to collective intentionality.

To see the importance of this question, consider Tarskian renditions of each type of attribution. First, "'Ellen has the Background capacity to utter assertions' is true if and only if Ellen has the Background capacity to utter assertions." Second, "'Charles has the collective intention to execute a pass play' is true if and only if Charles has the collective intention to execute a pass play."

With respect to the first sentence, the attribution seems clearly to be a dispositional one. Ellen has uttered assertions in the past, may be doing so now, and is likely to do so in the future. We may tell a complicated story about how Ellen learned and internalized various speech-act rules, but there is no suggestion that in saying she has the capacity to assert things, we are saying that she knows the rules for uttering assertions and consciously follows those rules each time she asserts something. In fact, if Ellen were consciously following the rules, we likely would not say she has the capacity to assert things, because the sense in which we normally attribute the capacity is one that connotes competence. Otherwise we might say – of a two-year-old Ellen, for instance – that she is learning to make assertions and so acquiring the capacity.

It seems that all that Searle can point to, as the fact to which the attribution of the Background capacity corresponds, is just that Ellen has made assertions, may be doing so now, and will likely make assertions in the future. But unlike dispositions like solubility, there is nothing about Ellen's physical state that we can describe as that in virtue of which, given certain conditions, she can utter an assertion. One alternative is to say that we still do not know enough about the brain to say what is the case to enable Ellen to make assertions, but this is more evasion than explanation. Admittedly, Searle does not say that having a particular Background capacity is the presence of a particular state in the brain; however, his position does seem to entail that there is such a state.

Searle might argue that Ellen's dispositional behavior is all we need; that the fact to which the attribution corresponds is just Ellen's having uttered assertions, doing so now, and likely doing so in the future, but so arguing does not help, because if all that true attribution of a Background capacity corresponds to is Ellen's dispositional behavior, it makes saying that she has a Background capacity to utter assertions redundant and robs it of explanatory force.

The second sentence is somewhat trickier because Charles has both individual and collective intentions. He has the collective intention to execute a pass play, but in order to have that collective intention, not only does he have to have the individual intention to block one or another opposing player to do his part in executing the pass play, it seems he also has to have the individual intention – his own intention, as it were – to execute a pass play. That is, Charles's individual intention to block the defensive end requires that Charles also individually, as well as collectively, intend to execute a pass play. The collective intention to execute a pass play seems too general. It seems Charles must also individually intend to execute a pass play, to the extent that he intends to block the defensive end, because the collective intention to execute a pass play does not specify Charles's part in its execution, namely, blocking the defensive end.

Searle is rather quick about how individual and collective intentions relate to one another yet remain different. While individual intentions are just that, individually had, collective intentions must be communal, despite individuals possessing them. Searle's whole point is that each of us, as a member of a coactive group, has the relevant collective intention all the other members have, which makes the activity coactive. But it seems all we get hold of in describing "the fact" of a collective intention is individual intentions. As we saw in the case of Jill's change of mind, when Jill stopped having her individual intention to take a walk with Jack, the collective intention to take a walk together, which she and Jack initially shared, surely cannot survive her change of mind. It would be bizarre and certainly false to continue to attribute the collective intention to take a walk together to only Jack, so whatever fact the true attribution of the collective intention corresponded to, that fact evaporated with Jill's changing her mind. Nor would it help in these cases for Searle to argue that collective intentions, as intentional states, are irreducible to physical states, so that the facts that make their attribution true cannot be sought in the brain. The problem precisely is that while we know well enough what it is for individual intentions to exist as intentional states, it seems we do not know what it is for collective intentions to exist as intentional states.

As indicated above, the point here is not to attempt to rebut Searle's contentions; it is to explore questions in order to better understand those contentions. With respect to contentions about the Background and collective intentionality, the questions most relevant to the present project have to do with what it is that makes attribution of Background capacities and collective intentions true. What prompts these questions is the relational nature of Searle's conception of truth: true sentences are made true by how things are, rather than, as for Foucault, by discursive sanctions. We need, therefore, to look more closely at Searle's conception of truth.

Searle on Truth

As we have seen, Searle's position on truth is steadfastly relational; true sentences are true in virtue of how they relate to states of affairs; it is states of affairs or "facts" that make sentences true. Because of this, Searle may be thought to endorse the correspondence theory of truth, as I maintained elsewhere (Prado 2003a). But as noted, Searle rejects attribution of correspondism to himself, accepting correspondence only as trivially true and noting how few recent defenses of correspondism there are (Searle 1999, 168). He is trying to reject the hopeless idea that he thinks integral to the correspondence theory, which is that we should be able to compare sentences and states of affairs as discrete *relata*. Referring to the confirmation of a belief, Searle asks, "Do I hold the belief in my left hand and hold reality in my right hand and look to see if they correspond?" He adds, "That is not my picture at all." Where he does speak of beliefs and sentences corresponding to the facts, he remarks that establishing correspondence is applying disquotation: "The correspondence theory in action is applied disquotation" (personal correspondence).

I believe that Searle's characterization of the correspondence theory is tendentious. No correspondist I know of thinks that establishing correspondence is a matter of comparing beliefs or sentences and reality in the way Searle describes in the foregoing remarks and describing correspondence as "absurd" (Searle 1995, 207). However, this is not of immediate importance at this juncture, and I return to the point below. What is important here is the relational nature of Searle's conception of truth. True sentences may correspond to how things are only in a trivial sense, but they do relate to states of affairs; it is how things are that makes beliefs and sentences true. And though Searle may avoid the problems plaguing the traditional correspondence theory, he does face the problem of identifying just what it is that makes a belief or sentence true in the sense that Williams captures when he observes that "[t]here is no account of facts that at once is general enough" to enable us to clearly identify just what it is that true sentences relate or correspond to, and at the same time "does more than trivially reiterate the content of the sentences for which it is supposed to be illuminating the truth conditions" (Williams 2002, 65).

To continue clarifying Searle's conception of truth, it merits quoting at some length a number of things he says. The first is from the debate between Searle and Rorty. At one point Searle is trying to clarify the notion of a fact in response to Rorty's rejection of the correspondence theory of truth. Rorty basically argues that we do not understand the relation of correspondence and that the theory cannot handle negative facts. To clarify his own understanding of facts, Searle first states his view of truth:

Look, Aristotle said, "To state the truth is to say of that which is that it is and of that which is not that it is not." And that I take it is the first statement of the correspondence theory. . . . [T]he idea of the correspondence theory is that when you say something you will succeed in having said something true if independently of your having said it there is a way that things are in the world and you accurately report or state or describe or represent how they are. . . . [W]e didn't get the contemporary formulation of it, which is something like this: "A statement is true if it corresponds to the facts" [u]ntil recently.

To explain facts, or what it is that true sentences correspond to, Searle claims a certain novelty for the contemporary understanding of facts in explaining this recent formulation.

[W]e hadn't done this trick with this Latin verb *facere* whereby you make it into a noun, it means a doing, so the fact is the done thing and to say that the statement corresponds to the facts is to appeal to what in French would be the *fait accompli*, it is that which is done or established. I think that's the formulation, that a statement is true if it corresponds to the facts, that leads to a lot of these puzzles, because people then think we have two entities, we have the statement over here and the fact over there, and the statement over here is true because it corresponds to this complex object over there, and then they look for some kind of mirroring relation or some sort of matching relation.   (Rorty and Searle 1999, 34–35)

Searle then contends that

the puzzle about facts is strictly an artifact of a certain philosophical confusion. We have a noun, "fact," and so we think it must name a type of object. Whereas in fact, what the word "fact" evolved to do was to provide us with, so to speak, the nonlinguistic counterpart of true statements stated in language. So there has to be an exact match between true statements and facts for the trivial reason that the word "fact" evolved precisely to make that match, that is, the word "fact" evolved so that you would have a word for the nonlinguistic counterpart of the statement in virtue of which the statement is true.   (Rorty and Searle 1999, 35)

Whether or not these remarks are effective against Rorty's worries, and however suggestive they are that Searle is defending some form of correspondism after all, the remarks make clear that Searle's is a relational position. Searle is not making the mistake some make of thinking that the world contains facts along with everything else, or that reality comes parceled up in convenient cognitive or doxastic chunks. Nonetheless, that the word *fact* denotes "the nonlinguistic counterpart of the statement in virtue of which the statement is true" means that even if Searle does not invoke the correspondence theory in saying that a true statement "corresponds to the facts" in the first of the above quotes and elsewhere, it remains the case that sentences do relate to something other than themselves, where that something is not so many more sentences. This makes his view relational in just the way Foucault's is not.

However innocent of theoretical correspondence Searle's conception of truth may be, and however unwilling he is to reify facts, the relational nature of his conception of truth is evident in that he does not hold facts to be linguistic. The widespread view that facts are what true sentences state, rather than what they relate to, is unacceptable to Searle. He argues that it is "a use-mention fallacy to suppose that the linguistic . . . identification of a fact requires that the fact identified be itself linguistic in nature." Searle adds that since facts are what make sentences true, they cannot be "identical with their linguistic descriptions" (Searle 1999, 22). Since facts are what make sentences true, facts cannot be only what true sentences state.

The second passage that merits quoting at length amplifies some of the foregoing and affords a summary of Searle's position on truth. Searle describes the disquotation account as holding that "for any sentence s used to make a statement p, s is true if and only if p" (Searle 1995, 208). With respect to his claim that correspondence is trivially true, Searle maintains that the disquotation account and the correspondence theory, stated as "a statement p is true if and only if the statement p corresponds to a fact," actually are "at bottom the same, because if the sentence quoted on the left-hand side . . . is true, then it is true because it corresponds to the fact stated on the right-hand side" (Searle 1995, 208).

The proffered summary comprises nine items, but only four are immediately relevant to the present discussion. Of special import is Searle's notion of "fit":

1. "True" is the adjective for assessing statements (as well as, e.g., beliefs, that . . . have the mind-to-world or word-to-world direction of fit). Statements are assessed as true when . . . the way they represent things as being is the way that things really are.
2. The criterion of reliability is given by disquotation. This makes it look as if "is true" is redundant, but it is not. We need a metalinguistic predicate for

assessing success in achieving the word-to-world direction of fit, and that term is "true."

3. Statements are made true by how things are in the world that is independent of the statement[s]. We need general terms to name these how-things-are-in-the-world, and "fact" is one such term. Others are "situation" and "state of affairs."

4. Because statements determine their own truth conditions and because the term "fact" refers to that in virtue of which statements are true, the canonical way to specify the fact is the same as the way to specify the statement, by stating it.   (Searle 1995, 219)

The thrust of the first point is that when we judge a belief or sentence to be true, we judge it to accurately represent how things are. The question of "fit" has to do with whether the statement assessed is one that conforms to how things are, as in the case of a true description, or requires that something be changed to conform to the statement, as in the case of a command or desire. The second point tells us that the criterion of truth is given by disquotation; the sentence "'It is ten o'clock' is true if and only if it is ten o'clock" says what it means to say that the embedded sentence is true. In this connection, though, Searle rejects the idea that attributions of truth are redundant and that it suffices to assert the sentence described as true. His claim is that we require a metalinguistic term to acknowledge that a belief or sentence does portray how things stand.

However, this is not a simple observation about terminology; the thrust of the remark is rejection of the redundancy theory of truth. *The Cambridge Dictionary of Philosophy* tells us that "[a]ccording to Frege's so-called redundancy theory, corresponding instances of 'It is true that p' and 'p' have exactly the same meaning" (Audi 1996, 813). On the redundancy theory, saying "It's true that we landed on the moon" says nothing more than does "We landed on the moon." But Searle does not accept that predication of truth in sentences of the type "p is true" adds nothing to utterance of p, or that predicating truth of the embedded sentence is only reassertion of the embedded sentence. The reason is straightforward: if being true is corresponding to the facts, then saying that a sentence corresponds to the facts cannot be mere reiteration of the sentence in question, because it is the assertion that a relation exists between the sentence and a fact, and that is not part of the sentence's meaning. It must be possible to say that that relation exists, and that cannot be done by merely repeating true sentences. It is notable that this point is somewhat at odds with Searle's endorsement of disquotation. It is actually a point more in line with Foucault's views, for whom attribution of truth does more than reiterate the true sentence.

The third point again tells us that – contra Sellars, Davidson, and Rorty – beliefs and sentences are "made true by how things are in the world." They are made true by facts in the way that a painting is made a portrait by being a likeness of an actual person. The third point reiterates that the world is quite independent of all the beliefs and sentences that it makes true, and asserts that we require a way to refer to states of affairs in that world and that *fact* is a term that denotes states of affairs. It seems, then, that despite the remarks about the Latin verb *facere*, we are again being told that facts are extralinguistic; facts are how things stand, so true sentences relate to facts, rather than facts being what true sentences state. For Searle, then, phrases like "the facts," "states of affairs," and "how things are" are equivalent because they have a common referent, namely, how things stand in the world.

The fourth point is a little tricky. What must be kept in mind is that regardless of how often he speaks of statements corresponding to facts, Searle rejects both that facts are "in the world" and that facts are purely linguistic. He insists that "facts are not complex objects, nor are they linguistic entities; rather they are conditions, specifically, they are conditions in the world that satisfy the truth conditions expressed by statements" (Searle 1995, 211). "Conditions in the world," the conditions that "satisfy the truth conditions expressed by statements," are states of affairs in the objective world. The force of denying that facts are complex objects is that the objective world is not parceled up in compilations of things and events constituting facts *separate from* our designating some relatively temporary dispositions of parts of reality as specific states of affairs. It is *we* who delineate some aspect of how reality is disposed as "a fact" when we articulate a descriptive or demonstrative sentence. On the other hand, when we do articulate a descriptive or demonstrative true sentence, we are not simply creating a linguistic item; we are correctly describing or pointing to some part of reality.

This all makes clear that the problem some see in our inability to identify a fact independently of the sentence that states it is not seen as a problem by Searle. He notes that "statements determine their own truth conditions." That is, a sentence states what, if it exists, makes the sentence true. So rather than it being a problem that we cannot identify a given fact except with the sentence that it makes true, Searle maintains that "the canonical way to specify the fact is the same as the way to specify the statement, by stating it" (Searle 1995, 219). Here it is more evident why Searle sees disquotation and correspondence as coming to the same thing, and why he considers the correspondence account to be trivially true.

Searle offers a formula intended to capture how disquotation and correspondence essentially are the same. Despite his rejection of the correspondence theory as absurd, he describes his formula as "a version of the correspondence theory." The formula runs: "For any s, s is true if and only if s corresponds to the fact that p." Searle qualifies, though, by saying that the correspondence theory "is not an attempt to define 'true' without using other semantic notions" (Searle 1995, 203). The reason is that if offered as a definition, the theory would be circular.

What is of greatest relevance here is that while Searle rejects the idea of a relation between statements and facts as peculiar entities, he clearly posits a relation between beliefs and sentences and their objects, where those objects are states of affairs or "the facts." Recall that "[s]tatements are made true by how things are in the world." To say how things are in the world, we need to talk of facts; we need to talk about facts because we require "general terms to name these how-things-are-in-the-world, and 'fact' is one such term" (Searle 1995, 219). This is how reference to a fact is reference to "the nonlinguistic counterpart of the statement in virtue of which the statement is true" (Rorty and Searle 1999, 35).

In a similar way, the term *corresponds* is not one entailing a specific theoretical understanding of the relation between a true sentence and a fact. The term simply is, like *fact*, an ordinary word that refers to how a belief or sentence relates in such a way to some state of affairs that it is made true by articulating that state of affairs. Searle notes that as far as correspondence is concerned, to say a sentence corresponds to the facts "is just a shorthand for the variety of ways in which statements can accurately represent how things are, and that variety is the same as . . . the variety of assertive speech acts" (Searle 1995, 213). In brief, a sentence has truth conditions that must be satisfied for it to be true, and those conditions are satisfied when reality is so disposed that it contains a delineable state of affairs that satisfies the sentence's truth conditions. When this is the case, the sentence corresponds to that delineated state of affairs, and the sentence is true.

Searle's conception of truth, then, is fundamentally and inescapably relational in that truth is the correspondence of beliefs and sentences to "the facts." We are left with the question of just how his conception differs from the correspondence theory, and it is tempting to conclude that it does so only in virtue of Searle's caricaturizing the correspondence theory he rejects as requiring us to compare sentences and states of affairs as we would compare swatches of cloth. But again, the point here is not refutation but exposition.

To proceed, then, the question that arises is this, Regardless of how we might articulate correspondence, how *else* might truth be understood? It is, therefore, time to travel to the other end of the philosophical universe and consider Foucault.

3

Foucault

Discipline and Power

Foucault enjoys a degree of fame that extends well beyond the spheres of philosophy and history, the two disciplines that most justifiably can claim him as their own. James Miller says that "[a]t the time of his death. . . . Michel Foucault was perhaps the single most famous intellectual in the world" (Miller 1993, 13). Alan Ryan does not qualify, saying that at his death Foucault "was the most famous intellectual figure in the world" (Ryan 1993, 12). David Macey makes the more modest claim that Foucault "was without doubt France's most prominent philosopher," but adds that Foucault's international reputation "almost eclipsed his reputation in France" (Macey 1993, xi).

Foucault is a thinker whose canon was shaped by the work of Nietzsche and Heidegger, Husserl and Saussure. His intellectual growth took place in a context rich in philosophical alternatives, most of them influenced by Marxism. And as Searle was personally influenced by Austin, a major contributor to analytic philosophy, so Foucault was personally influenced by Canguilhem, an important contributor to Continental philosophy. These various influences prompt Hubert Dreyfus and Paul Rabinow to argue that to understand Foucault one must triangulate him among phenomenology, hermeneutics, and structuralism (Dreyfus and Rabinow 1983).

Foucault's thought and intellectual options were most immediately shaped by Merleau-Ponty's interpretation of Husserl's phenomenology, Gadamer's Heideggerian hermeneutics, and Lévi-Strauss's Saussurean structuralism. But what Dreyfus and Rabinow see as a fruitful intellectual environment, most North American analytic philosophers see as muddling currents ultimately more disruptive than productive of rigorous thought. They see Foucault's work as compromised by ideological and political factors and thus of little value or interest. This perception explains why Didier Eribon can observe in his biography of Foucault that though Foucault "drew huge crowds" on his visits to North America, he was "completely ignored by most American philosophers" (Eribon 1991, 313). But there is more at work here than indifference. Most analytic philosophers do not ignore Foucault's work because they see it as in a different canonical tradition or even because they think it is bad philosophy. They simply do not think Foucault's work *is* philosophy. If they consider it at all, they see his work as a kind of ideological history of no relevance to their own work (Miller 1993). For instance, with respect to the issue of truth, Robert Nola describes Foucault as having "nothing to say" about "philosophical theories of truth and knowledge" (Nola 1994, 3). Nola says this in spite of all that Foucault does say about truth and his explicit claim that no one could claim to be a philosopher if he or she "didn't ask . . . 'What is truth?'" (Foucault 1980b, 66).

More serious than indifference and neglect is that many analytic philosophers see Foucault as subverting philosophy because he expounds postmodern views that they consider inimical to intellectual inquiry. Rorty notes that "a distinguished analytic philosopher," who I understand was D. M. Armstrong, "urged that 'intellectual hygiene' requires one not to read . . . Foucault" (Rorty 1982, 224).

What the bulk of analytic philosophers most object to in Foucault's work are his relativism, his alleged irrealism, and his rejection of ahistorical rationality. But unlike most of his postmodern peers, who offer only criticism of traditional methods, objectives, and assumptions, Foucault's conception of power relations makes his relativism and his rejection of objective standards worthy of serious consideration. His is not only a dismissive critique of philosophical inquiry conceived as governed by ahistorical standards and capable of discerning conceptual truths, but also of scientific inquiry conceived as capable of limning objective empirical truths. In his genealogical analyses Foucault offers detailed accounts of the genesis of such conceptions as that of ahistorical truth and rationality, and of how they come to achieve their regulatory dominance. But Foucault is not concerned only to reject established ideas, though that is sometimes his aim. Instead he tries to "make visible" the interrelatedness, the mutually determining and enabling roles, of power and knowledge. He tries to show that rather than knowledge yielding power through accurate description and the enabling of manipulative control, "power perpetually creates knowledge and, conversely, knowledge constantly induces...power" (Foucault 1980b, 51).

The challenge Foucault's work poses is his account of how power relations define disciplines, their contents, and, above all, the procedural standards and practices of disciplines. That is why Arac says that "to defend a subject against Foucault requires redefining the subject" (Arac 1991, vii). What I hope to show is that Searle's defense of a relational theory of truth requires redefining the subject when one factors in Foucault's conception of truth. However, as noted at the outset, the scope of the present project limits what I can say about Foucault, just as it limits what I can say about Searle. What follows, then, is a series of highlights, and the reader is again urged to look at one or both of the books recommended earlier.

The Three Domains

Foucault's early work was structuralist in character despite his denials that he was ever a structuralist (Hoy 1986, 4). In his "Foreword to the English Edition" of *The Order of Things*, Foucault complains that "half-witted" commentators label him a structuralist, adding that he has been "unable to get it into their tiny minds" that he used "none of the methods, concepts, or key terms that characterize structural analysis" (Foucault 1973, xiv). However, these remarks are at odds with Foucault's own statement of purpose in *The Order of Things* (Foucault 1973, xx–xxii). Additionally, speaking of the reception of the book, Miller remarks that the reviewer for *L'Express* "never used the magic word 'structuralism' because she did not need to"; Foucault's "structuralist sympathies" are evident in his "system" talk and references to Lévi-Strauss (Miller 1993, 148). Perhaps Foucault could not countenance the idea that his work was derivative; this may have more to do with his dubious rejection of structuralism than the methods and terms he used at the time.

The Order of Things and *The Archaeology of Knowledge* certainly seem to be intended as contributions to a successor discipline to epistemology, which is precisely what structuralism was supposed to be (Dreyfus and Rabinow 1983; Hoy 1986). The key point regarding the undeniable structuralist elements in these two works is that, in both, discourse is conceived as determining cognitive and social practices, and the heart of structuralism is that language or linguistic structure determines both.

However, in the late 1960s, Foucault abandons the sort of theorizing that aims at discerning underlying determinants. He does so less explicitly than by a change of emphasis. Dreyfus and Rabinow say that earlier, Foucault "used variants of a strict analysis of discourse," but that particularly after 1968 "Foucault's interests began to shift away from discourse." He began to focus on power relations, which "had not been previously thematized" (Dreyfus and Rabinow 1983, 104). In *Power/Knowledge*, Foucault himself remarks that his earlier work lacked "the problem of 'discursive regime,' the effects of power" (Foucault 1980b, 105). In focusing on power, Foucault discards his inclination "to treat language as autonomous and as constitutive of reality," and so rids himself of the traces of idealism that "lurk in the structuralist suggestion that discourse organizes . . . all social practices and historical epochs" (Hoy 1986, 4).

Whether or not deemed to have been a structuralist at one time, Foucault is thought of as a *post*structuralist by most contemporary Europeans because of his move away from conception of discourse as the determinant of cognitive and social practices. The structuralists see cultural phenomena as determined by underlying formations or configurations best understood on the model of rule-bound systematic interrelations of signs. Contrary to this, the post-1968 Foucault sees cultural phenomena as the results of power relations. The structuralists see the individual subject as a product of constitutive logical relations. Most importantly, these relations are supposedly discernable and capable of being mapped, at least in principle. The post-1968 Foucault sees the subject as emerging from basically accidental discursive and behavioral practices and from equally fortuitous interaction with equally emergent others.

In the end, labels do little to promote understanding of Foucault's work. As Dreyfus and Rabinow rightly stress, Foucault is a truly innovative philosopher. And if the "structuralist" and "poststructuralist" labels are of limited consequence, it is more important to appreciate that facile characterization of Foucault as a Derridean deconstructivist is quite mistaken. Even describing Foucault as a postmodern calls for qualification, as will become clear as we proceed. In particular, Foucault does not share postmoderns' implicit or explicit irrealism.

With respect to his originality, perception of Foucault as a disciple of Nietzsche is also too simple, and it is prejudicial if used to dismiss Foucault on moralistic grounds or as too unrigorous to be taken seriously. It is with regard to truth that Foucault owes the most to Nietzsche, but the debt is primarily for the questions Nietzsche raises, rather than his positive views. Foucault acknowledges this, saying that his debt to Nietzsche has to do with the question of the value of truth: "What I owe Nietzsche, derives mostly from the texts of around 1880, where the question of truth, the history of truth and the will to truth were central to his work" (Foucault 1988a, 32; Allen 1993).

Whatever intellectual debts he may owe to Nietzsche, Heidegger, and others, Foucault is an original thinker whose stock-in-trade is the over-turning of accepted histories and "truths," and it is in so doing that he invites mischaracterization as a table-turning deconstructivist. In *Madness and Civilization*, Foucault's doctoral dissertation and first major work, he shows himself capable of disturbing novelty of thought by arguing that madness is an *invention* (Foucault 1965). He portrays psychiatric reforms, such as those of Tuke and Pinel, as an "insidious new form of social control" that created a class of malady and then assigned it a negative moral status (Miller 1993, 103, 113). In *Discipline and Punish*, Foucault recasts penal reform as the imposition of extensive manipulative control (Foucault 1979). And in *The History of Sexuality, Volume 1*, he rethinks nothing less than human sexuality as imposed or "deployed" subject defining and as regulating a large collection of interrelated practices and types of expertise (Foucault 1980a).

Unlike Searle's work, where the methodology remains constant and the stages in his thinking are defined by fairly specific questions and problems, Foucault's work is characterized by different approaches that themselves shape the questions and problems he addresses. Hinrich Fink-Eitel describes Foucault's career as divisible into four stages that corre-spond roughly to the 1950s, 1960s, 1970s, and 1980s. In the first stage, Foucault "was especially oriented to Heidegger's philosophy," and was engaged more in beginning to define himself than in contributing to one or another debate. In the second stage, Foucault "became an archae-ologist of knowledge and wrote a 'theoretical' philosophy of objective, autonomous . . . discourse and knowledge formation." This is the period during which Foucault is most reasonably read as a structuralist. In the third stage, Foucault focuses on "the genealogy of power." In the fourth stage, Foucault "became an ethical writer" (Fink-Eitel 1992, 72).

So long as we are careful not to take useful but rough distinctions too literally, we can set aside the first stage, during which Foucault was still forging his philosophical identity, and work with the other three stages, which Arnold Davidson calls "domains of analysis" (Davidson 1986, 221; Miller 1993, 37–65).

The first domain of analysis is *archaeology*, which most character-izes Foucault's earlier books, published from 1961 to 1969. The sec-ond domain is *genealogy*, which most characterizes the books published from 1971 to 1976. The third domain of analysis is *ethics*, which most characterizes Foucault's last two books, both published in 1984, the year of his death. (Note that "ethics" is used in a special sense by Foucault; his concern is with ethics as self-directed, not other-directed.)

Some think it is important not to think of these domains, especially the first two, as separate or as wholly superseding one another; Dreyfus and Rabinow emphatically insist that "[t]here is no pre- and post-archaeology or genealogy in Foucault" (Dreyfus and Rabinow 1983, 104). I think this somewhat problematic. Some set great store by Foucault's assessment of his philosophical progression, but that assessment tends to be overly optimistic regarding the continuity of his work and especially regarding his own reflective clarity on the integration of the problems he addressed. But our concern here is less with holistic exposition of Foucault than with understanding his views on truth. What is of greatest interest in the present context is the domain of genealogy, as that is where Foucault presents his most significant challenge to the traditional conception of truth. How genealogy relates to archaeology and ethics is not of immediate concern. As for genealogy, it can best be situated relative to archaeology by citing Arnold Davidson's succinct descriptions of these two domains. He describes archaeology as analysis of "systems of knowledge" and genealogy as analysis of "modalities of power" (Davidson 1986, 221). Foucault himself offered something like this characterization with specific reference to the social sciences, saying that his work included investigation of forms of inquiry "which try to give themselves the status of sciences," and investigation of "the objectivizing of the subject" (Foucault 1983, 208–9).

The shift from archaeological analysis, in which discourse is deemed to shape practice, to genealogical analysis, in which discourse and practice are deemed to shape one another, is best understood by asking what question the concept of power or power relations is an answer to, what problem it solves. Putting things very simply, what Foucault eventually found inadequate in his own earlier views, and in structuralism, was conception of discourse's determination of cognitive and social practices as unilateral and asymmetrical. His break with whatever structuralist ideas he held and used came with realization that cognitive and social practices have a reciprocal influence on discourse. The concept of power or power relations explains that reciprocal influence. To better convey how this works, and to attempt to do some justice to a salient aspect of Foucault's thought, I consider archaeology briefly in the next section, before turning to genealogy and what is most relevant to the contrastive comparison with Searle on truth.

Archaeology

Foucauldian archaeology is a form of inquiry focused on the human sciences as systems of knowledge. It is a critical investigation of disciplinary systems of knowledge with the goal of understanding the discursive practices that produce and sustain those systems of knowledge. The archaeologist's interest is in disciplinary discourse, in expert pronouncements and idioms. To appreciate the point, though, it must be kept in mind that, for Foucault, disciplines and disciplinary discourses are systems of control as well as fields of study.

Concern with expert pronouncements and idioms involves understanding how they constitute disciplines or learned practices and how they shape the behavior of their participants. But archaeological investigation proceeds without concern as to whether what its target systems "say is true, or even . . . make sense." Archaeology "must remain neutral as to the truth and meaning of the discursive systems it studies." It is concerned with mapping "all disciplines with their accepted concepts, legitimized subjects, taken-for-granted objects, and preferred strategies, which yield justified truth claims" (Dreyfus and Rabinow 1983, xxiv). Archaeology's aim is not to assess the truth of claims made in knowledge-systems, but to understand how those claims come to be claims in knowledge-systems and how some of them come to constitute knowledge within those systems. There is no attempt to confirm or disconfirm the claims themselves, as the archaeological enterprise is a metasystemic one.

As to how archaeology actually works, "[a]rchaeological comparison does not have a unifying but a diversifying effect" (Foucault 1972, 159–60). That is, archaeology may unearth hidden similarities in and between systems of knowledge, but primarily it undermines accepted continuities. Archaeology is diversifying in the sense that it disrupts conventional views. It is comparative, but its focus is differences between established systems of knowledge and superseded or suppressed ones. Archaeology also has a diversifying effect in that it deliberately tries to fracture the smooth totality of disciplines' pictures of themselves and of their histories. The objective is to unearth, to excavate factors such as overlooked discontinuities, disruptions, anomalies, and suppressed items in disciplines and their fields and histories; the aim is to yield a new picture of what has previously been taken as definitive knowledge in the target disciplines.

The archaeological Foucault is most concerned with exhuming the hidden, the obscure, the marginal, the accidental, the forgotten, the overlooked, the covered-up, the displaced. His subjects for investigation, then, are whatever is taken as most natural, obvious, evident, undeniable, manifest, prominent, and indisputable. Foucault relies on detailed empirical research to supply the material to implement his basic strategy, which is to retell the history of a discipline or institution or practice. He highlights and connects previously marginal and obscured elements and events, and presents a different picture of that discipline, institution, or practice. In archaeology, Foucault's targets are disciplines or sciences, but he does not engage in abstract debate about operant theories. Instead he probes key elements of the subject matters and procedures of established disciplines. Instances of his early targets are psychiatric conception of madness and establishment and use of the asylum, and medicine's conception of illness and establishment and use of the clinic.

The diversifying effect of archaeological investigation is not limited to particular disciplinary practices. It is also operant on a grander scale in mapping what Foucault calls *epistemes*. These are the conceptual frameworks or dominant paradigms of an epoch or culture. *Epistemes* are holistic frameworks that define disciplinary problems and the nature of their potential resolutions; *epistemes* constitute views of the world comprising the most fundamental identificatory and explanatory notions.

An example of different *epistemes*, and of the shift from one to another, is found in *The Order of Things*. There Foucault discusses the difference between the "Renaissance" and "Classical" conceptions of language, specifically the difference between "trinary" and "binary" conceptions of the relation of signs to what they signify. In the pre-Cartesian *episteme*, the conception of the relation between signs and what they signify was trinary in that the relation included the sign, the thing signified, and an assumed essential resemblance between them. This was a conception of language as naturally or intrinsically, rather than conventionally, related to its referents. It was a conception that distinguished among "that which was marked, that which did the marking, and that which made it possible to see in the first the mark of the second" (Foucault 1973, 64).

The resemblance between sign and thing signified, central to the Renaissance *episteme*, is a matter of signs being natural correlates of things rather than arbitrarily assigned labels. With Descartes, and we should add Locke, words and things "were separated from one another"; the idea of natural resemblance was abandoned. Though discourse "was still to have the task of speaking that which is, [it] was no longer to be anything more than what it said" (Foucault 1973, 43). The assignation of signs becomes wholly volitional and conventional, thus undercutting the *episteme* in which linguistic reference is enabled by intrinsic resemblance.

Moreover, Descartes makes assignation of signs contingent on an epistemologically problematic relation between ideas and their putative causes. Foucault concludes, therefore, that Descartes's binary conception of signification and isolation of consciousness means that "Hume has become possible" (Foucault 1973, 60).

Archaeology, then, is the investigation of discontinuities, and particularly those that reveal abandonment of one conceptual framework and the adoption of another. It also is the unearthing of abandoned frameworks and the comparing of them with presently dominant ones. It is the meticulous mapping of established and excavated frameworks with a view to understanding how they are produced and how they work. But as illuminating as any positive characterization of archaeology is one that says what happens when archaeology goes wrong. Archaeology goes wrong when it turns into a theory about how things are and pretends to transcend its historical place by claiming discovery of hidden determinants that underlie phenomena. These pretensions are what Foucault rejects in structuralism. When archaeology takes a structuralist turn, its focus is "deflected from an interest in the social practices that [form] both institutions and discourse to an almost exclusive emphasis on linguistic practices." One consequence is ill-conceived objectivization of discourse as the determinant of cognitive and social practices. Another is "neglect of the way discursive practices are themselves affected by the social practices in which they and the investigator are embedded," and this latter is what invites Foucault's conception of power relations (Dreyfus and Rabinow 1983, xii).

Foucault did, for a time, think archaeology capable of discerning underlying realities. He entertained the ambition to get beyond practices and construals to something primitive that underlies even discourse. In 1961, he wrote that we "must try to return to that zero point . . . at which madness is an undifferentiated experience" before it is shaped and categorized by discourse and practices (Foucault 1965, ix). This is the sort of remark that makes Rorty and others think Foucault was mistakenly trying "to make archaeology the successor subject to epistemology" (Hoy 1986, 3). But there is no trace of archaeology so conceived in *Discipline and Punish* and *The History of Sexuality*. In fact, by 1977 Foucault is scornful of his own earlier epistemological ambitions to "rediscover the things themselves in their primitive vivacity" (Foucault 1988a, 119).

To reiterate, archaeology is the detailed, descriptive, assessment-neutral investigation of disciplines and expert idioms, of "knowledge systems." It does not claim to get behind appearances to ahistorical determinants of these systems or of anything else. Archaeology aims to exhaustively track down and disinterestedly describe factors and events that enabled the emergence of the discipline or institution that is its subject of inquiry. It begins by discounting received opinion and proceeds by rendering problematic what is least questioned in a knowledge system and reconstruing the apparently obvious and natural as suspect. Archaeology next searches out the discontinuities that mark shifts between conceptual frameworks, inventorying the disparate and accidental elements that result in the formation of conceptual frameworks and in the acceptance of something as knowledge. In brief, archaeology offers a restructured history of its target disciplines or knowledge systems by redescribing their elements in light of data that "hardly anyone else . . . noticed" (Hacking 1981, 28). The result is "a reordering of events . . . not perceived before" (Hacking 1981, 29). The aim of the reordering is to lay bare "the empirical conditions under which [expert] statements come to be counted as . . . true" (Hoy 1986, 3). This is achieved by providing an alternative account in which the accepted truth of those expert statements is revealed as one possible set of construals rather than as the unique articulation of objective truth.

The heart of Foucault's archaeological and genealogical analyses is what Ian Hacking describes as an effort "to rethink the subject matter." In archaeological investigation, this means beginning "from the ground up, at the level of tiny local events where battles are unwittingly enacted by players who do not know what they are doing" (Hacking 1981, 29). Hacking does not mean that individuals do not know what they are doing in the sense of acting blindly or without thought. Foucault himself puts the point succinctly: "People know what they do; they frequently know why they do what they do; but what they don't know is what what they do does" (Dreyfus and Rabinow 1983, 187). In other words, individuals do not know the consequences of their actions on others' actions, and those consequences are determining influences on the development of archaeology's *epistemes* and genealogy's disciplinary techniques.

It may look to many readers that archaeology is the Foucauldian domain of analysis most pertinent to contrasting Searle and Foucault. Certainly archaeology is of greater interest than genealogy to analytic philosophers familiar with Foucault's work. Archaeology deals with, if not quite the justification of knowledge, then the origins of what is deemed knowledge (Machado 1992). For this reason, it is the part of Foucault's work that is closest to the interests of analytic philosophers and is both most accessible and appealing to those who do delve into his work. However, it is in Foucault's genealogical analytics that we find his most direct challenges to analytic philosophical assumptions and methodology. That is where we find truth, knowledge, and rationality reconceived as products of power, so that is where we find those Foucauldian views most opposed to Searle's own. Therefore, I turn now to a brief consideration of genealogy, the domain of analysis that Dreyfus and Rabinow define as Foucault's investigation of "that which conditions, limits, and institutionalizes discursive formations" (Dreyfus and Rabinow 1983, 104). Genealogy is the domain of analysis that reconceives truth as nonrelational, as wholly discursive, and as a product of power.

Genealogy

Nietzsche's inversion of the particular over the universal was a philosophical revolution as momentous as Kant's "Copernican" inversion of the subjective over the objective. Foucault emulates Nietzsche with three inversions of his own. He inverts the priority of the significance of the marginal over the ostensibly central, he inverts the priority of the constructed over the supposedly natural, and he inverts the priority of the accidental over the allegedly inevitable in originative accounts. These inversions constitute the core of what is novel in Foucault's thought.

Foucault develops Nietzsche's idea that history is misconceived as "an attempt to capture the exact essence of things," arguing that history is wrongly done if conducted as a search for "origins" in the sense of essential beginnings (Foucault 1971, 78). Genealogy is the alternative to history so conceived; genealogy "opposes itself to the search for origins" (Foucault 1971, 77). The heart of the idea is that there are no essences to be discerned behind historical developments, no essences that explain why things developed as they did. A paradigm of what genealogy opposes is the Augustinian view of history as recording a divinely scripted, teleological, and linear sequence of events. For Augustine, history is a scripted, unfolding story defined by a specific beginning (the Creation), a middle (the Incarnation), and an end (the Last Judgment). Any historical inquiry must be shaped and guided by recognition of the divine script or prove ineffective in discerning the causes of events. Genealogy repudiates this idea that there is behind events a guiding hand or set of regulating principles that determine how things progress and explain why the present is as it is. Genealogy "does not pretend to go back in time to restore an unbroken continuity." It does not try to make out a harmony in past events that reveals hidden forces that "animate the present, having imposed a predetermined form [on] all its vicissitudes" (Foucault 1971, 81).

Foucault insists with Nietzsche that "if the genealogist refuses to [do] metaphysics," what he or she finds underlying historical events is "not a timeless and essential secret, but . . . that they [events] have no essence or that their essence was fabricated" (Foucault 1971, 78). Genealogy does not attempt to limn the elements and connections of a chimerical progression; instead it "operates on a field of entangled and confused parchments, on documents that have been scratched over and recopied many times" (Foucault 1971, 76).

The core of the genealogical inversion of the accidental over the allegedly inevitable is that rather than discerning underlying, organized continuity, history traces randomly discontinuous perpetuation. Rather than history being a searching through the past's myriad details for present- and future-determining design, genealogy is a tireless sifting out of disparate and adventitiously related causal components that our interests and priorities turn into episodes in an orderly progression we impose on events of interest to us. The contrast here is not simply one between striving to find universal, teleological determinants, on the one hand, and attending to essentially unrelated microparticulars, on the other. The contrast is between conceiving of microparticulars as components of a broader process, and understanding those particulars as exhaustive of history's subject matter. Genealogy is thoroughly Darwinian; it is not, nor can it be, concerned with *ultimate* origins; it is and can be concerned only with relative ones.

One of the broader implications of Foucault's Nietzschean rejection of the quest for origins is that reason itself is denied transcendent status. Reason is not a universal we instantiate; Foucault contends that an examination of reason's history reveals that rather than being some Platonic form in which we participate, reason or rationality "was born . . . from chance," that historical compilations of complex practices "slowly forged the weapons of reason" (Foucault 1971, 78). As we saw earlier, Putnam and others, and certainly Searle, are adamant in their rejection of this historicization of reason or rationality. The trouble with this rejection is that, as Putnam puts it in the passage quoted previously, the argument against the historicization of reason turns on the claim that historical standards "presuppose reason . . . for their interpretation" (Putnam 1987, 227). But Foucault's response would be that, *of course* that is how it appears, *if* we begin with conception of reason as ahistorical. The result is an impasse, and what we see in this impasse is something important about Foucault's claims, something to which I return, and this is that, strictly speaking, genealogy cannot simply make categorical counterclaims against "total-izing" history. Genealogy can only offer alternative accounts. *Alterity* is what is central to genealogy, not correctness. Perhaps the best indication of the importance of this point is how Foucault himself seems to forget it, and sometimes sounds as if his genealogical analyses *set things right*, something that would turn genealogy into that replacement for episte-mology threatened in his structuralist period, and thus vitiate Foucault's poststructuralist claims.

In any case, genealogy, properly conceived, attempts to "identify the accidents, the minute deviations . . . the reversals . . . the errors, the false appraisals, and the faulty calculations that gave birth to those things that . . . have value for us" (Foucault 1971, 81). The thrust of genealogical methodology and strategy is that the more discontinuous and disassoci-ated details are excavated, the harder it is to impose a grand synthesis on the past or to see the present as the product of an inexorable progression.

A key point about genealogy that relates closely to Foucault's con-ception of truth is his emphasis on the role of the body. The body "is the inscribed surface of events (traced by language)." It is the body that bears and manifests the effects of regulating discourses in its gestures, its postures, but above all its habits. A major task of genealogy is "to expose a body totally imprinted by history" (Foucault 1971, 82). It is also geneal-ogy's task to show how the body is "the locus of a dissociated self (adopting the illusion of a substantial unity)" (Foucault 1971, 83). The body sup-ports a self, an emergent, constructed subject, but a self that does not recognize itself as emergent and takes itself to be an essence prior to the effects of discourse, of socialization, and of the internalization of prac-tices. Genealogy carefully exposes the tiny influences on bodies that, over time, produce subjects defined by what they come to take as knowledge about themselves and their world.

Foucault's account of the role of the body is another of his inversions: an inversion of the priority of the behaving body over the supposedly controlling mind. As such, the account may be seen as a restatement of behaviorism. In *Discipline and Punish*, Foucault describes how the penal system reshapes inmates through the application of discipline to them as so many "docile bodies," bodies that have been made submissive by incar-ceration and behavioral control. What is crucial is that application of discipline is not only prohibitive management, but it is also the employ-ment of habit-instilling techniques that impose on the body a host of schedules, restrictions, obligatory comportment, and constant diagnostic and evaluatory examinations. The aim of discipline is not only to control inmates; it is to *change* them and, by changing them, to control them during and beyond their incarceration.

Foucault describes disciplinary techniques in the context of the penitentiary, but it is one of his main contentions that the intent behind the development and application of disciplinary techniques is less a matter of rehabilitating wrongdoers or redressing wrongs than of increasing efficient subjugation and control. The prison, then, is a crucible for development of techniques whose broader application came to characterize the late twentieth century and the beginning of the twenty-first, namely, large-scale management of people. The disciplinary techniques discussed in *Discipline and Punish* are evident in all institutions involved in the management of large groups: corporations, schools, barracks, hospitals, factories, and so on (Foucault 1979, 135–228). Foucault argues that the ubiquity of the techniques represents a historically recent reconception of people as not only susceptible to being physically constrained, but also internally malleable through the application of discipline. This is the importance of the inversion of the behaving body over the controlling mind: bodies are malleable because they are habit-formed, and if they are primary, subjects, as emergent, are malleable.

The idea of instilling controlling habits and value-sustaining self-images through the imposition of discipline on the body, the central notion in *Discipline and Punish*, is not new. It has been around, though in less potent form, at least since Aristotle. It is an idea readily found in abstract psychological treatises and in popular clichés, a paradigm instance being: "As the twig is bent, so grows the tree," a corruption of Pope's "Just as the twig is bent, the tree's inclin'd" (*Oxford Dictionary of Quotations* 1980, #12, 377).

The basic idea is that imposition of behavioral habits on an individual shapes that individual's self-image, perspectives, attitudes, values, desires, and objectives. Modification of behavior alters every aspect of who we are: what we think and feel, our attitudes, our values, our aspirations. What Foucault adds to this idea is that modification of behavior serves not only to control subjects, but to *manufacture* them. He adds that the instilling of habits, values, objectives, and self-images is, on the whole, largely unintentional, coincidental, and impersonal. Only some results of imposed discipline are intended and anticipated, because we are shaped and reshaped, not only by the deliberate efforts of those who exert control over our bodies, but also by the accidental, the fortuitous impact that others' and our own actions have on us. Much of what makes and shapes particular subjects is neither planned nor purposive, and to say how this is the case requires Foucault to employ his notion of power relations.

Power explains how subjects emerge as they do, how they are shaped by discipline. But Foucauldian power is not domination or coercion of individuals by other individuals; it is the complex network of acts within which some acts are acts of domination and coercion, of submission and resistance. As a network, as opposed to instances of domination or coercion, power constrains *actions*, not individuals. Power is all about people acting in ways that blindly and impersonally condition others' options to act. *Some* of the acts comprising the network are intended, but they never effect only what is intended; all acts have unforeseen consequences for the actions of others.

This is not the place to pursue it, and certainly not without a fuller description of power relations in a given society, but there is an intriguing parallel between Foucault's notion of power relations and the notion of a "multi-agent system" in computing science. As Katia Sycara summarizes, "[t]he characteristics of MASs [multi-agent systems] are that (1) each agent has incomplete information or capabilities . . . and, thus, has a limited viewpoint; (2) there is no system global control; (3) data are decentralized; and (4) computation is asynchronous" (Sycara 1998). "Agent" here is used anthropomorphically in that each element referred to is a bit of program code, but the key to the parallel with power relations is that "agents" in multi-agent systems model individuals in networks of Foucauldian power relations.

What is of greatest importance here regarding Foucauldian power is the connection between power and truth. Power, in shaping subjects, determines what they come to hold true, and power, in the imposition of discipline and practices, *produces* truth. This is because, as we will see in greater detail, power determines discursive currency.

We can best begin consideration of Foucault's concept of truth by considering perspectivism's role in the relation between genealogy and traditional "totalizing" history. We are told that a key trait of genealogy is "its affirmation of knowledge as perspective" (Foucault 1971, 90). In contrast to traditional history's conception of its inquiries as aiming at objective knowledge, genealogy is avowedly perspectival. It never forgets or obscures its own temporal and cultural situatedness. Genealogy rejects the idea that history can be done objectively, that it can be conducted from no particular point of view or at least buffered against perspectival influences. Genealogy casts traditional history's invocation of "objectivity, of the accuracy of facts and of the permanence of the past" as a mask for vested interests operant in the production of holistic narratives (Foucault 1971, 91). This is perhaps the point at which Foucault is closest to the sociology of Mannheim and his successors (Allen 2003, 37–38, 40–41). The import of this is that here we see one of the reasons why so many analytic philosophers dismiss Foucault. Mannheim, who is believed to have coined the term *relativism* in developing the sociology of knowledge, is read by many as concerned not with truth itself, but with what passes for truth, for ideological reasons. This is an interpretation commonly but wrongly imposed on Foucault's views despite his denials (Foucault 1980b, 118). I return to this point in the next section.

As we turn to more a detailed consideration of Foucault's nonrelational or wholly discursive conception of truth, it is important to remember that genealogical reconception of intellectual inquiry casts it as a series of diverse practices governed by thoroughly historical standards. A corollary of this reconception is that the actual workings of these practices are masked from their participants. They view their inquiries and communicative activities as regulated not by historical standards, but by ahistorical ones, seeing the fruits of their inquiries as ongoing discernment of objective truth and acquisition of unprejudiced knowledge. Moreover, the acquisition of knowledge is taken to be a progressively cumulative understanding of how things are.

Foucault seeks to unmask the historicity of truth, to show that truth is not how things are, but is instead the highest-order value in a discourse and set of practices. Knowledge, then, is not the learning of how things are; it is the highest-order category in a discourse and set of practices, in a "regime of truth." In like manner, rationality is not ahistorical principles that govern the discernment of truth and the acquisition of knowledge. Instead, rationality is a notion that functions as a regulatory touchstone for individual discourses and sets of practices. Whatever our illusions, therefore, truth relates to nothing outside discourse; it is not mimetic with respect to objective or extralinguistic reality.

Truth in Five Parts

Foucault does not offer a definition of truth; rather, he provides a multifaceted characterization. The fundamental claim is that truth is *produced* "by virtue of multiple forms of constraint." He amplifies by contending that "the 'political economy' of truth is characterised by five important traits." These traits are not offered as constitutive elements of truth, but as illustrative of the production of truth. From the outset, then, Foucault's treatment of truth focuses on how truth is "manufactured" in discourse, and there is no attempt to give an account of truth as a relational property.

Foucault maintains that truth (1) "is centred on the form of scientific discourse and the institutions which produce it." In Western culture, established scientific certainties are the paradigm of what is true. However, truth (2) "is subject to constant economic and political incitement (the demand for truth, as much for economic production as for political power)." There is constant change in what is deemed to be true in a given discourse in response to needs generated by political and economic developments. Truth also (3) "is the object, under diverse forms, of immense diffusion and consumption (circulating through apparatuses of education and information whose extent is relatively broad in the social body . . .)." Discipline-manufactured truths are constantly being disseminated in the service of political, social, and economic objectives, which themselves are conditioned by the production of truth. Moreover, truth (4) "is produced and transmitted under the control, dominant if not exclusive, of a few great political and economic apparatuses (university, army, writing, media)." This is the governance of the production and dissemination of truths, the management of disciplinary truth. And (5) "lastly, [truth] is the issue of a whole political debate and social confrontation ('ideological' struggles)" (Foucault 1980b, 131–32).

These five traits make up the specific content of Foucault's claim that "[w]e are subjected to the production of truth through power and we cannot exercise power except through the production of truth" (Foucault 1980b, 93). To clarify this characterization, and to show that Foucault's relativism is not facile postmodernism and does not entail irrealism, I proceed by winnowing out several different ways Foucault uses "true" and "truth." The objective is to show that his conception of truth is pluralistic. The five characteristics just mentioned apply to different degrees to the uses I distinguish, which coincidentally are also five in number. These uses or senses are fairly readily distinguishable, though not altogether separate from one another. As I argue, though, neither are they different aspects of a single sense. This is part of what makes Foucault's conception of truth difficult: it is multifaceted, and understanding how the several facets fit together requires abandonment of the entrenched traditional conception of truth as simple and unitary.

Foucault says much about truth because it is basic to his project to counter the traditional objectivist conception of truth. Foucault also says a lot about truth because he is aware that many think he espouses an irrealist postmodern relativism and denies truth in some holistic way. He feels it necessary to avow his concern with truth, describing those who take him to be denying truth as "simple-minded" (Foucault 1989, 295). The trouble is that Foucault says many different things about truth, and is quite explicit about the pluralistic nature of the concept of truth, insisting that "there are different truths and different ways of saying [the truth]" (Foucault 1989, 314). Unfortunately, some of the different things Foucault says or implies about truth look to many to be mutually inconsistent. Moreover, though he describes truth as historical because it is relative to discourse and is a product of power, Foucault compounds apparent inconsistencies by sometimes seeming to make ahistorical objectivist truth claims in his writings.

Because Foucault does not offer a theory of truth, his claims about truth cannot be checked for consistency against specific principles definitive of his position. Moreover, the question of whether what he says about truth is consistent is complicated by the fact that it is precisely one of Foucault's objectives to impugn the traditional relational conception of truth. Therefore, we cannot assume that uses of truth that may be at odds with one another according to the traditional understanding of truth are at odds in Foucault's revisionary and pluralistic conception of truth. The best way to proceed is, as indicated, to separate as clearly as possible the most significant ways Foucault uses truth. Once one is clear on how his uses of truth differ from one another, it is easier to understand how those uses hang together. What follows, then, is an analytic list of Foucault's uses of truth. It is important to keep in mind, however, that while the uses in question differ in the ways I outline, they nonetheless are interrelated, overlapping, and complementary.

The first of Foucault's uses of truth is what I call the *criterial* use (Prado 2000, 118). This is the use operant in the claim that every society "has its regime of truth." Each society has "types of discourse which it accepts . . . as true"; each has "mechanisms . . . which enable one to distinguish true and false statements" and "means by which each is sanctioned"; each has "procedures accorded value in the acquisition of truth" and "those who are charged with saying what counts as true" (Foucault 1980b, 131). The criterial use is clearly relativistic and, taken in isolation, is a version of cultural relativism. It is misperception of Foucault's criterial use as exhaustive of his conception of truth that prompts analytic philosophers to summarily dismiss his views and contentions as instancing fashionable but ill-conceived irrealist postmodern relativism. To reject Foucault's views on truth in this way is to miss that the criterial use is only one of several interrelated uses, and that it has to do specifically with what counts as true in a disciplined or learned discourse or, more broadly, in a given culture. In fact, the criterial use may be compatible with an objectivist view of truth, but what is important here is that if the criterial use is wrongly taken as exhaustive, not only do Foucault's views on truth look uninterestingly modish, some of the things he says about truth then are inconsistent. However, the criterial use is only one of five uses.

The second, and textually most prevalent, of Foucault's uses of truth is the *constructivist* use. It embodies the central idea that power produces truth. Whereas critics err by focusing on the criterial use to the exclusion of others, adherents make too much of the constructivist use and avail themselves of it too readily and often indiscriminately. What needs to be appreciated, to prevent both errors, is the relation between the criterial and constructivist uses. Briefly, Foucault's constructivist use explains how a claim or proposition comes to be a candidate for truth in a discourse, while the criterial use explains the conditions that are met by that claim or proposition in coming to be true in a discourse. This interrelation becomes clear once the criterial nature of the first use of truth is appreciated. In short, the criterial idea is that truth is discourse-relative; the constructivist idea is that the power relations that generate and define discourses produce truths. This candidacy-establishment interplay is the way that we are constantly "subjected to the production of truth through power" (Foucault 1980b, 93).

The constructivist notion of truth as a product of power baffles some and alienates others, but mostly it prompts misinterpretation. The most important misinterpretation is the construal of power's *production* of truth as only ideological *distortion* of underlying truth. Many followers and critics alike read Foucault as implicitly distinguishing between power-produced truth and ideological truth. This is not the case; Foucault denies the idea that ideological distortion of underlying ahistorical truth is the object of his analysis (Foucault 1980b, 118).

However, the mistaken reading of power-produced truth as only distortion of underlying truth is useful to consider, because it brings out how Foucault's different uses of truth qualify and limit one another. Foucault contends that it is wrong to interpret power-produced truth as only what passes for true in a discourse and actually contrasts with underlying truth (Foucault 1980b, 118). His constructivist use does not allow a distinction to be drawn between underlying truth and apparent truth; the constructivist use deals with the production of *all* truth. The criterial use of truth, which has to do with what counts as true in a given discourse, might have allowed a distinction between ideological truth and underlying truth, but it cannot when teamed with the constructivist use. What counts as true according to the criterial use cannot contrast with anything that is objectively true because nothing is true in discourse that is not a product of power, and there is no truth other than discursive truth. Though initially the criterial use appears compatible with some understanding of discursive truth as different from objective, underlying truth, the constructivist use eliminates that possibility. The constructivist use disallows that there is more to truth than what genealogy inventories.

Understanding the criterial and constructivist uses of truth and how they fit together requires appreciating that in Foucault's relativization of truth to discourse, a discourse is like a Wittgensteinian form of life; it is a set of practices, an integrated collection of things we say and do, including elements that are not themselves verbal, notably gestures, actions, and silences. A discourse, like a form of life, also has conventions that determine who may speak and when, and in what contexts verbal expressions, gestures, actions, and silences constitute the establishment or acknowledgment or assertion of something as true. In Foucault's terms, these conventions are the "mechanisms . . . which enable one to distinguish true and false statements," the "techniques and procedures accorded value in the acquisition of truth." These conventions also establish persons deemed expert and "charged with saying what counts as true" (Foucault 1980b, 131). These mechanisms, techniques, and procedures jointly constitute the structure and limits of a discourse. It is in the environment provided by these practices that the specific content of a particular verbal expression, gesture, action, or silence counts as what Searle would describe as a commissive, directive, assertive, expressive, or declarative speech act.

However, understanding discourse as a form of life must remain Wittgensteinian and not become Kantian. A tempting way to make sense of how Foucault makes truth relative to discourse is to construe discourses as "conceptual schemes," and their truths as functions of how conceptual schemes organize noumenal reality. This is a trap with respect to understanding Foucault's relativism. It is a move similar to thinking that what he means by discourse-relative truth is ideologically distorted truth. Foucauldian power does not produce truth by generating "categories" that organize our awareness of reality. Power does not produce truth in any systematic way; power produces truth blindly and randomly. It produces truth through actions that enable or inhibit other actions and that occur "at the level of tiny local events" (Hacking 1981, 29). Power is not like Kantian categories of the understanding; power is not anything separate from what people say and do. Power is no more than individuals' employment of language and engagement in various practices. It is not a conceptual filtering system that organizes a Jamesian blooming, buzzing confusion. Power just is people acting and so constraining others' actions.

At base, the truth power produces is the correctness of certain discursive acts, in the broad sense, in a given discourse. And "correctness" here is to be understood in the same way that applies to moving a pawn or a knight on a chessboard in accordance with the rules of chess. Speaking the truth is making the right move in a discourse, where what is right is what is dictated or allowed by a truth regime's correctness criteria. A discourse's truths are moves sanctioned by that discourse's mechanisms for distinguishing truth and falsity; moves that conform to the discourse's expert judgments that have been codified as disciplinary principles or their corollaries.

This last point brings us to a crucial question raised by Foucault's constructivist contention that power produces truth, which is, How do the truths of a discourse become what individual discourse-participants actually believe, as opposed to what they merely adhere to and profess? How do discourse-participants come to hold power-produced truths instead of merely accepting them as one might adopt conventions for prudential reasons? For instance, how do penitentiary inmates and sexed social beings accept disciplinary truths as defining their own essences, as opposed to being so many behavioral requirements? This is, in effect, the large question of how subjects are manufactured, and raises myriad issues about how imposed routines inculcate habits that in turn reshape subjectivity. Foucault's answer is the whole of *Discipline and Punish* and the whole of *The History of Sexuality*, but something considerably more compact is needed here.

What is central to the question about the internalization of discursive truths is that while discourses are obviously sustained by individuals' participation in them, discourses present themselves to subjects as environments fully on a par with the physical environment. Both environments are inescapable and demanding. Most individuals are unreflectively ensconced in their discursive environments. Only a very few, the Darwins and the Freuds, manage to play a role in radically changing their discourses, initiating development of new discourses. The question about the internalization of discursive truths, then, presupposes an answer to a prior question, namely, How is a discourse, while not anything in itself, encountered as an environment so that its truths are internalized?

Differently put, how are a discourse's truths presented to subjects as objective rather than as simply others' beliefs? The answers to these related questions turn on the next of Foucault's uses of truth.

The third of Foucault's uses of truth, the *perspectivist* use, is the most difficult. This use derives from Nietzschean perspectivism, which makes truth a function of interpretation and denies that there is anything but interpretations (Nietzsche 1968, 267, 330). This is the use of truth that, though not normally recognized as distinct, gets Foucault dismissed as an irrealist. Understanding Foucault's perspectivist use first requires appreciating how his perspectivism differs from the extreme irrealism-entailing relativism usually attributed to him. The crucial difference is that, as we will see in considering the fifth use of truth, Foucault is mostly silent on the question of extralinguistic or extradiscursive reality.

Contrary to the common assimilation of Foucault's Nietzschean-derived perspectivism to extreme relativism, his perspectivism is differently conceived. Foucault's perspectivism is not simple leveling of all truth claims to the same status, a leveling consequent on the abandonment of conception of truth as ahistorical, abandonment that usually entails denial of objective reality. The perspectivism of Foucault's perspectivist use is denial of the possibility of descriptive completeness.

Radical relativism denies that any particular truth claim can be justified by recourse to anything objective or "extraperspectival," so it reduces all truth claims to expressions of opinion no one of which is better than any other. Radical relativism makes perspective the sole ground of assertion. But radical relativism cannot stop at the epistemological position that whatever objective reality there may be is not accessible to us. Radical relativism immediately slides into the ontological position that there is no reality other than that defined by perspective. The idea of a reality *other* than a perspectival one ceases to have content. There are, then, as many realities as there are perspectives – and solipsism seems unavoidable. Central here is that the question of reconciling or rationalizing perspectives does not arise for radical relativism. Any agreement of any two or more perspectives can only be coincidental.

Against this, Foucault's perspectivist use of truth is limited to the idea in Nietzschean perspectivism, which is denial of the possibility of a global or holistic description of the world within which diverse perspectives could be reconciled or "rationalized" as so many true but incomplete points of view. The crucial difference here is that Foucault simply is silent on the issue of extralinguistic or extradiscursive reality. In this, as we will see, he is of a mind with Rorty.

Reading the perspectivist use as radically relativistic is not the only common error impeding the understanding of this use. Another distortion of the perspectivist use is an ontological version of the epistemic construal of relativism as holding truth relative to conceptual schemes. The distortion occurs with introduction of a noumenal, or "thing-in-itself," world as what perspectives are perspectives on. An example is found in Todd May's treatment of Foucault's genealogical analytics. Following Nehamas, May describes perspectivism as not necessarily vulnerable to arguments against extreme relativism, because perspectivism only denies that "there could ever be a complete theory or interpretation of anything, a view that accounts for 'all' the facts" (Nehamas 1985, 64). May argues that perspectivism does not claim "that the world contains many meanings but, rather, that every view upon the world is an interpretation, a limited and revisable perspective" (May 1993, 80). He adds that it is "perspectives which are plural, not the world," but then expands Nehamas's account by claiming that Nietzsche held that "the world is ontologically indeterminate" and so supports an unlimited number of interpretations. May then goes on to say that what interpretations interpret cannot itself "be rendered in any interesting sense" (May 1993, 79). By speaking of something that supports interpretations but cannot be "rendered" or described, May implies that a noumenal something underlies interpretations. But Nietzsche explicitly maintains that "[t]he antithesis 'thing-in-itself' and 'appearance' is untenable." His perspectivism is not one in which interpretations are phenomenal organizations of a noumenal world not knowable in itself; neither Nietzsche's nor Foucault's perspectivism is an ontological or metaphysical position (Nietzsche 1968, 298).

Whatever it may come to, Nietzsche is clear that there are *only* interpretations. Hard as this claim may be to make out, it should not be made more palatable by supplying a noumenal world to bear interpretations. However we might read Nietzsche, certainly Foucault's perspectivist use of truth should not be understood as May interprets it. Positing a noumenal world to support diverse and possibly incommensurable discourses is positing an unknowable absolute of precisely the sort genealogy expressly opposes. Foucault is adamant in rejecting posited "conditional" transcendencies. He says of genealogy that it works "without . . . reference to a subject which is either transcendental in relation to the field of events or runs in its empty sameness throughout the course of history" (Foucault 1980b, 117). We need to come to grips with the perspectivist use of truth as wholly discursive and not entailing the positing or denial of anything that is not discursive.

Appreciating the discursive nature of the perspectivist use of truth enables better understanding of Foucault's agreement with Nietzsche that we should press the question, "After all, why truth . . . Why are we concerned with truth?" (Bernauer and Rasmussen 1988, 15). Though most traditional philosophers would reject this question out of hand, taking it as frivolous or perverse, the question arises as a serious one when perspectivism denies any possibility of an interpretation-rationalizing description of the world. Given that denial, it becomes necessary to explain why we have "the will to truth"; it becomes necessary to understand why we are driven to establish a single perspective as the uniquely correct one. Following Nietzsche, Foucault contends that "instead of trying to find out what truth . . . is," we would be better advised to try to understand why we accord traditionally conceived truth ultimate value, and place ourselves "absolutely under its thrall" (Foucault 1988a, 107).

Foucault's Nietzschean question about the value of truth must not be interpreted superficially. He is not asking why we value the truth in cases where a falsehood, an illusion, or an evasion would prove more useful. To think that is to assume what is at issue: that there is always an objective truth distinct from truth in discourse. Nietzsche's question, in part, is why we think that there is always just one correct interpretation, and, in part, why we give the highest priority and value to achieving that uniquely correct interpretation. Note that it will not do to say that we do so for utilitarian reasons, because we can best manipulate things if we know their precise disposition. If this were the reason for the value put on truth, it would be largely acceptable. But it is not the reason. Intellectual history is full of declarations of the ultimate value of truth *for its own sake,* declarations that invariably put truth over utility (Allen 1993; Williams 2002).

The reason for the will to truth is that our intellectual tradition has it that there can be no higher value than attainment of truth *for itself.* Having the truth may well facilitate achievement of our ends, but that is incidental. We strive to know truth regardless of whether it is applicable to our ends, and most of the truth our tradition aspires to possess is of no practical use. The whole point is to *have* it. This is what Nietzsche questioned.

Foucault's Nietzschean perspectivism primarily denies that we can meaningfully assert that things are a certain way independently of how we take them to be, and it denies the corollary that we should strive to achieve the one true perspective. His perspectivism, then, is not a positive thesis about the nature of truth; it is the rejection of the possibility of referring to and discerning a determinate state of being beyond our interpretations. Appreciating this enables us to return to the question of the appropriation of discourse-relative and power-produced truth by discourse-participants. The answer to this question depends on seeing how what is appropriated as truth is sustained in discourse and presented to discourse-participants as objective, as *not* perspectival.

Writing about Nietzsche and William James as perspectivists, Gilles Deleuze says that theirs is not the familiar sort of relativism, that it is not "a variation of truth according to the subject." That is, their perspectivism is not subjective relativism or relativization of truth to individuals' beliefs. Their perspectivism is not, in short, extreme relativism. Though Nietzschean perspectivism "is clearly a pluralism," it is not the fragmentation of truth into so many instances of individuals holding something true (Deleuze 1993, 20).

Some of the concern expressed by Deleuze focuses on how there can be intersubjective discursive or cultural constructs – constructs not reducible to individual beliefs. The task is to say how these constructs are "objects" presented to individuals, but without reifying them into mysterious entities. The aim is to say how power-produced truths, as cultural artifacts, are sustained in discourse, and so can be intersubjective and encountered and adopted by individuals. In this, Deleuze is doing something very like what Searle does in explaining the intersubjective nature of the elements of social reality.

An example of a cultural construct that is intersubjective and not reducible to beliefs held by individuals is a stereotype. Stereotypes are intersubjective to the extent that though fairly well defined, they elicit different responses from different individuals. For instance, the same negative racial stereotype may elicit amused contempt toward the relevant racial group in one individual, and virulent antipathy toward the same group in another individual, but the stereotype is not identical with either the contempt or the antipathy.

The idea of intersubjective cultural constructs has a parallel in sociobiological debate. Dawkins facilitates his Darwinian account of culture by introducing the concept of "a new kind of replicator." He thinks there are cultural artifacts that are intersubjective and capable of cultural transmission comparable to genetic transmission. These ideational items contribute to the content of a culture and survive independently of particular individuals' beliefs and attitudes. Dawkins calls these cultural artifacts *memes*, playing both on the Greek *mimesis* (imitation) and on *gene*. Examples of *memes* are "ideas, catch-phrases, [and] fashions," as well as practices such as "ways of making pots or of building arches" (Dawkins 1976, 206). Dawkins's contention is that "as genes propagate themselves . . . via sperm or eggs, so memes propagate themselves . . . via a process which, in the broad sense, can be called imitation" (Dawkins 1976, 206).

Dawkins offers the example of how a scientist who has a good idea passes the idea on to colleagues and students. The idea is then used in articles and lectures and "if the idea catches on, it can be said to propagate itself" (Dawkins 1976, 206). This "catching on" is Rorty's notion of "uptake" on a new metaphor or vocabulary, and is presented as analogous to natural selection. Following Dawkins, Rorty maintains that "[m]emes are things like turns of speech, terms of aesthetic or moral praise, political slogans, proverbs . . . stereotypical icons, and the like." *Memes* "compete with one another . . . as genes compete" with one another, and different "batches of both genes and memes are carried by different human social groups" (Rorty 1991b, 4).

What is important in the present context is that a culture's discursive components, its constructs, its *memes,* are presented to the culture's members in the process of enculturation as realities on a par with the physical environment. Individual members of the culture form perspectives not only on their physical environment, but on their cultural environment as well. The constructed components of the cultural environment, such as stereotypes, show how something can be a power-produced element in a culture or discourse, and so become something about which individuals can form beliefs. But these constructs are not anything in themselves; they are sustained in discourse by being elements in repeated practices. The concept of an objective sexual nature is a relevant example. For Foucault, our supposedly objective sexual nature actually is a cultural construct, a power-produced artifact integral to the governance of sexual behavior through the "deployment" of certain conceptions of normalcy, values, and self-images. The successful governance of sexuality requires positing an underlying objective nature, so that diverse sexual behavior can be presented as the manifestation of that nature or its perversion. Learned or disciplinary discourse propagates the idea that a sexual essence underlies our desires and acts and so "explains" them. Individuals are taught about human sexual nature and form their own interpretations and beliefs of what is presented to them as fact but actually is discourse-constructed and sustained. In this way, individuals inhabit a reality in which the components are constructs as well as physical objects and events. With this idea of intersubjective cultural constructs in place, we can better understand how individuals appropriate power-produced truths as their own.

Appropriation of power-produced truths, then, occurs when individuals take constructed truths as matters of fact and form beliefs and attitudes about and toward them. Just as individuals form beliefs about physical things and events, they form beliefs about cultural constructs presented to them in various ways, ranging from expert accounts to texts to advertisements to remarks made in passing. Individuals are inundated with multifarious presentations of "scientific facts" and "common knowledge" directly through formal and informal schooling. They are swamped by indirect presentation of what "everyone knows" through implication, innuendo, and confirming or adverse reactions to what they say and do.

The bombardment of individuals' senses by the physical world is equaled by the barrage of cultural constructs that assails them. They need to deal with cultural constructs as much as with any physical thing or event that they encounter and must manipulate, navigate around, be present at, or avoid. Individuals, then, appropriate the truths of their discourse in dealing with cultural artifacts as unproblematic givens, in dealing with them as so many more bits of reality. To the extent that this is the case, Foucault's genealogical tracing of the production of cultural constructs, as well as Searle's application of collective intentionality to social reality, could be as important as empirical science.

The foregoing explanation of the intersubjectivity of cultural constructs may be resisted because of our Cartesian epistemological tradition. Some find it hard to see what discourse-relative, power-produced truths could be, if not so many particular beliefs formed and held by particular individuals. They find it difficult to see how cultural constructs could be present in discourse without simply being particular expressions of particular beliefs held by discourse-participants. Searle faces basically the same opposition in explaining how the various discursive institutions that comprise social reality, such as money and contracts, are sustained by collective intentionality.

Whether or not Foucault or Searle ultimately can make their respective versions of the claim that social constructs are not identical with nor reducible to so many particular beliefs or intentions, two things seem clear: first, their efforts are intriguingly parallel and, second, with respect to Foucault, separating power-produced truths as cultural artifacts from individuals' beliefs facilitates understanding his thinking about power's productivity. Conceiving of social or cultural constructs as intersubjective items amenable to individual interpretation allows there to be objects in discourse about which beliefs may be formed by individuals to whom these items are presented. It is then clearer how disciplinary techniques shape subjects: they do so by presenting regimented individuals with constructs as realities. Those individuals, in the process of dealing with them as the applied disciplines require, must acknowledge and internalize said constructs.

Perhaps the salient example is human sexuality. Though Foucault describes it as a social construct, it is dealt with as an objective nature by psychology, psychiatry, social psychology, penology, and other disciplines. Individuals who are analyzed, counseled, and otherwise governed regarding sexual behavior by the application of disciplinary practices are constrained through the imparting of "facts" and the inculcation of habits to accept that their problems or concerns relate to an objective nature that defines their sexuality and which they may be distorting or violating. This is how it comes about that, as Susan Hekman puts it, "subjects fin[d] their 'truth' in their sexuality" (Hekman 1990, 70).

Four central points should now be clearer. The first is how Foucault's criterial use of truth has to do with what counts as truth in a discourse. The second is how his constructivist use has to do with the production of truth in discourse. The third is how his perspectivist use has to do with the appropriation of discourses' truths by individuals. And the fourth is that subjectivities are shaped by power through individuals being constrained to treat the constructs of power as established realities. Together, these four points illuminate how the criterial, constructivist, and perspectivist uses of truth fit together in Foucault's thought. However, there are two more pieces to the puzzle.

Lawrence Kritzman observes that "Foucault was concerned, above all else, with the idea of experience" (Kritzman 1988, xviii). Aside from the criterial, constructivist, and perspectivist uses of truth, Foucault has a fourth use he characterizes by distinguishing between truth resulting from inquiry (*l'enquête*) and truth resulting from test or trial (*l'épreuve*). As he applies it, the contrast is between what is learned through investigation and what is not so much learned as realized in a challenging experience. I call this the *experiential* use of truth. This use basically is what we have in mind when we talk about realization and resolution, as when we realize that we believe something we had not articulated before, or when a previously ambiguous idea or situation is resolved by something we learn. In both realization and resolution, what we understand or learn is not something we acquire by questioning or examining anything. Rather, it is how cognitive elements reassemble themselves, how we see something *differently* because of a striking and provocative experience. The experiential use of truth is about realization or resolution achieved through the cognitive dissonance and reflection that various sorts of crises force on us.

According to Foucault, what we achieve in "limit experiences" is truth that "does not belong to the order of that which is, but rather of that which happens: it is an event" (Miller 1993, 271). The examples Foucault offers of experiential truth are alterations of perspective occurring when undergoing torture to establish innocence or trial by combat to establish rightness of action. In such cases, individuals may wholly reconceive who and what they are and value, or some other part of what defines them as persons. In these cases, truths are established in how a subject is redefined by crisis-prompted realization or resolution. Less dramatic but more useful examples are cases of experiencing the pressing need to understand occurrences that impugn much or all of what we believe and cherish, as when we lose religious or political faith or are betrayed by a friend.

The experiential use of truth will seem anomalous to traditional philosophers. It looks to be about changes of mind due to emotional rather than rational factors. That is, experiential truth appears to be change or realignment of beliefs due to causal rather than reasoned grounds, and so not philosophy's concern. Foucault himself acknowledges this, describing experiential truth as "repugnant to both science and philosophy" because it is neither propositional nor the consequence of reasoning or articulable insight (Miller 1993, 270).

However, the experiential use is neither as philosophically irrelevant as it first appears nor as alien to philosophy as Foucault might like. Experiential truth is basically the outcome of what Alisdair MacIntyre calls "epistemological crises." These are circumstances where individuals find themselves not only forced to question something they previously accepted without hesitation, but to question the evidential criteria they previously used to resolve similar perplexities (MacIntyre 1977). The result of the need to forge and apply new or reexamined evidential criteria in dealing with a pressing perplexity is just the sort of cognitive change Foucault claims is found in "limit experiences." To put the point in more mundane terms, some truths are gained or established because of how things "come together" during cognitive turmoil rather than as conclusions drawn on the basis of reasoned inquiry.

We might note in passing that while he does not explicitly say so, there is little doubt that Foucault thinks of his own achievements in rethinking madness, penality, and sexuality as acquisition of experiential truth. There is even less doubt that he saw his work as providing others with the opportunity for limit experience and so acquisition of experiential truth. Speaking of his books, Foucault claims that truth "is not found in a series of historically verifiable proofs; it lies rather in the experience which [a] book permits us to have" (Foucault 1991b, 36).

Like the perspectival use, the experiential use of truth has more to do with the appropriation of truth than with truth's production by power. Individuals appropriate a large number of discourse-sustained, power-produced truths in the process of being reared and enculturated, and then in dealing with others throughout their lives. But unless their lives are wholly placid and unremarkable, there will be times when encounters with new discourse-sustained truths and novel situations generate serious intellectual turmoil. For example, consider a young adult whose religious beliefs clash with some newly encountered idea or situation. Raised as a conservative Catholic, a young woman may rethink and reaffirm or abandon her previously unreflective moral condemnation of abortion when challenged by an unwanted pregnancy. Again, raised as a fundamentalist Baptist, a young man may rethink and reaffirm or abandon his previously unreflective creationism when challenged by exposure to Darwinian evolutionary theory.

These are instances of major cognitive clashes and consequent changes in beliefs and attitudes, but what is crucial about such cases is that the changes in beliefs and attitudes will be perceived as achievement of insight occasioned by deeply disruptive intellectual trials. The insights may be deemed positive or negative; they may be seen as enlightenment resulting in personal growth or as revealing personal failure. However, what matters here most is that individuals who embrace new truths after great agitation, indecision, and anguished reflection will consider their hard-won new truths to be epiphanies: revelations of how things *really* are with them, whether those new truths enhance or diminish them as persons in their own or others' eyes. Whether positively or negatively, the individuals in question will have been changed by their limit experience. In MacIntyre's terms, the wresting of new truth from deeply challenging bewilderment is adoption of new correctness-criteria and acceptance of new self-images and reformed perceptions of how things stand.

We might sum up much of the foregoing by saying that Foucault's criterial, constructivist, and perspectivist uses all have to do with power's production of truth in discourse and with the appropriation or internalization of discursive truth. What emerges as most noteworthy about experiential truth is that it *opposes* power-produced truth. It does so in that experiential truth wrung from the cognitive and emotional disruption of a limit experience offers the only counter to the ever-tightening grip of power. This is because experiential truth is in large part determined by individuals' particular histories, situations, and how they cope with power's shaping of them. The experiential use of truth is a kind of balance to the others: it explains why the production of truth and its appropriation by individuals are not wholly determining of what those individuals believe and of what they are as subjects.

If we could stop here, understanding Foucault's views on truth would be simpler than it is. For one thing, his position would be wholly relativistic and, if the worse for that, at least it would be consistent. However, there is a fifth and rather elusive use of truth still to be considered.

The fifth of Foucault's uses of truth is what I call the *tacit-realist* use. This is the use that critics think is inconsistent with Foucault's account of truth as produced by power (Nola 1994). This use occurs in comparatively few textual remarks, but that it occurs at all is what raises questions. The remarks in question look to many philosophers as clearly inconsistent with a historicist account of truth or, more specifically, with the criterial and constructivist uses. The reason is that truth seems to be used objectively in the remarks.

Perhaps the most notable example of these remarks is Foucault's assertion that when he speaks of truth he does not mean "the ensemble of truths which are to be discovered and accepted," and that what concerns him is "the ensemble of rules according to which the true and the false are separated and specific effects of power attached to the true" (Foucault 1980b, 132). Dreyfus and Rabinow render this passage more perspicaciously, translating the passage as that by truth Foucault does not mean "those true *things* which are waiting to be discovered" (Dreyfus and Rabinow 1983, 117; my emphasis). What matters at this juncture is the contrast drawn, and I note the different translation only to highlight what precisely it is that Foucault has in mind, as I will discuss forthwith.

The passage does suggest that Foucault inconsistently distinguishes power-produced or historical truth from discoverable objective or ahistorical truth. Nor is this instance unique. There are other passages that play on the contrast between power-produced and objective truth. In responding to a question about how truths are articulated, Foucault answers that expressing the truth in one way or another "does not mean . . . that what [is said] is not true" (Bernauer and Rasmussen 1988, 17). This distinguishes clearly between truth and how it is articulated, implying just as clearly that how truth is articulated in different discourses and at different times differs from *what is true*. Again, speaking of censorship and propaganda, Foucault condemns any "political regime that is indifferent to truth" (Foucault 1988a, 267). More worrying still is his contrast of "the constraints of truth" with prohibitions that are "arbitrary in origin" and develop "out of historical contingency" (Foucault 1972, 217–18).

We seem, then, to return to the idea that power's production of truth is the ideological distortion of underlying truth. There are also references to truth "about oneself" that suggest that there is, after all, something about oneself as a subject that is not a product of power relations (Dreyfus and Rabinow 1983, 212, 214; Foucault 1988a, 240). So it does look as if Foucault "intends to distinguish . . . objective, i.e., discovered, truth from his own use of the term" (Nola 1994, 39). If this is the case, the dilemma is that he either is inconsistent in doing so or is talking only about ideologically distorted or ideological truth, despite his denials that he is doing so.

Passages referring to or implying objective or ahistorical truth enable critics to conclude that Foucault "needs the distinction between what is true and what we take to be true" in order to unmask the power relations that "he alleges determine our discourses about what we believe to be true or false" (Nola 1994, 39). Even Rorty agrees that genealogy cannot claim to expose the deployed nature of dominant truths without implying that it reveals suppressed truths (Rorty 1986, 41–49). Rorty's point has some force, especially given the tone of Foucault's genealogical works, which is usually that of revelations being made.

It seems, then, that the most straightforward way to make sense of the problematic remarks referring to or implying truth that is not a product of power is to ignore his denials and take it that Foucault's power-produced truth is, after all, ideological distortion of truth. But this is a major interpretive step, and quite at odds with Foucault's expressed views. He was well aware of this common misreading, joking that when he asserts "a relation between truth and power," many say with relief, "'Ah good! Then it is not the truth'" (Foucault 1988b, 17). Foucault adamantly rejects interpretation of his work as only about ideology, pointing out that ideology "always stands in . . . opposition to something else which is supposed to count as truth," that is, to supposed discourse-independent ahistorical truth, which is precisely what genealogy denies (Foucault 1980b, 118).

I need to sort out the apparent inconsistency between the fifth or tacit-realist use of truth, present in the remarks in question, and the other uses of truth, especially the constructivist use. This can be accomplished with a number of clarifications. The first clarification requires appreciating that

Foucault is not offering a theory of truth. One of Foucault's objectives is to show that theories about truth are historical products pretending to ahistorical import. Critics err if they think Foucault's criterial, constructivist, perspectivist, and experiential uses of truth are parts of a theory about the nature of truth, and hence that the tacit-realist use is an inconsistent element of that theory. This is why I have been careful to speak of the ways Foucault *uses* truth, as opposed to speaking about parts or aspects of a theory.

The trouble is that there is a strong tendency to believe that since *true* has the same force in different uses and contexts, whatever is said to be true in those diverse ways must be true in the same way – most notably by "corresponding to the facts." It is generally assumed, then, that philosophizing about truth begins with theorizing about just what it is to be true. As Rorty points out, however, "'true' resembles 'good' . . . in being a normative notion, a compliment paid to sentences that seem to be paying their way." In other words, when we use *true* to describe a sentence we use "a term of praise" (Rorty 1982, xxv; 1991c, 127).

The first clarification, then, is that the commendatory force of *true* may be acknowledged as the same across different contexts without postulating a theoretically explicable essence that explains that common force. The parallel is to *good*. All sorts of things are described as good, from points to plans to persons, but the criteria for judging points made, plans proposed, and persons' behavior as good vary greatly. There is no essential way of being good that a theory might discern and that would explain how things as diverse as a point made in discussion and a soufflé are both good. Foucault's various uses of *true* need not have anything more in common than commendatory force, and if that is all that they have in common, they will not be inconsistent in a philosophically worrying way.

A second clarification is that the appearance of inconsistency in Foucault's occasional invocation of the tacit-realist use of truth is partly due to his own terminology. Foucault should not speak of "truths" when expressing disinterest in "the ensemble of truths which are to be discovered," because he is not talking about *truths* at all. As the Dreyfus – Rabinow translation makes clear, what Foucault is talking about are "things" or states of affairs. To speak of "truths" is wrong because referring to an ensemble of truths waiting to be discovered conflates linguistic truth and extralinguistic states of affairs or how things are or the world. What Foucault actually is setting aside in the passage at issue is not *truths* about the world, but the *world*. That is, he is not interested in the disposition of the world, in what is the case outside of language; his concern is with what governs objectification and description of the world *in* language. Foucault is in agreement with Rorty's contention that though the world plays a causal role in our awareness of it, it plays no *epistemic* role. To paraphrase Davidson, the world is not what makes truths true (Rorty 1982, xxv; Davidson 1985, 194; Rorty 1991c, 81, 127).

Rorty speaks of the world as "the ineffable cause of sense." He thinks the notion of "the world" is either a vacuous notion or simply everything that "inquiry at the moment is leaving alone" (Rorty 1982, 15). Foucault is engaged in an inquiry into truth that leaves the world alone; he is setting aside the world, or the ineffable cause of sense, as not relevant to what he wants to say about truth. However hard it is for some to understand, Foucault is trying to say something complicated about truth that separates truth from the world. In particular, he is rejecting the idea so basic to Searle's thought, which is that the world is the guarantor, the "maker" of truth. This will seem paradoxical to many, but it is crucial to understanding Foucault on truth to see that he is trying to talk about truth without thereby talking about how things are. Therefore, rather than denying the world by implication in describing truth as constructed in discourse, Foucault simply is not talking about the world or extralinguistic reality.

Despite the foregoing clarifications, the tacit-realist use of truth does pose a problem that has to do with what we might call ordinary conversational uses of truth. For instance, Foucault would not answer as a genealogist when asked if it is true that he visited Tunisia. But in answering that it is true that he did visit Tunisia, in speaking as a participant in discourse, it is not clear what he can have in mind or be implying when he uses *true* in this ordinary way. The question that arises is prompted by Searle's claims about our intuitions regarding truth, and is basically whether the ordinary use of truth in everyday conversations entails that true sentences are true because they accurately portray the world. This is to ask if ordinary uses of *true* and *truth* are inherently relational, as Searle believes, in always implying that it is the world that makes things true. If ordinary uses of *true* and *truth* imply that the world is thus-and-so, Foucault's ordinary conversational use of *true* is not innocuous and is likely inconsistent with his relativism and especially his constructivism.

This point becomes more pressing if we change the example. If Foucault is asked not if he visited Tunisia, but if it is true that water expands when it freezes, it is not clear that he can say that it is true, even in ordinary conversation, without implying that the sentence "Water expands when it freezes" is true in virtue of water's behavior rather than because purely discursive criteria are met. Foucault might intend to say only that *in our present regime of truth* the sentence "Water expands when it freezes" counts as true, but the trouble with this particular example is the lack of plausible alternatives. That is, if the intention is to describe a sentence as true but restrict oneself to the current discourse, it seems a fair question to ask after the content of the implicit claim that the sentence might not count as true in another discourse. But it is difficult to imagine a discourse in which "Water expands when it freezes" would be false, or perhaps nonsensical, and "Water contracts when it freezes" would be true. The sentence about water expanding on freezing seems to be an instance of a claim or expression that establishes a Searlean relation between a sentence and the world, as well as being an instance of a claim or expression that looks as if it would have to be true in any discourse on Earth.

The upshot regarding the tacit-realist use of truth is a dilemma. We can read Foucault as a tacit realist, which excludes him from the charge of irrealism laid against postmoderns and deconstructivists who explicitly or by implication espouse some form of irrealism – usually linguistic idealism. But this possibly generous reading appears to require that we reduce Foucault's constructivist claims about power producing truth to claims about ideological distortion of objective truth. This is because realism commits him to Searle's view that things are just one way or another, and it seems that truth is all about saying how things are. But reducing Foucault's claims about the production of truth by power to claims about ideological distortion is contrary to his explicit avowals, as well as to the holistic nature of his relativization of truth to governed discourse. On the other hand, we can dismiss Foucault's tacit-realist uses of truth as so many unfortunate slips, but doing so not only admits significant inconsistency into his thought, it makes his relativistic conception of truth vulnerable to charges of irrealism.

In my view, Foucault is a realist, albeit a tacit realist, so I think the only option is to try to understand how truth is wholly discursive, hence is a product of power, but without its being so entailing a denial of objective reality. As indicated, the key to this understanding is appreciating that, contrary to tradition, and certainly contrary to Searle's view, objective reality plays no epistemic role in sentences being true because truth is not relational; true sentences are not propositional renditions of how things are in the world, so, pace Searle, the world is not what makes true sentences true.

Summing Up

Foucault uses *true* and *truth* in at least five distinct, though interrelated, ways. His criterial, constructivist, and perspectivist uses of truth depend primarily on whether his concern is with discourse-defining practices, the role of power relations, or the appropriation and value of truth. His experiential use of truth has to do with radical perspectival change and adoption of belief. The tacit-realist use of truth is Foucault occasionally alluding to extralinguistic states of affairs, which he takes as unproblematic and as not figuring in his analyses. Extralinguistic states of affairs do not fit into consideration of power-produced truth because Foucault's account of truth is not a relational one: truth is not accurate rendition of the world.

Foucault's five uses of truth do not constitute a theory of truth; they do not jointly describe an essential way sentences are true, as does the theory holding truth to be a relation of correspondence to the facts. However, while Foucault's uses of truth do not collectively constitute a theory, they nonetheless constitute a new perspective on truth. The uses offer a pluralistic perspective that counters the traditional view of truth as monolithic. For Foucault, truth is not monolithic; it is several different things in that we attribute truth to sentences in a least five different ways. But those different ways are not themselves fixed or unchanging. Truth has been different things at different times and is different things at the same time. Truth is historical and heterogeneous.

In this connection, it might be thought that Foucault offers little that others have not offered. For instance, Rorty claims that Foucault offers nothing more than Dewey did in the latter's pragmatic account of truth (Rorty 1982, xviii; 1991c, 193–98). But this is mistaken; the role of power is new. Foucault's account of truth is not only pluralistic, it offers an explanation of the mechanics that produce the different sorts of truths in disparate discourses and epochs. Against this, the pragmatic view deals with truth simply in terms of utility and varying contexts; the only reason given for why something is true is that it works. "What works," though, is simply what we deem useful or productive at any given time; however, some take the Peircean line that "what works" is what we eventually all will agree is useful or productive at some future point when disagreement about what is and is not useful comes to an end. Against this, Foucault offers genealogical mappings of uses of *true* and *truth* that provide quite specific accounts as to why something is counted as true in a given context and at a given time. Foucault's concern is not merely with a general explanation of how *true* and *truth* work; he is concerned with explaining how *true* and *truth* work and come to work as they do in diverse discourses or, as we might put it, different forms of life.

This may be the place to note that Foucault seems precluded from adopting or endorsing a disquotational understanding of truth because attribution of truth in four of Foucault's five uses of truth is never only reiteration of the subject sentence. In the criterial use, there is always allusion in attribution of truth to a sentence to the discursive conditions the sentence meets; in the constructivist use, there is always allusion to power's productive role; in the perspectivist use, there is always allusion to a particular standpoint or point of view; in the experiential use, there is always allusion to an individual's particular history. The tacit realist use appears to allow disquotational understanding.

Central to most of what I have said in this chapter is that Foucault detaches truth from how things are, claiming that truth is produced within discourse and so does not constitute or represent some relation to how things are. Many find this a difficult idea and try to interpret it in ways they find more acceptable. For example, May argues that we have to draw a distinction that "Foucault neglected in his epistemic inquiries: the distinction between justification and *truth in an ultimate sense*" (May 1993, 71; my emphasis). But this is not a distinction Foucault's thought can accommodate. Ironically, the problem with May's claim is the same as Foucault's own when Foucault says he is not concerned with an ensemble of discoverable truths. Neither Foucault nor May should refer to "ultimate" or discoverable *truth*, because to do so is to conflate truth with extralinguistic reality.

To close this chapter, it is enough to say that what holds Foucault's first four uses of truth together, what makes them all uses of *truth*, is their shared commendatory force. What separates the uses into four distinct uses are the factors that determine how each use of *is true* is justified. The experiential use is a special case, because in it the factors in question are, in the main, exclusive to individuals, since the use has to do with individuals' predispositions to respond in various ways to epistemological crises or the effects of power. The experiential sense is the closest Foucault comes to the subjective relativism that many wrongly think he holds.

The fifth or tacit-realist use is also a special case, though actually less so than one initially might think. This use falls outside Foucault's genealogical mappings because it is one that is essentially allusive in nature, that is, the tacit-realist use is less a use of truth than it is an allusion to what lies beyond language and hence does not figure in Foucault's consideration of truth.

Given the foregoing descriptions of Searle's and Foucault's positions in this and the previous chapter, I now need to address the issue on which they are most at odds, namely, the connection between truth and reality: between beliefs and sentences deemed true and the disposition of the world. To proceed, and to avoid futile excursions into metaphysics, I address the truth/reality issue arising from Searle's and Foucault's work in terms of their positions on the confirmation of beliefs and assertive or descriptive sentences.

4

Truth, Reality, and Confirmation

Truth and the World

The foregoing chapters on Searle and Foucault raise many questions, and chief among them is one about what epistemic role Searle and Foucault respectively attribute to extralinguistic reality. For Searle, truth is inextricably related to how things are in the world in that beliefs and sentences are true when they accurately depict how things are, when they square with "the facts." For Foucault, extralinguistic reality is tacitly acknowledged and put aside in considering truth, because truth is wholly linguistic; truth is discursive currency, and true sentences neither depict nor are made true by states of affairs in the world.

Searle's problem with extralinguistic reality is that the epistemic role it supposedly plays in making beliefs and sentences true eludes satisfactory theoretical articulation. This difficulty is perhaps most evident in Searle's frequent reliance on very simple examples to explain how true beliefs and sentences square with states of affairs. By using simple examples, like the one I consider below about believing one's keys are on a table, Searle in effect precludes the necessity to consider interpretative, identificatory, and descriptive subtleties. In simple examples, the claimed relation of truth to the disposition of the world appears self-evident and difficult to challenge. It is hard to explore issues of interpretation, identification, and description if one is limited to simple examples and has to resort to artificial devices, such as raising issues about what is meant by "keys" or "table." It is quite a different matter if the proffered example of a true sentence is "Light is both a wave and a particle-stream" or "The repressive hypothesis was a major element in the deployment of human sexuality."

In these examples, the apparent clarity of the relation of "The keys are on the table" to keys on a table evaporates and we see the difficulties of the relational conception of truth.

Foucault's problem with extralinguistic reality is that the claim that it plays no epistemic role in confirmation is counterintuitive. The strength of Searle's employment of simple examples is precisely that it seems bizarre to say that the truth of the sentence "The keys are on the table" is wholly linguistic or discursive and independent of plainly seeing the keys on the table. Moreover, as I will consider later, Foucault's problem with reality's alleged irrelevance to truth or discursive currency takes a special form in his work, because Foucault presents his genealogies as intellectually compelling in a way that goes beyond proposing their discursive currency and internalization by individual subjects. As we have seen, Foucault also faces the problem that divorcing truth from reality prompts many to think that he must believe that there is no way that things are, that things are as we believe and say they are. As a consequence, Foucault is wrongly lumped with postmoderns who are linguistic idealist or irrealists of some stripe.

There is unquestionably a tension in Foucault's work regarding the relativization of truth and a number of problematic remarks. Aside from the tacit-realist use of truth and the polemical tone of his writings and lectures, there are passages where Foucault maintains that genealogy is "a form of history which can account for the constitution of knowledges, discourses, domains of objects, etc."; there are also passages where he maintains that his books must assert what is true to be of value (Foucault 1980b, 117; 1991a, 36). If truth is internal to discourse, genealogies should be presented only as alternative ways of construing some or all of the dominant principles and histories of their respective discourses. Genealogies should not be presented as extradiscursively true of their own or any other discourses. Foucault should offer his genealogies as alternative interpretations and justify them pragmatically in terms of particular intradiscourse objectives. Instead, Foucault presents his genealogies as compelling and goes so far as to challenge his critics by asking whether any of them has shown that his genealogical accounts are "*false* [or] *ill-founded*," clearly implying that his accounts are true and well founded (Foucault 1980b, 87; my emphasis).

Sympathetic commentators and unsympathetic critics, like Hoy and Habermas, press the question of how Foucault can be a historicist relativist regarding truth, yet present his genealogical analyses as intellectually compelling. Like Rorty, they think that Foucault actually fails to maintain his detachment of truth from reality because he presents his analyses as if he were discerning *deeper* truths (Hoy 1986; Habermas 1987, 273–74). Given his principles, all that Foucault should do is present his genealogies as opportunities for his readers to have productive interpretive experiences, which may, but need not be, similar to his own in developing the genealogies he presents.

Foucault goes only a little way toward resolving this apparent inconsistency, basically doing no more than acknowledging that there is a problem: "What historical knowledge is possible of a history which itself produces the true/false distinction on which such knowledge depends?" (Foucault 1991a, 82). As he sees it, the issue is the truth status of a given genealogical analysis of a particular history, such as that of penality. But what he offers in response is thin indeed, being only that sorting out "the difficult relation with truth" must begin with "the way in which truth is found used inside an experience" (Foucault 1991b, 36).

In responding in this way, Foucault seems to be appealing to the experiential use of truth and the internalization of discursive truths in limit experiences, as described in Chapter 3. The thrust of the appeal is that after due consideration, we should understand that we only see and speak about our internalized truths as objective because they are what we have internalized *as* truth. After all, at the heart of relativization of truth is the collapse of the distinction between subjective and objective truth. The knowledge gained, or the truth internalized, about a particular history, then, is what we "find" in an experience such as, for example, reading *The History of Sexuality*. If that reading produces a limit experience, one of MacIntyre's epistemological crises, and if in resolving the crisis we appropriate what Foucault presents as the history of sexuality, and reject "the repressive hypothesis," then we internalize his genealogy of sexuality as *true*. Henceforth, barring a new limit experience, we will speak of the deployment of sexuality as the true or correct history of sexuality and reject the repressive hypothesis as false, as a ruse of power.

With respect to Foucault's role in this appropriation, as an author he wrote *The History of Sexuality* as a consequence of thinking differently about the dominant history of sexuality as repressed since the Victorian era, and in the process himself internalized his own genealogy of human sexuality. But more than that, in writing the book he seeks to have *us* internalize his genealogy. It seems, then, that with respect to presenting his genealogies as intellectually compelling, genealogies that *he* has internalized in the process of developing them, Foucault has every right to speak about what he has internalized as truth in the most forceful way – especially if his intention is to get others to think differently.

The immediate response to this characterization of what Foucault is doing in presenting his genealogies as he does is that it will not work in Foucault's case because he presents himself as a genealogist, as one who understands the relativity of truth, and so understands that what he has himself internalized is historical and does not support categorical claims. However, there is a crucial point to be noted with respect to this response. Foucault's interest in offering his genealogies is not limited to revealing the workings of power in the development of institutions and the like. I think this is what Rorty, Habermas, and Hoy underestimate in contending that Foucault violates his own principles in presenting his analyses as cogent and so intellectually compelling.

The key point is that Foucault is as much interested in *changing* things as he is in tracing genealogies. Perhaps his deepest commitment is "to shake up habitual ways of working and thinking, to dissipate conventional familiarities" (Foucault 1989, 305). As I discuss in more detail below, Foucault's commitment to novelty of thought is total, so it is not enough for him to present genealogies as options in construal of institutions, disciplines, or histories; genealogies must be presented in a forceful, vigorous manner if they are to be effective in changing habitual ways of thinking. Reconstrual of dominant histories of institutions or practices is insufficient to prompt new thinking; dominant histories must be impugned, and that can only be done by presenting competing genealogies as compelling. But doing so does not entail that the proposed genealogies are presented as depicting objective realities that have been distorted by the histories the genealogies are intended to displace. All that need be entailed is that what has been internalized as truth, and become current and dominant in discourse, is or has become oppressive and supports power relations that stifle new thought.

Once it is seen that Foucault's manner of presenting his genealogies has to do with novelty of thought and anticipated productivity, rather than claimed discernment of underlying truth, it becomes clear that the cogency genealogy claims is not a matter of accordance with a reality conceived of as the measure and bestower of truth. Instead, that claimed cogency is a matter of promised productive alterity. What this means is that Foucault's implicit and occasionally explicit claims of the correctness of his genealogies are not claims about *reality*, not claims about deeper truths unearthed by his analyses, but rather claims regarding what we *ought* to internalize. They are claims about the experiential truths we *should* adopt. Foucault's polemics, then, may open him to a charge of arrogance, but not one of inconsistency.

Once we better understand how Foucault is dealing with truth and reality as separate from one another in the sense that the former is not measured nor dictated by the latter, and that he does not violate this separation in his polemics, we can see that his position is not undermined by inconsistency. This is not to say that there are no problems with Foucault's detachment of truth from reality; however, the problems he faces, like Searle's problems with saying just how true beliefs and sentences relate to states of affairs, are philosophical ones, not preclusive logical errors.

To proceed, I need to address how Searle and Foucault's views on truth and reality were enabled. There were developments in the debate on truth that shaped contemporary conceptions of truth. We could go back to Plato and Protagoras to trace the major contributing factors, but it is more practical and fairer to current debate to go back only to Kant and Nietzsche. They are the thinkers who most enabled contemporary conceptions of truth; in particular, they made it possible for thought about truth to take the relativistic direction it did in the work of Foucault's predecessors and peers, but also in the work of some of Searle's predecessors and peers – most notably James and Dewey, Goodman and Rorty.

The crux of Kant's contribution was philosophical recognition that asking if our view of the world is correct prompts realization that, as Williams puts it, "we cannot step entirely outside our . . . conceptions and theories so as to compare them with a world that is not conceptualized at all, a bare 'whatever there is'" (Williams 1998, 40). Once the inescapability and implications of conceptualization are grasped, it becomes clear that reality is knowable only from one conceptual perspective or other. The most serious consequence of this is that our beliefs and assertions cannot be assessed for truth by straightforward comparison with a reality accessed from no point of view. In assessing our beliefs, and consequent assertions, about how things are in the world, our perception of how things are is always conditioned by the very beliefs we are trying to assess.

Another consequence is that reality itself becomes problematic by a likely inevitable epistemic division between naive "direct" and sophisticated "indirect" forms of awareness of reality. The unreflective realist, who unquestioningly accepts that the world consists of mind-independent and accessible bright suns, marmalade pussycats, and clattering railroad cars is told that "all there really is . . . is what 'finished science' will say there is," and the world seems to slip away (Putnam 1987, 4).

These two consequences are, of course, of a piece, because it begins to look as if what there is really can only be some thing-in-itself reality that conceptualization or our "manifest image" serves up in various mind-dependent ways, and that is describable only with aspectually conditioned sentences (Putnam 1987, 4). Nonetheless, the Kantian realization might not have been enough to push doubts about truth and verification to the extreme idea that perhaps there is nothing "out there" at all, an idea that fostered the radical relativism that is now current in some quarters. Coherence theories might have remained more Davidsonian than Goodmanesque, pragmatism might have remained more Deweyan than Rortyan, and postmodern constructivism might have remained peripheral. Instead, relativism burgeoned into various extreme forms (Krausz 1989). What made the crucial difference was Nietzsche's contribution.

Nietzsche asked after the value of truth; as noted, he asked why we give the highest priority to achieving a uniquely correct description of how things are. Whatever else prompts this question, it seems inescapable in light of the Kantian realization that the world is unknowable except under some conceptualization, and the post-Kantian realization that conceptualizations may vary. Nietzsche's question raises the issue of whether "the world" is any way at all, independently of how we represent and describe it, since it becomes problematic whether the notion of a noumenal reality, of a "bare 'whatever there is,'" is coherent. The next step is not a legitimate one, but many find it unavoidable in the circumstances, and it is a move from the epistemological admission that we are limited to our conceptual framework, to the ontological position that the contents of that framework exhaust what there is. Given his realist inclinations, Kant's only option was to posit a directly unknowable noumenal reality, but as noted earlier, Nietzsche forcefully argued that "[t]he antithesis 'thing-in-itself' and 'appearance' is untenable," maintaining that truth is not linguistic portrayal of "the facts" because "facts [are] precisely what there is not." Again as was noted above, according to Nietzsche, there are "only interpretations," and the world – what there is and what true sentences supposedly portray – "is not a fact but a fable" (Nietzsche 1968, 267, 298, 330).

The combination of Kant's realization and Nietzsche's question enabled a paradigm shift in philosophical thinking about truth and what truth supposedly is about. Pilate's question ceased to be a rhetorical evasion and became a philosophical problem; Protagoras's old claim that we are the measure of what there is gained new depth as language became our Newtonian universe; Derrida's "axial" proposition

"There is nothing outside of the text" became conceivable (Derrida 1976, 159).

What is most significant to a comparison of Searle and Foucault about the foregoing has to do with confirmation of beliefs and claims. That is, as we will see in the next chapter, Searle and Foucault are not opposed metaphysically; both are realists and there is little to say about their views regarding reality or the world per se. What needs.to be considered here is how Searle relates truth to states of affairs, while Foucault makes truth wholly linguistic. Searle's relational conception of truth requires understanding how we square beliefs and sentences with the reality they putatively describe and in virtue of which some are true. This question is best addressed, with respect to Searle, in terms of how we determine the word-to-world "fit" of beliefs and sentences or how we confirm beliefs and sentences; with respect to Foucault, the question is best addressed in terms of how sentences circulate in discourse independently of the disposition of the world.

This radical difference between Searle and Foucault on the truth/ reality connection is interestingly reflected in how touchstone philosophical reference works define truth with or without reference to objective reality. *The Cambridge Dictionary of Philosophy* defines truth in the traditional way, and in line with Searle's view, as "the quality of those propositions that accord with reality, specifying what is in fact the case" (Audi 1996, 812). However, *The Oxford Companion to Philosophy* is more circumspect, saying that "[t]he term 'truth' seems to denote a property," and going on to consider if it is a property of sentences, statements, or propositions. It then describes correspondence as "the best known theory of truth" without committing itself to it (Honderich 1995, 881). A. R. Lacey's *A Dictionary of Philosophy* and Blackwell Publishing's *A Companion to Epistemology* both avoid offering a definition of truth in terms of a relation to reality and instead describe the various substantive and "deflationary" theories (Lacey 1990, 245–48; Dancy and Sosa 1993, 509–14). The *Concise Routledge Encyclopedia of Philosophy* offers definitions only of particular theories of truth: the correspondence, coherence, pragmatic, and deflationary theories (Routledge 2000, 899–900). Beyond discipline-specific reference works, the *Oxford English Dictionary* conforms to tradition – and Searle's view – and defines truth as "(II. 5.) conformity with fact; agreement with reality" (*Oxford English Dictionary* 1971, 3424). *Webster's Unabridged* follows suit, defining truth as "2. . . . that which conforms to fact or reality" (*Webster's* 1979). However, *The Fontana Dictionary of Modern Thought* defines truth without mention of reality as "[t]he property implicitly ascribed to a proposition by belief in or assertion of it" (Bullock, Stallybrass, and Trombley 1986, 876).

Conception of truth as relational, so of confirmation as entailing comparative reference to reality, is, as we saw in Chapter 1, what Allen calls the "classical" conception of truth. Allen's characterization has four elements: "the priority of nature over language, culture, or [history]"; "the idea that truth is a kind of sameness ... between what is said and what there is"; the "derivative character of the signs by which truth is symbolized"; and the unquestioned value of truth (Allen 1993, 9–10). As will emerge, the two elements most relevant to a contrastive comparison of Searle and Foucault are the first, nature's priority, and the second, truth as a sameness of what is thought or said and how things are.

Allen's characterization applies directly to Searle, despite the latter's rejection of the traditional correspondence theory. As argued above, what Searle rejects is a too-literal understanding of the establishment of correspondence. In any case, he does however hold that how things are, "the facts," are prior to and independent of their portrayal and of how culture or history might affect their portrayal. As we saw in Chapter 2, facts are not linguistic for Searle; they are not simply what true sentences state: Searle tells us that "the word 'fact' evolved so that you would have a word for the *nonlinguistic counterpart* of the statement in virtue of which the statement is true" (Rorty and Searle 1999, 35; my emphasis). For Searle, then, the "sameness between what is said and what there is" is just that true sentences mirror objective states of affairs when they correspond to the facts. This point holds regardless of his rejection of correspondence as a one-to-one comparison. Searle does explicitly commit himself to "the idea that truth is a matter of correspondence to the facts," arguing that a statement "will be true or false depending on whether things in the world really are the way the statement says they are." For him, therefore, truth is "a matter of accuracy of a certain sort of linguistic representation" regardless of how we go about establishing the accuracy of representation or correspondence (Searle 1995, 199–200).

As for the derivative character of signs, not only are facts temporally and logically prior to their representations, since Searle's position on intentionality is unequivocal on only consciousness being inherently intentional, but signs can only be derivatively intentional. Signs point to what they signify only in virtue of what *we* intend. As for the value of truth, Searle never questions it.

Foucault, on the other hand, rejects all four of Allen's elements. As we have seen, Foucault does not offer a theory of truth; he uses truth in five different ways and is explicit that "there are different truths" (Foucault 1989, 314). Truths are collected under a single label or concept only because of commendatory force and similar discursive and sociocognitive roles. What Foucault does offer is a good deal on how power relations produce truths and on how discursively current truths comprise regimes with particular standards and practices regarding the currency of sentences: "Each society has its regime of truth ... that is, the types of discourse which it accepts and makes function as true; the mechanisms ... which enable one to distinguish true and false statements; the techniques and procedures accorded value in the acquisition of truth; the status of those who are charged with saying what counts as true" (Foucault 1980b, 131).

Searle, Conceptual Relativism, and Confirmation

With respect to confirmation or justification, Searle's relational conception of truth is that truth is the squaring of beliefs and sentences with reality, with his extralinguistic "facts." This is diametrically opposed to Foucault's understanding of confirmation as a matter of establishing or recognizing the currency of a sentence in a discourse. What makes Foucault's discursive-currency view implausible, and makes Searle's relational view plausible, is that it seems intuitively clear that determining the truth of a belief or sentence *is* a matter of squaring it with reality. This is a powerful intuition, and its force explains why the relational conception has been so persistent in thought and debate about truth for so long.

However, things are not as straightforward as intuition suggests. The nagging question remains of just how we confirm the replicatory accuracy of a belief or sentence. In Searle's terms, the question remains of how we establish the word-to-world fit of a belief or sentence, how we determine that a belief or sentence does correspond to the facts. Doing so, on the one hand, seems to be obviously *some* kind of comparison but, on the other hand, we understand that doing so cannot be a one-to-one comparison because we have no independent access to states of affairs other than through the beliefs we hold and the sentences we utter.

Still, it seems that true beliefs and sentences do and must relate to reality, to the disposition of the world. Consider how it may initially appear that Foucault and Davidson are in accord with respect to the discursive nature of truth. Davidson tells us that "[n]othing, ... no thing, makes sentences and theories true: not experience ... not the world, can make a sentence true." However, this comment is preceded by Davidson saying that, with respect to establishing something as true, "all the evidence there is is just what it takes to make our sentences and theories true." Davidson's point is that there is no truth-making relation between states of affairs, on the one hand, and beliefs and sentences, on the other, but that is not to say, as Foucault maintains, that the truth of beliefs and sentences is wholly discursive. Davidson acknowledges that "facts, if we like to talk that way, make sentences and theories true." What puts Foucault closer to Davidson than to Searle is what Davidson adds in saying that the point about facts in some sense making sentences and theories true "is put better without mention of facts." He then articulates what seems to separate him from Foucault: "The sentence 'My skin is warm' is true if and only if my skin is warm." And even though he adds that "[h]ere there is no reference to a fact, a world," what he says is enough to separate his from Foucault's wholly discursive understanding of truth (Davidson 1985, 194).

In these comments, Davidson is clearly thinking about the disposition of the world, as Searle insists we should. Despite Davidson's denial that the warmth of his skin *makes* "My skin is warm" true, his skin being warm is still very much the key factor regarding the truth of the sentence. This sounds very like Searle's insistence that squaring sentences and "the facts" is not a matter of establishing some esoteric relation of correspondence, but rather a matter of saying how things are. Can Foucault, in relativizing truth as he does, deny that "My skin is warm" being true has to do with my skin being warm?

To clarify, and as anticipated in Chapter 2, I need to return to the point about how Searle conceives of establishing a confirmatory relation between a belief and how things are. Consider the full passage from which I quoted earlier. In response to my describing him as a correspondist in "Correspondence, Construction, and Realism" (Prado 2003b), Searle explains how he understands confirmation as follows:

Suppose I believe my car keys are on the dining room table. Now, how do I find out if this belief is true or false? Do I hold the belief in my left hand and hold reality in my right hand and look to see if they correspond? That is not my picture at all. Rather, my picture is that I look for my car keys. If they are on the table, then my belief is true, otherwise not. In accord with disquotation, the way to find that it is true that p, is to find that p. The correspondence theory in action is applied disquotation. (personal correspondence)

The difficulty with this account is that though Foucault could hardly disagree with it, for him Searle's explanation of how we confirm a belief is simply not to the point. Foucault, faced with the foregoing account, would say, "Of course, but that is not the issue."

To appreciate why Searle's account is beside the point, and to better understand the closeness of Foucault to Davidson and the distance of both from Searle, notice that Searle is discussing confirmation of a *belief*, and, as his account runs, it is a belief that almost certainly is not articulated. That is, Searle's example about the keys does not require that the belief that the keys are on the dining room table be articulated in thought or orally, and is very unlikely to be articulated in ordinary situations. The case in point is just a matter of Searle getting ready to leave the house, proceeding to the dining room, and picking up his keys from the table. This is confirmation of the truth of his belief only in an extended sense, because the belief is at issue only in the practical way that Searle might end up looking for his keys, or wondering where he left them, if they are not on the dining room table. In short, going to the table and picking up the keys may confirm his unarticulated belief or expectation, in the sense that Searle's intention to drive somewhere is not interrupted by failure to find his keys, but successfully picking up the keys does not confirm a belief in the sense of confirming or justifying a claim.

The importance of the foregoing clarification is that the contrast Searle tries to make, between a naive correspondist idea of comparing a belief or sentence with a state of affairs, and an instance of "applied disquotation" showing how the belief that-p is confirmed by p, does not work. The reason is that, in effect, we do not have a belief that-p to be confirmed; what we have is only a behavioral disposition, as we might put it, to retrieve the car keys from a particular place. And if Searle *did* articulate the belief, and say to himself or someone else, "My car keys are on the dining room table," and did, in fact, find his keys on the dining room table, we would be back to square one with respect to what to say about the relation between the sentence articulating his belief about the keys, and the location of the keys. Differently put, the force of the keys being where they are sought goes no way at all toward resolving the issue of how the truth of a *sentence* is established; all the account provides is an instance of a behavioral sequence that is not thwarted by an expectation's failure.

Davidson refers to "sentences and theories" in the foregoing quoted remarks. In the case of a sentence or theory, we have an item, a simple or complex proposition, that purports to describe how things are. In Searle's terms, we have an item that purports to correspond to the facts. In the keys-on-the-table case that Searle describes, however, it is arguable that we have nothing that needs squaring with reality *other than* in terms of whether or not a behavioral sequence is thwarted and a new one initiated, namely, looking for the keys. We certainly may speak of this as confirmation of the belief, as Searle does, but the debatable claim that he does not provide a case of "applied disquotation" robs his account of philosophical force.

The basic problem with Searle's attempt to illustrate confirmation with an instance of "applied disquotation" is that he presents how we substantiate beliefs and assertions by recourse to the world as too straightforward a matter and uses an example that is too simple. We cannot attempt a "confrontation between what we believe and reality," which Davidson rejects as "absurd" (Davidson 1986a, 309). We certainly do not, and should not, think in terms of holding a belief or sentence in one hand and reality in the other to compare the two in confirming one of the former, but it does seem too quick to say that establishing word-to-world fit can be adequately explained by describing a clear-cut and uncomplicated case of finding something where we are disposed to collect it – especially if it is a case that does not require, or likely even involve, anything propositional.

It seems, then, that the sort of practical example Searle offers does nothing to prevent Foucault's rejection of the idea that confirmation is a matter of establishing correspondence between sentences and states of affairs. If so, Foucault is not in the impossible position of having to deny the case Searle describes. In fact, the example's failure to cut philosophical ice raises anew a question about Searle's position, rather than impugning Foucault's. The question is just how different Searle's understanding of correspondence as "applied disquotation" is from the traditional correspondence theory.

Searle's insistence that correspondence is only trivially true, once we understand disquotation, is supposed to distance his conception of confirmation from the impossible correspondist idea of pairing off what we believe or say and reality. Referring to *The Construction of Social Reality*, Searle responded to my correspondist characterization of his views by saying, "You think that I am defending a version of the old fashioned correspondence theory. I am not. That is a view I characterize as 'absurd'" (personal correspondence; Searle 1995, 207). Unless we accept the very simple characterization of correspondist confirmation as a matter of holding a belief in one's left hand and holding reality in one's right hand, and looking to see if they correspond, however, the question persists about how he avoids correspondism's dilemmas.

Nor am I alone in reading Searle as a correspondist. Fotion's exposition of Searle's views on truth includes the admission that correspondism "has come upon hard times lately," but Fotion goes on to say that Searle "seems to be resuscitating the old correspondence theory of truth"

(Fotion 2000, 233). This is a cautious attribution more than adequately grounded in such Searlean remarks as: "I . . . defend the idea that truth is a matter of correspondence to facts" and one of the things "we all know to be true" is that "statements are typically true if they correspond to facts" (Searle 1999, 9).

Searle no doubt would respond by pointing out that he is using "correspondence" and "correspond to" in innocuous ways, given his contentions about disquotation and the triviality of the correspondence theory. This response is weakened, though, by one of the main problems with the correspondence theory, which is that there is no clear, unequivocal definition or account of just what correspondence *is*, so it is difficult to say one is using "correspondence" and "correspond to" in a way *other* than as used in exposition of the correspondence theory, if the way it is used in that theory eludes clear articulation.

My cautious description of Searle's conception of truth as being *relational*, as opposed to *correspondist* in nature, may not, in the end, mark a significant difference. If Searle's description of the correspondence theory as trivially true, and as merely applied disquotation, fails to avoid correspondism's problems with confirmation, it becomes unclear how he is not a correspondist. In any case, what matters for Searle is that confirmation does involve somehow squaring sentences and states of affairs or facts, while, for Foucault, confirmation is wholly discursive. The upshot is that, in light of Searle's and Foucault's views, questions persist about reality's role with respect to truth.

We are not likely to make much progress on the question of just how Searle can explain confirmation while avoiding correspondism's dilemmas; that is an issue with which he must deal, despite obviously being of the opinion that he has dealt with it. In any case, the thrust of the foregoing remarks has less to do with Searle's position than it does with showing that the intuitive appeal of Searle's position does not preclude Foucault's position. Foucault's views are not vitiated by the need to deny the obvious, if only because the apparently obvious is not quite that. We can proceed, then, by noting that what emerges is that Searle and Foucault are primarily divided on reality's epistemic role in confirmation of propositional truth candidates. The core of the division is Searle's resistance to, and Foucault's endorsement of, problematization of confirmation of the truth of sentences as the checking of those sentences against objective reality.

Davidson puts the basic problem clearly in describing his coherence theory of truth and knowledge. He explains that "there is a question how we can know that [truth] conditions are satisfied, for this would appear to require a confrontation between what we believe and reality." As we saw, Davidson goes on to say that this idea of a comparative confrontation is absurd (Davidson 1986a, 309). To Davidson's statement of the problem, we can add Williams's related characterization of our suspicion of truth as due, first, to recognition that awareness is aspectual and second, to past experience that apparent certainties prove false (Williams 2002, 1).

Earlier consideration of Kant and Nietzsche reminded us that we cannot climb out of our conceptualization of the world to gain a neutral position from which to compare our beliefs and sentences to the disposition of the world. This is the underlying reason why Davidson adds to his remarks about truth conditions the contention that "nothing can count as a reason for holding a belief except another belief" (Davidson 1986a). This is also why, despite his various disagreements with Rorty, Davidson acknowledges that he concurs with Rorty's claim that "nothing counts as justification unless by reference to what we already accept, and there is no way to get outside our beliefs and our language . . . to find some test" (Rorty 1979a, 178). We seem, then, to be pulled in Searle's direction by our intuition and at least in Foucault's general direction by contemporary thought on truth. What can we say about confirmation to resolve whether Searle and Foucault are hopelessly at odds on truth or are only talking past each other?

Nagel's Poser

The best articulation that I have found of the issue of epistemic confirmation or justification is Nagel's, who articulates the issue, and the more general contemporary doubts about truth, as the question of "where understanding and justification come to an end." Nagel describes the central problem as being whether understanding and justification "come to an end with objective principles whose validity is independent of our point of view," or whether they "come to an end within our point of view."

There is little doubt that the latter idea seems to predominate in our time, when so many take it that "ultimately, even the most apparently objective and universal principles derive their validity or authority from the perspective and practice of those who follow them." Though he does not refer to Searle or Foucault in particular, Nagel captures the heart of the opposition between them in saying that the new question, "in a nutshell, is whether the first person, singular or plural, is hiding at the bottom of everything we say or think" (Nagel 1997, 3).

For Foucault, we are at the bottom of everything we think and say. Therefore, for him, confirmation cannot be a reaching out of language or discourse to a reality that – precisely because of its independence and objectivity, its extralinguistic nature – remains separate from the practices we employ to count sentences true. Searle cannot accept this. For him, the very independence and objectivity of reality make it inescapably what is at the bottom of everything we think and say, and so what determines the truth of what we think and say.

Searle begins his rejection of relativism based on the aspectual nature of awareness, or what he calls "conceptual relativism," by admitting that our concepts "are made by us" and acknowledging that "[t]here is nothing inevitable about the concepts we have for describing reality," explicitly affirming that thought and perception are inescapably aspectual (Searle 1992, 131; 1999, 22). But Searle staunchly maintains that the aspectual nature of awareness and the possible variation of concepts do not entail that "external realism is false because we have no access to external reality except through our concepts." Searle goes so far as to say that he is "embarrassed" by the contention that the aspectual nature of awareness precludes external realism, describing the idea as "remarkably feeble" (Searle 1999, 23).

To make his position, Searle uses an example about different ways of counting the things in a room. According to the example, in one "conceptual scheme," the furniture in a room may be counted as a number of individual pieces, while in another conceptual scheme the furniture may be counted as one set (Searle 1999, 23). Note that Searle uses the phrase "conceptual scheme," clearly indicating that he considers the two ways of counting furniture as illustrating a conflict between different conceptual frameworks. The importance of this is that, as I consider below, some would not consider the two described ways of counting furniture as the relevant sort of conceptual difference, if what is at issue is conceptual relativism.

Searle then argues that, with respect to conceptual conflict, "[t]he appearance of a problem derives entirely from the apparent inconsistency in saying there is only one object and yet there are [several] objects." He maintains that "once you understand the nature of the claims, there is no inconsistency whatever. They are both consistent, and indeed, both are true." Searle adds that there are "many such examples in daily life. I weigh 160 in pounds and 72 in kilograms. So what do I weigh really? The answer is, both 160 and 72 are true depending on which system of measurement we are using." His conclusion is that "[t]here is really no problem or inconsistency whatever" in seeming conceptual diversity (Searle 1999, 23).

The main flaw in this argument is, as above, Searle's choice of examples. Here he characterizes conceptual relativism in a way that simply excludes the possibility of genuine conceptual diversity, and so precludes philosophically significant conceptual incommensurability. Searle's examples are supposed to establish that conceptual diversity does not rule out universally true descriptions of how things are, but the examples *presuppose* commensurability. What Searle tries to establish with his examples is that discrepancies among different descriptions generated by what he takes to be divergent conceptual schemes are only apparent, and therefore do not preclude descriptions of the world being true despite the use of different organizing concepts. What he offers as conceptual diversity is simply not that.

The core of Searle's argument is that descriptions generated by different conceptual frameworks only appear inconsistent because of the use of different inclusion criteria and measurement systems. This claim presupposes external realism, which is supposedly what is at issue, in reducing conceptual diversity and conflict to confusion about inclusion criteria and measurement systems. What underlies Searle's claim is his unshakable conviction in virtue of the world being just one way, and wholly independent of how it is represented, that the descriptions in his examples *must* be ultimately compatible despite the application of different organizing concepts and measurement systems.

While Searle is surely right about there being a single, objective reality, recall that his argument is intended to rebut the claim that the aspectual nature of awareness, by preventing "direct" access to the world, precludes external realism. That is the claim Searle describes as "remarkably feeble" and which he takes himself to be rebutting (Searle 1999, 23). The response to the claim seems just as feeble, to the extent that it is question-begging regarding conceptual diversity. But the main trouble here is that Searle's charge that the aspectual nature of awareness is used to ground irrealism is as dubious as his rebuttal. No doubt there are some who argue as Searle suggests, but Foucault certainly does not argue that because awareness is aspectual, the world does not exist or is a product of discourse. To return to what has emerged as an underlying theme in the foregoing, it is the *epistemic role* of the world that Foucault problematizes, not the world, and that is what most divides him from Searle.

It merits mention that Searle is not merely equivocating in arguing as he does against conceptual relativism, as it might appear. His characterization of conceptual relativism is not disingenuous; it is dictated by his realism because his realism essentially prevents Searle from taking conceptual incommensurability seriously. This perhaps is clearest with respect to empirical inquiry. Searle is what some call an "inevitabilist"; he believes that science is a human artifact defined by how "its object of inquiry determines the shaping of the artifact itself." Therefore, Searle sees science "as bound to be as it is . . . because of the inherent structure of the universe" (Baruchello 2001, 103). This point applies equally to truth, not that Searle thinks truth is an artifact, as Foucault does, but because "the facts" determine what is true in thought and language. Interestingly, the point seems to apply to Foucault's tacit-realist use of truth. His dismissal of the "ensemble of truths" that are to be discovered can be read as Foucault saying that his lack of interest in these "truths" – but recall the inappropriateness of the term "truths" – is due to how they are not "truths" produced or altered by power because they just are how the world is.

For Searle, then, humans, Martians, and intelligent spiders all inevitably would discover Boyle's Law or Avogadro's Number, regardless of how their respective conceptual frameworks might differ, since any impartial science is molded by "the facts," and not by operant concepts or systems of representation. Furthermore, history, philosophy, and the social sciences also are molded by "the facts" because, as we saw above, eventually all social constructs are built on and must "bottom out" in brute reality or what is "not itself an institutional construction" (Searle 1995, 191). So incompatibility of description or conceptual conflict can only be apparent and must be ultimately resolvable, either by determining that descriptions vary because they use different measurement systems or the like, or by showing that some descriptions are true and others are false. This "inevitabilist" view is contrary to Foucault's constructivism, which casts science as "a goal-oriented . . . artifact reflecting specific ends as well as determinate social and historical conditions," though not contrary to his tacit-realist use of truth (Baruchello 2001, 103).

Searle's treatment of conceptual relativism turns on the fact that, for him, conceptual frameworks organize a single reality, not experience. This is clear in his contention that "[e]xternal realism allows for an infinite number of true descriptions of the same reality made relative to different conceptual schemes" (Searle 1995, 165). In Searle's view, diverse conceptual frameworks structure our construals of the world; they determine what we make of it, what we emphasize, what we value, what we ignore, and so on. But what is diversely construed is one world, one world that is as it is regardless of how we choose to think and speak of it.

What Searle misses is what Davidson points out, which is that conceptual relativism is about the structuring of *experience*, not the world. Briefly put, conceptualization's objects are the constituents of awareness, not the causes of awareness. Though he rejects the scheme/content distinction, hence conceptual-scheme relativism, Davidson makes clear that the point of conceptual-scheme relativism, as a philosophical position, is the central proposition that "[t]here may be no translating from one scheme to another," that conceptual frameworks may be incommensurable, because "[r]eality itself is relative to a scheme: what counts as real in one system may not in another" (Davidson 1973/1974, 5). This understanding is absent in Searle's examples of conceptual relativity; those examples amount to no more than application of different inclusion criteria and different measurement systems. If you jog a mile at 7:00 AM in sixty-degree weather, while I run 1.6 kilometers at seven hundred hours in fifteen-degree weather, we are not operating with different conceptual schemes; we are using different measurement systems. If we meet and chat after our exercise, we would hardly need to employ field-linguist techniques to understand one another about what we had just been doing.

Searle is quite right that there is no deep inconsistency generated by the use of different inclusion criteria and measurement systems, as becomes evident when we correlate civilian and military time, Imperial and metric measurement, and Fahrenheit and Celsius scales, but neither is there conceptual relativity in these cases. Weighing coffee in pounds and kilograms is not an instance of applying different conceptual schemes. Conceptual relativity, if it exists at all, is present in very different cases: Tycho Brahe and Johannes Kepler watching the dawn, with the former seeing the sun rising while the latter sees the horizon dropping; a physicist taking his cooling coffee to be losing caloric fluid while another takes his to be dropping in mean kinetic energy; a theist anticipates death as a transition while an atheist anticipates it as annihilation. And even these cases fall well short of the conceptual incommensurability we might encounter in trying to communicate with an intelligent light-year-long cosmic cloud.

Fotion tries to make Searle's position more plausible by offering a more sophisticated example than Searle's furniture and weight ones: "One historian characterizes a people as mainly industrious, another as mainly selfish, still another as mainly religious. It appears as if there is no one way to describe them. It also appears as if the feature each historian picks out is . . . a function of the ideology brought to the description" (Fotion 2000, 214). The inclusion of ideology helps, but Fotion's example still falls short. His three historians likely would be divided by no more than disagreement as to whether the character of the people in question is better captured by describing them *first* as industrious, as selfish, or as religious. No one would argue that these characterizations are mutually exclusive, much less incommensurable.

The upshot is that what Searle offers as examples of conceptually different descriptions fails because he construes conceptual relativism only as variation in organization of a common reality, rather than as variation in organization of experience. Searle's acknowledgment of the aspectual nature of perception and his admission that "[t]here is nothing inevitable about the concepts we have for describing reality" do not amount to acknowledgment of the kind of conceptual relativism that poses serious philosophical problems. This is because the possibility of incommensurability among conceptual frameworks is precluded by the fundamental position that "[w]e live in exactly one world, not two or three or seventeen" (Searle 1999, 22).

If Searle's presupposition of realism in his consideration of conceptual relativism needs to be made even clearer, we only have to note his assertion that "the most fundamental features of [the] world are as described by physics, chemistry, and the other natural sciences" (Searle 1995, xi). There is no preparedness here to consider that there might be incommensurable differences among competing sciences. The point is not, of course, to assert that there *are* such differences, only to make clear that their possibility, which is what is at issue, is precluded because resolvable conflicts due to the employment of diverse inclusion criteria and measurement systems are the only sort recognized. It might be thought that Searle is not alone in conceiving of conceptual relativism in this tendentious way. Putnam often sounds very like Searle and uses examples very like Searle's object-counting one in his own treatment of conceptual relativism; however, Putnam does recognize what he calls "radical" relativism, which does tolerate incommensurability (Putnam 1987, 17–20).

The relevance of Searle's treatment of conceptual relativism to the confirmation or justification issue is that Searle is unwilling to seriously consider that we may not have conclusive access to the world or "the facts" to confirm articulated beliefs or justify claims. Searle is not simply precluding questions about incommensurability; his presupposition of an accessible, objective, single reality is not a naive one. What Searle is really doing is using what Rorty describes as a philosopher's ploy commonly resorted to in arguments against pragmatic and relativistic claims regarding the world and conceptualization.

In defending his pragmatic understanding of truth, Rorty says that such accounts are usually "met by changing the subject from truth to factuality" through an appeal to "hard facts" (Rorty 1991c, 80). He explains, "When Galileo saw the moons of Jupiter through his telescope, it might be said, the impact on his retina was 'hard' in the relevant sense." That is, regardless of how he and his supporters conceptualized the experience of looking through the telescope, objectively real moons had a causal impact on Galileo and his supporters' eyes, just as they did on the eyes of the Paduan astronomers. The fact that "[t]he astronomers of Padua took it as merely one more anomaly . . . whereas Galileo's admirers took it as shattering the crystalline spheres once and for all" supposedly changed nothing. The argument is that "the datum itself . . . is utterly real quite apart from the interpretation it receives" (Rorty 1991c, 81). Searle's own shift from truth to factuality is clear in the following passage, where he is driving home a point about the priority of how things are to how they are represented.

Think of the relation of realism and conceptual relativism like this: Take a corner of the world, say, the Himalayas, and think of it as it was prior to the existence of any human beings. Now imagine that humans come along and represent the facts in various different ways. They have different vocabularies, different systems for making maps, different ways of counting . . . etc. Next imagine that eventually the humans all cease to exist. Now what happens to the . . . Himalayas and all the facts about the Himalayas in the course of these vicissitudes? Absolutely nothing. Different descriptions of facts, objects, etc., came and went, but the facts, objects, etc., remained unaffected. (Searle 1995, 164)

This is all very well, but it is not what is at issue; it is just the change of subject Rorty describes.

As Davidson and Rorty observe in different ways, what is at issue regarding conceptual relativism is not brute reality but how conceptualization objectifies, qualifies, and conditions experience. The trouble is that Searle imposes on conceptual relativists his own presupposition that conceptual frameworks organize objective reality. The clearest instance of this is his claim that "conceptual relativity . . . seems to presuppose realism, because it presupposes a language-independent reality that can be carved up or divided up in different ways" (Searle 1995, 165). Searle is right only to the extent that some forms of conceptual relativism are Kantian in holding that there is a noumenal reality that is diversely conceptualized. However, the worrying sort of conceptual relativism, what Davidson is concerned to defeat, is Nietzschean, not Kantian, in that it rejects the thing-in-itself/appearance or scheme/content dichotomy as untenable or unintelligible. This sort of relativism, the sort Putnam calls "radical," dismisses the idea of a single, variously conceptualized reality as incoherent.

In sum, consideration of Searle's treatment of conceptual relativism reaffirms that, for Searle, confirmation ends in showing that a belief or sentence corresponds to the one reality by faithfully portraying how things stand in that reality, and this is so, regardless of how the belief or sentence is conceptualized. Searle endorses "the Enlightenment vision" of a universe amenable to accurate description, and it is a universe that "exists quite independently of our minds" (Searle 1999, 1–4). Searle is adamant that "there exists a real world that is totally independent of human beings and of what they think or say about it," so if we are to confirm or justify what we think and say about that world, we must square our beliefs and utterances with how it stands (Searle 1999, 13). In fact, given that realism is a condition of intelligibility, a Background factor, there is no coherent alternative to reality playing the epistemic role of guarantor of truth. We may describe truth as discursive, but ultimately any social construct "must bottom out in an . . . element that is not itself an institutional construction," so objective truth must underlie anything we circumscribe as discursive truth (Searle 1995, 182–91).

Discursive Confirmation

Foucault's treatment of confirmation is less textually evident than Searle's. There is no explicit denial of the Searlean claim that it is "intuitive" that true sentences are "made true by how things are in the real world" (Searle 1995, xiii). Foucault's position on the truth/reality relation is defined by his rejection of the second of Allen's elements, the idea that truth is a kind of sameness with the world. This entails something that perplexes many, as we have seen, because our intuition is that truth *is* some kind of sameness between what we think and say and how things are. Moreover, rejection of the second element makes it look as if Foucault is denying the priority of nature over language.

Foucault is denying that priority, but not in terms of the sheer existence of brute reality; he is denying that nature's or reality's objectivity and independence from language, culture, and history give nature priority in the sense of playing the decisive role with respect to truth. In short, Foucault is denying what Davidson denies and Searle asserts: that nature or the world or "the facts" *make* true beliefs and sentences true. Nature's objectivity and independence simply is a fact, and according to Foucault, it is a fact that does not bear on discursive truth. Nature or brute reality is "the ineffable cause of sense," and as such is something that genealogical analysis of truth "at the moment is leaving alone" (Rorty 1982, 15).

However, as has emerged, this is where things get complicated in trying to understand Foucault's views. What is difficult to grasp is not only that nature or the world or the things themselves are irrelevant to discursive truth, in the sense that they do not establish or guarantee what is or is not true; it is also that discourse is not about nature or the world or the things themselves, because discourse is not *about* anything. Discourse is, as we might put it, itself a reality that in a sense competes with the world.

A discourse is a very complex set of practices that constitute an environment in which participants have their social and disciplinary being. The sense in which discursive reality competes with extralinguistic reality is that discourse objectifies what count as things and events. Referring to essences that we think we discern, Foucault insists that we must "substitute for the enigmatic . . . 'things' anterior to discourse, the regular formation of objects that emerge only in discourse" (Foucault 1972, 47). His point is that brute reality, the world, does not contain clinical madness, judicial criminality, or human sexuality. Brute reality does not contain the second law of thermodynamics nor – as Foucault reminds us by recounting Borges's fictional taxonomy – does it contain phyla and species (Foucault 1973, xv). Ironically enough, Searle would agree that reality, the world, contains money, contracts, and marriage only as social constructs.

For Foucault, then, confirmation cannot extend beyond discourse, beyond language. This seems plausible enough with respect to justifying claims about the role of discipline and the imposition of a sexual nature, but what about things like believing one's car keys are on the dining room table and finding them there, or asserting that water expands when it freezes and finding that ice floats?

I can clarify the daunting idea that discursive truth is not determined by how things are by drawing a parallel to how truth is established in a court of law when juries issue verdicts and presiding judges accept those verdicts. Consider that prior to the issuing of a verdict, a defendant's actions may be described as criminally negligent by the prosecutor and as innocently injurious by the defense attorney. What is important, and not realized by many, is that, in law, the actions in question are indeterminate as to classification and culpability prior to the verdict. If the jury finds for the prosecution, what happens is that the actions in question then and only then are established as criminally negligent, and it is then and only then true that the individual on trial acted in a criminally negligent manner.

Most people think that the accused either did or did not act in a criminally negligent manner, regardless of the verdict, and that juries try to discern what really happened by considering the evidence. But despite appearances, that is not how the judicial system works. What the accused actually did is and remains a particular action, an event that took place at a certain time and place; however, prior to a "guilty" verdict, that action is not yet an act of criminal negligence from the legal perspective. That is precisely what the jury *decides*, not discerns. This is why, cynically put, innocence is no excuse in the courts, and why convictions need to be formally revoked when, say, someone else confesses to the crime for which some hapless defendant was convicted. It is the verdict that determines the reality of criminal negligence or of innocence, not the actions that took place.

The pivotal point is that there is no fact of the matter that is independent of the verdict, despite the actuality of the events that constituted the defendant's actions. The verdict does not conform nor fail to conform to the factuality of an act of criminal negligence; the verdict does not articulate the one correct description of the act at issue. There is a fact of the matter only *after* the verdict. It is the verdict, as the judgment of the court, that establishes that certain actions were an instance of criminal negligence or not, but to say this is not to deny the reality of the defendant's actions. The legal description and the actuality of the actions are separate things.

Foucault's position is basically that there are no truths, no facts of the matter, independent of societal and disciplinary truth-establishing practices. Foucault rejects Searle's idea that facts are "the nonlinguistic counterpart of true statements stated in language," that "the word 'fact' evolved so that you would have a word for the nonlinguistic counterpart of the statement in virtue of which the statement is true" (Rorty and Searle 1999, 35). Beliefs and sentences do not match up to *anything* extralinguistic in being true, whether "nonlinguistic counterparts," or reified facts. For Foucault, what determines sentences as true is entirely internal to discourse and consists of the practices that allow certain things to be said and disallow certain other things being said. Truth is a status given to some beliefs and sentences. This is the point of Foucault's claim that regimes of truth each have procedures and designated authorities that determine what is true (Foucault 1980b, 131). Establishing a sentence as true is not a matter of ascertaining that the sentence accurately represents something extralinguistic; instead, it is a matter of sanctioning a sentence's use in a discourse, including its use in sanctioning the use of other sentences.

What is implausible about Foucault's position, and plausible about Searle's, is that whatever we might say about the truth of sentences, our beliefs and remarks about keys on tables and water freezing seem undeniably to be about keys and water, not about whatever we might think or say about keys and water. However problematic they may be as a philosophically convincing account of confirmation, Searle's contentions about his belief that his keys are on the dining room table are credible with respect to how we ordinarily think about the confirmation of belief.

It is important to appreciate that, for Searle, consideration of truth does not begin with what we *say*; it begins with how the world *is*. The thrust of Searle's example about confirming the belief that his keys are on the table is that what we think about the world begins with our awareness of its disposition and our capacity to manipulate and move around in it. The great bulk of that is not articulated. Philosophizing about truth, then, does not begin with what we say; it begins with how things are and whether or not we get it right in awareness. The truth of our beliefs about keys on tables and water freezing appears to be fundamental, and confirmation of those beliefs does seem to be picking up keys and ice floating.

The only way to understand Foucault's indifference to states of affairs when considering truth is to see him as not concerned with something as fundamental as our ability to cope with our physical environment, and to see him as conceiving of philosophical consideration of truth as focusing on discourse. To clarify this, consider again Searle's example about his keys being on the table. Finding the keys on the table is a matter of a sequence of behavior being successful, or that sequence not being disrupted and another sequence being initiated. Searle's expectation is not the belief *that the keys are on the table*. That is, what supposedly is confirmed, the "belief," is a belief in the same sense we ascribe beliefs to animals, and is better described as a disposition: a state prone to produce certain behavior. As such, it is as much something in the world as the keys themselves. The property of *being true*, then, does not apply or fail to apply to this state or disposition. It is not until and unless the belief is articulated, even if only to oneself, that it becomes cognitive in the sense of something that is either true or false. It is only at the point, when the Searlean "belief" is captured in a sentence, that Foucault becomes interested, because that is when discursive truth is at issue.

Foucault rejects the conception of truth as beginning with those states of ours that are responsible for our navigating around the world and manipulating the things in it. The things themselves, including mental states, are real enough, and prior to language and culture, but they are prior only in the philosophically irrelevant sense that they exist independently of both. They are not prior in the sense of normative precedence. What exists prior to and independent of discourse is *brute reality*, Rorty's ineffable cause of sense, and brute reality does not lend its actuality to sentences.

For Foucault, an articulated belief or sentence being true is a matter of it achieving a certain status through complex discursive and practical procedures, not the belief or sentence corresponding to extralinguistic reality. As for basic beliefs about keys and water, if these are not articulated, they remain outside the purview of philosophizing about truth. What Searle considers confirmation of the belief that his keys are on the dining room table, that is, picking up his keys, is no more than one more operant causal factor in the series of events that comprise a particular sequence of his behavior.

True Genealogies?

However, if Searle faces a problem with respect to how we square beliefs and sentences with "the facts," one problem Foucault faces is that while his genealogies are not *supposed* to square with some extralinguistic reality, he usually presents them as if they do. Recall that Foucault insists that genealogy struggles "against the power of a discourse" and opposes the "functioning of an organized scientific discourse within a society" (Foucault 1980b, 83–84). The question is how Foucault's oppositional genealogies of penality and sexuality are *better than* the dominant histories they oppose, if they do not better discern and describe how things developed or are. This is the question Hoy, Habermas, Rorty, and others see as left unanswered and so as possibly vitiating genealogical analysis. Why should we listen to Foucault if his oppositional genealogies are, by definition, not current in discourse, but neither are – by his own principles – objectively true?

Supporters as well as critics of Foucault have pressed the question of how he can present his genealogies as better than the histories and accounts they oppose, while holding truth relative to concurrent and temporally successive discourses. Though he does not mention Foucault in particular, Searle himself puts this question to postmoderns. As Fotion observes, Searle makes the point "that it is not clear on what basis we should take any postmodernist pronouncements seriously," since, "[h]aving made all thinking relative to one or another conceptual scheme, one set of thoughts would seem to be as good as any other" (Fotion 2000, 217).

Robert Nola presses a version of the same question about Foucault's claims in his suggestively titled "Post-Modernism, A French Cultural Chernobyl: Foucault on Power/Knowledge." Nola asks how Foucault can maintain that truth is relative and also claim "that theories which rival his own are false" (Nola 1994, 37). Todd May, a much more sympathetic reader of Foucault, also makes the same point by noting that given his "radical questioning" of the traditional philosophical conceptions of truth and knowledge, Foucault owes us, but fails to provide, an account of why we should "accept his inquiries as justified and possibly true" (May 1993, 71). David Couzens Hoy, though a supportive expositor of hermeneutic and postmodern positions, notes that while relativizing truth to "what in Anglo-American philosophical vocabulary could be called a . . . paradigm or conceptual framework," Foucault seems to exempt his own pronouncements from that relativization (Hoy 1986, 5).

Certainly Foucault does not write as if he were only offering discourse-specific interpretive alternatives. His works are decidedly polemical and he is often scathing in his treatment of opponents, definitely writing as if he were right and they were wrong. The question is quite apt, then, as to what he is doing. I suggested earlier that the pivotal point here is that we may have no choice but to present to others what we have internalized as truth as being objectively true. I suggested further that Foucault's intent in presenting his genealogies as compelling analyses was that we should adopt them and internalize those genealogies as true. But even if these suggestions go some way toward resolving the question about the didactic manner of Foucault's presentation of his genealogies, he makes things worse by going further than relativizing truth to discourse and maintaining that rationality itself is historical, contending that "forms of rationality are created endlessly" (Foucault 1988a, 35).

If Foucault's genealogies are not assessable or confirmable by being squared with extradiscursive Searlean facts *and* our assessment of them is conducted by employing reasoning that is as relative to time and discourse as the genealogies themselves, it looks as if all Foucault can do is attempt to *persuade* others to adopt his genealogies. That is, Foucault's presentation of his genealogies of penality and human sexuality would not be a matter of establishing the cogency of those analyses, but only an effort to convince us of his opinions. When we add power to the equation, and recall how it shapes subjectivities as well as molding the operant rationalities Foucault historicizes, it seems that what we think are rational argument and assessment never rise above mere persuasion and rationalization, and that our standards change to accommodate our objectives and desires.

Some will say that this is precisely the situation, that Foucault is a typical postmodern who reduces intellectual inquiry and reasoned debate to interest-serving sermonizing. In a typical response to claims like Foucault's about the historicity of rationality, Putnam argues that rationality cannot be historical, that historical standards or developments "cannot define what reason is" because they "presuppose reason . . . for their interpretation" (Putnam 1987, 227). Putnam contends that rationality is "a regulative idea" that governs all inquiry and enables us "to criticize the conduct of all activities and institutions" (Putnam 1987, 228).

Putnam's is a familiar view of rationality as something that we manifest as thinking beings and cannot influence; rationality or reason is something we meet or fail to meet, not something we produce. This view is fundamental to conceptual and empirical inquiry, which presuppose that there are procedural standards that are independent of values or culture, and that it is only in virtue of their existence that we can achieve correct understanding of the world and ourselves. Ahistorical rationality is taken to be basic to intellectual and practical inquiry and what enables us to distinguish between the fruits of inquiry and mere opinion.

Foucault calls claims like Putnam's "blackmail," charging that philosophers counter "every critique of reason or every critical inquiry into the history of rationality" with application of what he considers a false dichotomy requiring one to "either . . . accept rationality or . . . fall prey to the irrational" (Foucault 1988a, 27). But Putnam and others do not see the dichotomy as false; they take it that to attempt to relativize rationality as Foucault does *is* to fall prey to irrationality.

However, the issue is not as straightforward as it might appear. Foucault's claim about the historicity of rationality can be clarified, even if not substantiated, by distinguishing practical from regulative rationality. Putnam is right to feel challenged, because Foucault's point is about regulative rationality. The point can be restated in Rorty's terms as the claim that there is "no criterion that we have not created in the course of creating a practice." Regulative rationality is "obedience to our own conventions" (Rorty 1982, xlii). Put this way, the point emerges more clearly as being that there is no rationality independent of our inquiry-defining practices, no divine or Platonic principles to which our practices must conform. Rorty is more appreciative of Putnam's objection than is Foucault, so he spells out what it means to claim that regulative rationality is historical.

Using the term *vocabulary* to refer to what Foucault would call a discourse, and others likely would call a conceptual framework, Rorty argues that we must accept "that there is no standpoint outside [a] particular historically conditioned and temporary vocabulary . . . from which to judge this vocabulary." Therefore, to say rationality is historical is to give up "the idea that intellectual . . . progress is rational, in any sense of 'rational' which is neutral *between vocabularies*" (Rorty 1989, 48; my emphasis).

The core of what Rorty is claiming is that we cannot achieve a history of vocabularies or discourses – for instance, of scientific paradigms – that reveals cumulative progress from one to another according to standards external to them all. Here Rorty is in accord with Kuhn and Feyerabend that the shift from, say, Aristotelian to Newtonian physics, though of practical benefit, cannot be judged an objectively progressive one in the sense of being an advance in our discernment of how the world really is (Kuhn 1970; Feyerabend 1978).

Rorty's formulation of how rationality is historical enables restatement of Foucault's claim about multiple rationalities and precludes Putnam's dismissal of the claim as simply wrongheaded. On the one hand, the heart of the matter is that there are philosophers committed to real progress in intellectual inquiry: to progress that is objective advancement across discourses and that is governed and may be measured by ahistorical regulative principles. These philosophers consider that shifts such as from Aristotelian to Newtonian physics are authentic, perspective-free advances, rather than only changes from one to another paradigm or conceptual framework. They believe that it is both *better* and *more rational*, quite independently of paradigms or frameworks, to have physics in which we need to explain why projectiles slow and drop to the ground, rather than physics in which we need to explain why projectiles keep moving and do not immediately drop to the ground. Explanatory recourse to momentum, gravity, propulsive force, and wind resistance is judged to manifest truer understanding of how things are than explanatory recourse to a natural tendency to fall to the center of the Earth and the contravening effect of air massing behind a projectile. Searle is one of these philosophers, believing in progress measured by cumulative discernment of truth about the world and ourselves (Searle 1999, 1–37).

On the other hand, we have Foucault and others, including Feyerabend and perhaps Kuhn, who see no way of establishing that a paradigm
shift is an objective advancement. These philosophers consider appeals
to truth, reason, and rationality in the process of trying to establish
real progress to be no more, though no less, than constitutive moves
in the production of norms and paradigm-relative truths. For these
thinkers, appeals to truth and rationality are either the establishment
of the conventions Rorty speaks of or application of those conventions.
For Foucault and Rorty, "progress" is always how sequences of events
or paradigm shifts look from within the present discourse or vocabulary or conceptual framework. There can be no recourse to extradiscursive criteria that could show judgments about progress to be right
or wrong, because we are unable "to step outside of our current theory
of the world" in order to evaluate its merits against competing theories
(Rorty 1979b, 85).

The internalization of standards to discourses, paradigms, vocabularies, or conceptual frameworks is basically the fundamental postmodern
idea that there is an inescapable "turning back" on our beliefs, language,
and practices in intellectual inquiry (Lawson 1985). Hilary Lawson characterizes the postmodern perspective's defining tenet and greatest problem as the recognition that there is an inherent circularity in intellectual inquiry, because inquiry ends up assessing itself and its progress by
applying standards that it itself generates. This is Rorty's more positively
put point about obedience to our own standards, and is what Foucault
acknowledges in asking what knowledge "is possible of a history which
itself produces the true/false distinction" (Foucault 1991a, 82).

Reference to Rorty in the present context may suggest that perhaps
the only way for Foucault to deal with the question of the cogency of
his analyses is to adopt Rorty's neopragmatism and maintain that utility is the only criterion for choosing among contentions, discourses,
conceptual frameworks, or, for that matter, Searle's and Foucault's
respective conceptions of truth. Unfortunately, utility is only a stopgap
measure.

The difficulty with appealing to utility as the ultimate criterion is that
the question immediately arises as to what ends utility *properly* or *best*
serves. As endless debates amply demonstrate, intractable conflicts arise
because of the generality of "pleasure" or "happiness," or some variation
on one of these as utility's ultimate end. Each of these is, notoriously,
wide open to varying interpretation, which takes us back to the lack of
recourse to external standards.

Foucault does not appeal to utility as Rorty does; he does something more heroic by stressing that genealogy's primary function is to constantly problematize established discourses and conceptual frameworks, dominant histories and disciplines. In so doing, Foucault appeals to *novelty* – novelty of thought and practice (Foucault 1980b, 85; 1988b, 265). Of course, we can raise the same question about novelty that we can raise about utility, What end does novelty serve? Foucault is silent on this, seeming to take it that novelty of thought and practice is worthwhile in itself. He asks what intellectual activity can consist of if not "the endeavor to know how and to what extent it might be possible to think differently" (Foucault 1986, 9). He tells us "[m]odifying one's own thought and that of others seems to me to be the intellectual's reason for being" (Foucault 1989, 303). As noted above, the job of the intellectual is "to shake up habitual ways of working and thinking, to dissipate conventional familiarities" (Foucault 1989, 305). Of his own work, Foucault tells us, "When I write, I do it above all to change myself and not to think the same thing as before" (Foucault 1991b, 27).

Miller portrays Foucault in his biography as valuing change for its own sake, as an end in itself (Miller 1993). But while this might initially look sophomoric, novelty of thought and practice plays a relatively precise role in Foucault's thinking, a role that imbues change with ultimate value in his thought. The crucial point is that novelty of thought and practice is the only effective resistance to power's increasingly constricting effects. Novelty is the only source of resistance to the conformity that is progressively imposed on us by power relations. Novelty of thought and practice, wrested from epistemological turmoil in limit experience, provides a counter to the constant "normalizing" influence of power relations because it enables new perspectives on established truths and procedures. Novelty keeps at bay what Foucault sees as the worst possible outcome of power's relentless efficacy: the homogenizing and total regimentation of human beings.

In "Two Lectures," Foucault offers a more focused account of genealogy's prime problematizing function when he maintains that his alternative histories are "anti-sciences." It is always "against the power of a discourse that is considered to be scientific that . . . genealogy must wage its struggle" (Foucault 1980b, 84). What genealogy does is oppose "the institution and functioning of an organized scientific discourse within a society" (Foucault 1980b, 83–84). *Scientific* here must be understood broadly, as referring to all that is taken to be disciplinary truth, where disciplines range from physics to psychiatry, from educational psychology to all manner of professional counseling. Genealogies are antiestablishment; they oppose *whatever* is current and dominant in a regime of truth. Therefore, though one genealogy cannot be preferred over others because of imagined greater closeness to ahistorical truth, it may be preferable because of the degree of dominance of what it impugns, and thereby of the magnitude of what it enables. A new genealogy makes possible novel construals of events and institutions, thus enabling resistance to the dominant influences that shape our collective truths and practices, and through them, our individual subjectivities. The more powerful the dominant influences, the better the opposing genealogy.

Recourse to novelty, then, goes some way to resolve the matter of how Foucault can present his genealogies as better than what they oppose. For example, his genealogical analysis of sexuality is given huge importance by the scope and supremacy of what it opposes. Moreover, Foucault's genealogy of sexuality seems to be unique. Where might we find a competing account that so challenges the dominant understanding of sexuality? Kinsey's work on sexual practices might come to mind, but it was more a development of the dominant view than a rethinking of it. Perhaps feminist critiques of sexual attitudes and values, taken together, constitute a competing genealogy.

However, in the end, just as Rorty faces the question of what ends utility should serve, Foucault faces the question of what end novelty serves. The question persists as to why we should prefer the thought and practices a problematizing genealogy enables over those established by what it displaces. The only answer is a fundamentally Nietzschean aesthetic one: power is increasingly constricting – we cannot escape power relations – but novelty of thought and practice can change the structure of power relations, and in that change we come as close as we can come to Nietzschean self-definition.

It merits mention, though, that the foregoing applies to Foucault's genealogical works; achieving change in the power relations that define our subjectivity is the only freedom we can attain. The point seems much more problematic with respect to Foucault's later ethical works. There, the subject rather mysteriously regains a measure of autonomy. Though of interest, this consideration is not of immediate relevance, as my comparison of Searle and Foucault focuses on the latter's genealogical "domain of analysis."

Novelty's ultimate value for Foucault, then, is ultimately a Nietzschean blend of aesthetic and ethical worth. However unsatisfactory this valuation of change for its own sake may be to many, Foucault's prioritizing of novelty explains the point I made earlier about his offering his genealogies as what we *should* internalize. The reason we should internalize them is that they are opportunities for us to think differently. Therefore, Foucault presents them as opportunities that are preferable to their competitors and to the dominant thought and practice those genealogies challenge.

Essentially, Foucault offers his genealogies as opportunities for us to think differently because they enabled *him* to think differently, and so to become a different subject. This reliance on the importance of his own intellectual development is part of the reason Rorty complains that Foucault mistakenly proceeds as if his philosophical project must be *our* philosophical project (Rorty 1991a, 198).

The foregoing will not satisfy readers who agree with Habermas, Hoy, Rorty, and others that Foucault is inconsistent in presenting his genealogies as intellectually compelling while relativizing truth to discourse. Nonetheless, the foregoing explanation of Foucault's assertiveness does enable us to proceed on the understanding that Foucault is being too zealous rather than preclusively inconsistent. Foucault is neither being simply inconsistent nor disingenuously presenting his genealogies as ahistorically true while historicizing truth. The source of his assertive presentation of his genealogies is his perception of them as compelling opportunities for novel thought, and that perception seems to suffice for them to be, in his view, better and more compelling than what they counter.

However plausible most of the above might be, a question remains that underlies everything said so far, and that is, again, how Foucault can separate truth from the world by internalizing truth to discourse and abandoning conception of truth as relational. Foucault is not alone in facing a persistent question about truth and reality. The question for Searle is how he connects truth and the world, how he relates beliefs and sentences to states of affairs in establishing truth. We now need to look more closely at the role realism plays in Searle's and Foucault's respective positions on truth.

5

Truth and Realism

One reviewer of *A House Divided* remarks that in my contribution, a lead-up article to this book, it is Davidson who emerges as "the real hero" (Prado 2003a, 2003b; Lackey, forthcoming). This is because, in considering the question of confirmation or justification and reality's role, Davidson, while never coming close to impugning realism, nonetheless cogently argues that the only reason we can have for holding a belief is another belief, and that there is no possibility of demonstrating the truth of a belief or sentence by comparing it with some bit of extralinguistic reality. Though more problematic in several ways, Foucault's position is importantly similar to Davidson's. The basic similarity between Davidson and Foucault is found in the latter's holding that discursive truth and the establishment of discursive truth in confirmation are separated from brute reality by the fact that brute reality plays no epistemic role in the determination of truth despite its essential role in the *causing* of belief.

Brute reality enters the confirmation picture only when we fail at what we try to do, when the world's disposition impedes or defeats action based on our beliefs and assertions. In Searle's example about his keys being on the table, the brute reality of the keys being on the table does not confirm his belief. The disposition of the world is as it is, and its role is limited to causing awareness and belief; the disposition of the world does not also play a confirmatory role. Reality figures in the example only to the extent that the local disposition of the world either enables Searle to pick up his keys and go on his way, or causes him to acquire new beliefs and consequently engage in different behavior, such as searching for the keys. As Rorty puts it, brute reality cannot make true sentences true because there is "no way of transferring this nonlinguistic brutality to *facts*, to the truth of sentences" (Rorty 1991c, 81).

Ironically, Foucault fumbles a key comment, quoted earlier, which if differently stated, would have made clear how his own separation of truth and reality is a putting aside of what plays no epistemic role in the confirmation of truth. As noted, Foucault misspeaks in saying that he is not concerned with an ensemble of *truths* waiting to be discovered (Foucault 1980b, 132). What he actually sets aside is not truths, but extralinguistic reality. It is Rorty's "ineffable cause of sense" that Foucault's genealogical inquiry "is leaving alone"; Foucault sets the world aside because he is of a mind with Rorty regarding our need to "see sentences as connected with other sentences rather than [with] the world," and with Davidson's view that "nothing can count as a reason for holding a belief except another belief" (Rorty 1982, 15; Davidson 1986a).

Foucault not only errs in speaking of truths, he also separates truth from brute reality in too offhand a manner, a manner taken by many as implying or entailing denial of reality. Foucault is interpreted as a linguistic idealist and as agreeing with Derrida that "[t]here is nothing outside of the text" or discourse (Derrida 1976, 159). However, thinking of Foucault as just another postmodern and lumping him in with "other French contemporaries . . . especially Derrida, is a disservice both to Foucault and to the important ideas that he can bring to North American philosophy" (Munteanu 1998, 153).

Foucault's pluralistic, discursive redescription of truth is an important idea and worth serious consideration, and it should not be summarily dismissed because of misinterpretation of it as irrealist in nature. Nonetheless, as has been evident in all of the foregoing, and as Searle would insist, it does seem counterintuitive to separate truth and reality. The problem, then, is to make good sense of how Foucault can be a realist – albeit a tacit realist – and still hold truth to be wholly discursive and nonrelational. As we have seen, this is the obverse of the problem we have with Searle, who poses the problem of how to make good sense of the way that states of affairs make beliefs and sentences true, and hence of how confirmation is establishment of some legitimating relation between beliefs or sentences and states of affairs (Searle 1995, 219).

In this connection, note that it will not do for Searle to claim that he does not face this problem because confirmation is not a matter of establishing a comparative relation between beliefs and sentences and states of affairs, as he does in the keys-on-the-table example. The fact is that however Searle may disparage as naive and ill-conceived the idea of comparative confirmation being establishment of correspondence of beliefs and sentences to states of affairs, if he insists that states of affairs make beliefs and sentences true, then he must be prepared to offer *some* theoretical account of how we confirm beliefs and sentences vis-à-vis the disposition of the guarantor states of affairs.

Mere reiteration of the disquotational view will not suffice because Searle does not accept that facts are linguistic in the sense of being simply what true propositions state, so facts persist as the "nonlinguistic counterparts" of true sentences. Therefore, if facts make sentences true, or true sentences correspond to facts, in however innocuous a sense of "correspond" Searle may favor, he owes us an account of how we establish the relation between true sentences and the states of affairs that supposedly make those sentences true. In short, his is a relational conception of truth, and whatever relation sentences bear to states of affairs, some account must be given of how we come to know that that relation exists.

What we need to do at this juncture is to clarify as well as possible how Searle and Foucault relate truth and reality, and that has less to do with how they do or do not relate *sentences* to reality than with the place of realism in their thinking. Searle's realism is explicit and unequivocal:

> I regard the basic claim of external realism – that there exists a real world that is totally and absolutely independent of all of our representations, all of our thoughts, feelings, opinions, language, discourse, texts, and so on – as so obvious and indeed as such an essential condition of rationality, and even of intelligibility, that I am somewhat embarrassed to have to raise the question and to discuss the various challenges to this view.   (Searle 1999, 14)

Being a realist, for Searle, is not a matter of endorsing a philosophical position; it is what we might call an *intentional stance*, to borrow a term from Dennett. What I mean by this is that Searle's view is that, as intentional beings, our awareness is determined by our taking most of what we are aware of as independent of us, as objective realities, and that it is only in virtue of our so doing that we can think as we do, communicate as we do, and deal with and move around in the world as we do.

Searle considers challenges to realism as rooted in what he calls "perspectivism," and sums up what is central to antirealist claims as being the idea that "we have no access to, we have no way of representing, and no means of coping with the real world except from a certain point of view, from a certain set of presuppositions, under a certain aspect, from a certain stance" (Searle 1999, 20). What Searle sees as the basic error in perspectivism is assuming that "knowing reality directly as it is in itself requires that it be known from no point of view" (Searle 1999, 21).

Searle rejects this assumption, arguing as follows: "For example, I directly see the chair in front of me, but of course I see it from a point of view." Nonetheless, he maintains, "I know it *directly* from a perspective. Insofar as it is even intelligible to talk of knowing 'reality directly as it is in itself,' I know it directly as it is in itself when I know that there is a chair over there because I see it" (Searle 1999, 21; my emphasis).

Despite variance in perspective, then, we have direct access to the absolutely mind-independent world whose disposition makes beliefs and sentences true. Whatever problems there may be with understanding just how beliefs and sentences relate to or derive their truth from states of affairs, and whatever might be decided about Searle's understanding of correspondence as trivially true, it is abundantly clear that Searle's realism is indisputable and unstinting. Nor does Searle's relational conception of truth in any way impugn his realism. In fact, given his realism, it is difficult to see how he could conceive of truth as other than beliefs and sentences squaring with the disposition of extralinguistic reality. It is Foucault who poses the problem with respect to realism, and whose position we need to examine more carefully.

Foucault, Realism, and the Complexity of Truth

Foucault's relativization of truth to discourse, and therefore his separation of truth from extralinguistic reality, can be further clarified as not being irrealist by considering the relativization and separation as two tightly connected but separate steps in one conceptual move. I can most briefly review the relativization step by using a passage from Allen's *Knowledge and Civilization*.

Allen remarks that in Foucault's thought, "[t]ruth-value is, in effect, 'monetarized.'" This is the point made earlier about truth being currency in discourse; Allen is simply making the point more literally. He tells us that "[l]ike prices or money, truth-values are purely . . . conventional, ultimately arbitrary structural artifacts of social economy. There is no more 'substance' behind the truth-value of statements than behind the price of commodities" (Allen 2004, 137).

But there is no linguistic idealism here, as so many assume. Referring to a sentence about witches, Allen tells us that equating truth with currency "is not to say the currency a . . . statement enjoyed in fifteenth-century Europe *made it true*, á la linguistic idealism" (Allen 2004, 137). He adds that "[p]ower cannot gear up, as it were, and make it go true that black is white, or two and two are five." To think this is to continue to understand currency and truth as different things, because it is to think that currency somehow *makes* something true, when *being* true simply is being current in a discourse; truth just is currency, "circulation in an economy of serious speech acts" (Allen 2004, 138).

Once truth is relativized to discourse, once being true is discursive currency rather than faithful depiction of the world, the second step seems inevitable and is the same one that Rorty and Davidson take, which is to deny, contra Searle, that the disposition of the world plays an epistemic role in the confirmation of beliefs and sentences and is the guarantor of truth in virtue of true beliefs and sentences corresponding to states of affairs.

This second is the step that offends realist sensibilities. The first, the relativization of truth to discourse, may be tolerated, especially if misconstrued as entailing that what is relativized is only what passes for truth in discourse, not "real" truth, as Foucault's position is often misinterpreted. However, when it is further claimed that the world neither guarantees the truth of beliefs and sentences nor makes them true by serving as their "original," as it were, then the relativization of truth to discourse together with the detachment of truth from states of affairs is taken as denial of the world.

Aside from rejection of linguistic idealism and irrealism, such as the above-quoted comment that he is not saying everything comes out of our heads, Foucault displays his realism in remarks that initially sound odd coming from him. On the same occasion as he makes the comment referred to, Foucault's interviewer asks him if perhaps truth is not a construct after all. Foucault responds somewhat surprisingly by saying, "That depends. There are some games of truth in which truth is a construct and others when it is not" (Foucault 1988b, 17).

This is a remark that would be taken as simply inconsistent by anyone unfamiliar with the various different uses of truth inventoried in Chapter 3, but it is not inconsistent, as I hope to have shown. However, to say it is not inconsistent is not to say that the remark is unproblematic.

The trouble is that while it is clear enough that truth is a construct in the criterial and constructivist uses, it seems just as clear that truth is not a construct in the case of the tacit-realist use. Given the difference between the criterial and constructivist uses of truth, on the one hand, and the tacit-realist use, on the other, it looks as if Foucault thinks that while some truth is wholly discursive, some truth is depiction of states of affairs. It then looks, yet again, as if Foucault either *is* concerned with what passes for true in discourse or "ideological" truth, despite his denials, or is being inconsistent.

I dearly would like to offer a decisive account here of how Foucault deals with this problem, but I cannot because I do not believe that he ever did resolve the issue. This is not to say that everything he says about truth must be understood as being only about what passes for true in social and disciplinary discourses. Foucault's position is very like Rorty's, and suffers from the same basic difficulty. While Rorty may talk plausibly about brute reality and the ineffable cause of sense, or what inquiry is leaving alone, he is much less plausible in maintaining that physics is just another *genre*, like history or art, and that its pronouncements only "pay their way" or are pragmatically utile, as are the pronouncements of other *genres*. Differently put, when beliefs and sentences about the world and its phenomena are in question, it is unconvincing to be told that they are described as true only in virtue of their utility in common or learned discourse. In the end, Searle seems right in claiming, as we will see below, that it is difficult for Rorty and Foucault to allude to objective reality, in rejecting charges of idealism or irrealism, while denying that some sentences are true in virtue of how things stand in the alluded- to reality.

We can make some progress by focusing on Foucault's above-quoted insistence that the possibility of an indefinite number of possible alternative genealogical descriptions "does not mean that there is nothing there and that everything comes out of somebody's head" (Foucault 1988b, 17; cf. Rabinow 1997, 297). This remark constitutes the first explicit point of contact between Foucault's and Searle's respective understandings of realism.

Just as Searle denies that variance in descriptive perspective entails impossibility of "direct" access to reality and so irrealism, Foucault denies that variance among genealogies entails linguistic idealism. For instance, opposing a genealogy of sexuality as constructed to the dominant history or conception of it as a discerned essence does not entail claiming that physical primary and secondary sexual characteristics are not objectively real and are mind- or language-dependent.

Searle is right that most postmoderns believe that perspective and the mediatory role of conceptualization jointly preclude "direct" access to the world. He is also right that they then erroneously conclude either that the world, because unreachable "directly," is only an empty abstraction or, notoriously, that there is no reality outside language. But Foucault's denial that genealogical variance means everything "comes out of somebody's head" and similar remarks should preclude interpreting him as another postmodern impugning the objective reality of the world.

Unfortunately, as is usual with Foucault, ambiguities – often deliberate – cloud the issue. In dismissing interpretation of himself as a linguistic idealist or irrealist, Foucault remarks, "some draw the conclusion that I said that nothing exist[s]" (Foucault 1988b, 17). However, what Foucault is referring to when he makes this remark is madness, not physical reality. He tells his interviewer, "I have been made to say that madness does not exist, although the problem was quite the contrary. It was a question of knowing how madness, under the various definitions that we could give it, could be at a certain moment, integrated in an institutional field which considered it a mental illness" (Foucault 1988b, 17).

Foucault's main concern in the relevant context is not objective reality, but rather how certain actions were collected as a particular type of behavior, and how that behavior, as a type, then came to be deemed perverse manifestation of an *essence*, and so capable of being an object of scientific study and therapeutic treatment. Foucault takes very seriously the alternatives that were open: to construe the behavior as so many disparate perverse or inexplicable acts or, for that matter, manifestation of divine possession or mere eccentricity. Because the Foucauldian genealogy of madness presupposes that things might have been, and still can be, different, it presupposes that the behavior at issue might be differently construed at different times and in different discourses. But this entails that the various acts that are collected as special behavior, and deemed madness in a particular regime of truth or economy of knowledge, be objectively real in order to be available for different characterization in a regime or economy. Foucault is not saying that madness does not exist *as a series of actions*; what he is denying is that the behavior is *by nature* of a piece, manifesting a discerned essence. Quite contrary to this, Foucault is claiming that the behavior-unifying "essence" is an *imposition*, something "deployed," in an economy of knowledge.

Foucault himself was at one time concerned to discern the sort of essence of madness that he later rejects as misconceived. As we saw in Chapter 3, what he sought to attain was the point "at which madness is an undifferentiated experience": the point prior to its being characterized by the various medical disciplines and its becoming a delineated feature of an economy of knowledge (Foucault 1965, ix). But we also saw that Foucault begins to abandon that ambition as early as the writing of *The Archaeology of Knowledge*. Abandonment of a search for the essence of madness is not denial of the objectivity of the acts that various disciplines collect as instances of madness; it is not espousal of the view that disciplinary discourses *create* the behavior in question.

Nonetheless, a certain ambiguity about brute reality persists. In Foucault's genealogical works, it is abundantly clear that truth is currency in discourse and that knowledge is sanctioned discourse, that there is "no more to 'knowing' than *who gets to say what*" (Allen 2004, 122). This, then, is a radical separation of truth and knowledge from brute reality, and it leaves one uneasy about Foucault's perhaps too-casual dismissals of linguistic idealism or irrealism.

Our counterpoint here is Searle's articulation of realism: "The world (or alternatively, reality or the universe) exists independently of our representations of it" (Searle 1995, 150). In Searle's case, there can be no separation of truth and knowledge from the world; it is the world that makes beliefs and sentences true, and knowledge is, for the most part, gaining and possessing knowledge of the world. Truth and knowledge are inextricably tied to the world.

As I maintain, what happens with respect to Foucault is that his denial of essences is taken as denial of the objective realities that supposedly manifest those denied essences. This is like thinking that denying a remark was malicious entails denying the utterance occurred as a sequence of muscle contractions and movement of air. The crux of the matter is that Foucault has little interest in things and events themselves. At the core of his relativistic account of truth is the idea that constraints on what we say are not imposed by the world or nature or states of affairs, but by all of the factors that define a regime of truth, a discourse, an economy of knowledge. As discussed earlier, sentences being true is not sentences mirroring states of affairs, but rather their gaining and maintaining currency due to application of the conventions and norms of particular discourses. It is the rules of discourse, not the world, that make a sentence true. This clearly is the point of greatest difference with Searle, who, as we saw, maintains that it is "intuitive," so one supposes not seriously deniable, that true sentences are "made true by how things are in the real world." Having knowledge, then, is not making the right moves in a discourse, but possessing beliefs and uttering sentences that accurately depict "the facts" (Searle 1995, xiii).

Foucault's relativization of truth to discourse, in breaking the traditionally assumed connection between truth and the world, at least looks like a slippery slope to irrealism. After all, knowledge of the world is mediated by neurophysiological goings-on and conceptualization, so the breaking of the connection that truth supposedly establishes between beliefs and sentences and the world seems to result in the world slipping beyond our epistemic grasp. Regardless of his dismissals of it, then, linguistic idealism haunts Foucault's position.

The first question we might ask at this point is why Foucault needs to separate truth from the world. Could he not, like Searle, admit conceptual diversity and relativize truth to discourse, but retain some form of acknowledgment that how things are determines what we properly can think and say?

Something of an answer begins to emerge if we, first, recall Foucault's tendency to be provocative – something he shares with Rorty – and, second, consider the following point. In Chapter 3, I described how Foucault uses truth in five ways that are differentiated by the contextual peculiarities of intradiscursive confirmation or the "means by which each is sanctioned" in a regime of truth (Foucault 1980b, 131). Using Davidson's terms rather than Foucault's, I propose that the five uses of truth result from how *being true* "is not a property of sentences," but instead is "a relation between sentences, speakers, and dates" (Davidson 1985, 43–44). Foucault needs his five uses to deal with the various ways that sentences, speakers, and dates relate to one another. This idea is supported by how Foucault's need is not unlike Davidson's need to deal with sentences in diverse "passing theories" (Davidson 1986b).

Once it is acknowledged that the truth of sentences is a function of their currency in the discourse in which they belong, of the context in which they occur, of who utters them, and of when they are uttered, it ceases to be possible to think of sentences as being true simply in virtue of replicating or depicting states of affairs. The most obvious reason for this failure is that, as Davidson recognizes, identification and description of states of affairs vary with sentences used, the speakers who use them, and when they use them. But this does not mean that because they are variously identified and described, states of affairs are metaphysically problematic. Searle is right about this much: objective compilations of things and events in the world may be described in unlimited and diverse ways, and the variety of descriptions in no way qualifies, much less jeopardizes, their mind- and language-independent objective existence. However, the likely rejoinder here is that this is all the more reason for Foucault to fall in line with Searle on the compatibility of conceptual or perspectival diversity and direct awareness and portrayal of extralinguistic things and events.

What Foucault sees is that truth is determined not only by the relations among sentences, speakers, and dates, but also by myriad historical and social factors that affect and define speakers and hearers as subjects, and that sanction some expressions and bar others. It is these latter conditions that Foucault attempts to describe when he inventories the components of regimes of truth and economies of knowledge, and when he traces the effects of discipline and power relations. This is why he feels that he needs to loosen "the embrace, apparently so tight, of words and things" in order to understand truth (Foucault 1972, 47). If some consequently read him as a linguistic idealist or other sort of irrealist, Foucault sees that as their problem, not his.

Foucault feels the need to attend specifically to the language games we play and the rules by which we play them, and believes that doing so has little or nothing to do with the world or Searle's "facts." The reason, as I have tried to make clear, is that he sees the disposition of the world as playing no epistemic role in how sentences become and continue to be current in a discourse or regime of truth.

The disposition of the world, as in the case of Searle's keys being or not being on the table, and how it relates to a belief or sentence, plays a role in whether or not Searle goes on his way or has to search his pockets for the keys. But it confirms nothing, in the sense of establishing a belief or sentence as true. The disposition of the world comes into the picture only when new beliefs are caused because the world is not as we say or believe it is. If we believe or say that our keys are on the table, the brute reality of certain objects being or not being in a certain place figures in consideration of the truth of our belief or utterance only to the extent that if the keys are *not* on the table, our belief or utterance will not support successful action, and a new belief will be caused. However, neither of these is an epistemic consideration bearing on the truth of the belief or utterance; both are indications of the value of the belief or the utterance, which is the gist of pragmatism and where Rorty is most right about beliefs or sentences "paying their way."

We can close this section by acknowledging the Davidsonian point that truth is a function of sentences, speakers, and times, but adding Foucault's contribution that there is a great deal of both a structural and "political" nature involved in something's being true. Foucault's loosening of the embrace between words and things is another matter, and one not easily resolved. Even though confirmation of the truth of beliefs and sentences involves other beliefs and sentences, not an impossible comparison to "corresponding" states of affairs, true beliefs and sentences are not all wholly unrelated to how things are in the world. Recall that despite his insistence on the linguisticality of truth, Davidson affirms that

the sentence "'My skin is warm' is true if and only if my skin is warm."
Davidson adds that "there is no reference to a fact, a world," but his doing
so in no way implies that the sentence "My skin is warm" is true or false
irrespective of his skin's temperature (Davidson 1985, 194).

Sentences like "My skin is warm" and "Water expands when it freezes,"
unlike those about penality or sexuality, pose a problem for Foucault.
Such sentences are instances of his tacit-realist use of truth, but saying so
only slots them into a problematic group. What persists is the inescapable
fact that these sentences are *about the world*, and hence that their truth
must bear some relation to how things are. Clearly, more needs to be said.

Separating Truth and the World

Much of the foregoing suggests that tackling Foucault's separation of
words and things head on is not a productive strategy. This is because, as
acknowledged earlier, he does not seem to have worked out the implications of his tacit-realist use of truth. We need, therefore, to proceed in a
more indirect manner.

As noted in the previous section, the first point of contact between
Foucault and Searle is that neither allows perspectival variance to imply,
much less entail, linguistic idealism or some other kind of irrealism.
Searle's arguments against the challenges to realism are based on his view
that variance in perspective does not preclude direct access to reality. In
Searle's view, then, the epistemological issue about the independent existence of a brute reality that is accessible only indirectly does not arise, and
if the epistemological issue does not arise, there is no basis for ontological denial of extramental or extralinguistic reality. For his part, Foucault
explicitly denies that variance in genealogical description entails that
"everything comes out of somebody's head." By implication, variance in
discourses does not entail linguistic idealism or irrealism either.

A second point of contact between Searle and Foucault is their shared
realism about *social* reality. We saw in Chapter 2 how Searle understands
the construction of social reality as the production and maintenance of an
integrated set of institutions that are objective with respect to individuals'
beliefs, in that they are enabled and maintained by collective intentionality. We also saw in considering Foucault's perspectivist use of truth in
Chapter 3 that social constructs are presented to subjects as objective
realities, and how it is that these constructs are maintained in, and so
constitute, our cultural and social environment. Social constructs are not
reducible to individuals' beliefs for Searle or for Foucault.

Useful in clarifying the objectivity of social reality in Searle's and Foucault's respective positions is a distinction between two different kinds of realism. On the one hand, there is a very Searlean "ordinary realism" that encompasses physical and social reality and holds "that the world, including the social world[,] subsists independently of our thought about it." On the other hand, there is a narrower "critical realism," which Frank Pearce and Anthony Woodiwiss describe as holding that "[w]hereas the non-human world in no way depends upon us thinking about it for its existence . . . the human and especially the social world is in large part so dependent" (Pearce and Woodiwiss 2001, 51–52).

Searle is clearly an "ordinary" realist in virtue of the role of collective intentionality. As for Foucault, application of the ordinary/critical distinction makes it "impossible to read him as a critical realist," because Foucault's thought manifests "an ontological insistence on the non-minded and material character of social reality" (Pearce and Woodiwiss 2001, 52, 61). As considered earlier, social reality is as objective an environment for individuals as is the physical world they inhabit.

What differentiates "ordinary" and "critical" realism with respect to Searle and Foucault is whether the elements of social reality are identical with or reducible to so many individual beliefs. Both Searle and Foucault deny that identity or reducibility, albeit in different ways and for somewhat different reasons. Neither believes that institutions like marriage and money are physical realities like moths and mountains, but neither believes that social reality is mind-dependent in the sense of being a compilation of individuals' beliefs. Admittedly, there are problems with what makes the social objective in both Searle's and Foucault's thought: collective intentionality and the Deleuzean objectivity outlined in Chapter 3. However, the point here is not whether Searle and Foucault are *right* about the objectivity of social reality, but rather that, for both, the social is a "second order" reality supervening on physical reality but not one reducible to so many beliefs held by individuals.

To return to the most bothersome question of Foucault's distancing of words from things, what needs to be appreciated is that in separating truth from the world, Foucault is primarily concerned with showing that what he calls some "things," that is, essences or natures, are manufactured in discourse rather than found in the world. Showing this to be the case is crucial to Foucault's account of how coming to hold something true shapes us as subjects of experience and as subjects of governance. His point is that most of what determines our subjectivity is manufactured and imposed, not given in brute reality. The point can be put this way: Foucault is not interested in whatever relations sentences may bear to the world or that we may establish between sentences and the world. What interests him is *how we relate to sentences*. The focus of his interest is on how we relate to the sentential elements of dominant regimes of truth or economies of knowledge, as well as how we might relate to the sentential elements of earlier or contemporary regimes or economies that have been obscured or suppressed by present dominant regimes or economies.

A recurring difficulty, though, is that loosening the connection between words and the world, making truth a function of discursive conditions, does sound as if it is Foucault focusing on what merely passes for true rather than on what actually is true, after all. And this is so despite his being adamant in rejecting interpretation of himself as concerned only with ideologically distorted truth. He insists that his genealogical treatment is of truth itself, not of "something else which is supposed to count as truth" (Foucault 1980b, 118). Certainly Foucault is not arguing, for instance, that human sexuality does have a discernable essence that has been distorted since the Victorian period; he is arguing that the truths of human sexuality are just what is current in the learned or disciplinary discourses that "deploy" the constructed essence of "human sexuality" throughout our culture.

If Foucault's rejection of the idea that he is concerned only with what passes for true is taken seriously, it emerges that the root of misperception of him as concerned with ideologically distorted truth is a conflation of truth and states of affairs. And when this point emerges, it becomes clearer that misperceiving Foucault's separation of truth from states of affairs as irrealism is also to conflate truth and states of affairs.

The conflation of truth and states of affairs is a consequence of giving the wrong answer to what Davidson calls "the essential question" posed by true sentences. That question is whether a true sentence "is the . . . place where there is direct contact between linguistic theory and events, actions and objects" (Davidson 1985, 219–23). Many philosophers take a true sentence to be the place where the envelope of language is thinnest, as it were, and where cognition and brute reality most directly connect. The basic and compelling idea is that in uttering truths, we achieve our most direct epistemic contact with objective reality.

This idea may be wrongheaded, but acknowledging that it is does not make it much easier to see true sentences as separable from the things and events many of those sentences purport to describe. What is it in

Foucault's thought that enables loosening the "embrace" of words and things; what is it that enables him to separate truth and the world?

Enabling the Separation

We can begin to understand what enables Foucault to separate truth and world by appreciating that his work on the development of institutions like the clinic, the asylum, and the prison, and on the introduction and use of exclusionary categories like "madness," "deviancy," and "normalcy," is all about *us*; it is about what we say and do. Foucault's work is about how we have taken ourselves as objects of study and how we have manufactured truths about ourselves; in this, his work is especially about what we *say* about ourselves. This point is evident in Foucault's work beginning with *The Order of Things*, which is subtitled "An Archaeology of the *Human* Sciences" (Foucault 1973; my emphasis).

The key point is that little of the content of the human sciences, those disciplines most concerned with words rather than things, with the social world rather than the physical one, fits or fails to fit brute reality. It is the content of the physical sciences that fits or fails to fit the world; it is the physical sciences that produce the sentences that may or may not have Searle's word-to-world fit. But the physical sciences are only peripherally relevant to Foucault's genealogical analyses; they are relevant only when their pronouncements encroach on or influence the human sciences.

Foucault "inscribes" truth in discourse to track and expose how psychiatrists, psychologists, penologists, vocational counselors, social workers, and others of their ilk construct natures and essences and their disorders and "syndromes" to explain human behavior. He wants to expose how these disciplines gerrymander our actions into protean categories generated by manufactured natures and essences, and ground the imposition of regimens, therapies, and medication to establish and maintain "normalcy." In this, Foucault is again doing what he did a little earlier when he worked to track and expose how historians, economists, linguists, and the like construct ahistorical governing principles and transcendencies to explain human historical and cultural developments. He attempts to expose how these disciplines structure and order events to lend them meaning and teleological direction to justify political actions and demands.

Foucault's objective is to comprehend and make clear how power relations function in the erection and maintenance of economies of knowledge, in order to understand how disciplinary truths and constraining and enabling influences define and redefine us as subjects of experience and governance, and as objects of study. Achieving that understanding has little to do with the truth of descriptions, such as of what happens when water cools to thirty-two degrees Fahrenheit. In yet another relevant but characteristically ambiguous passage, Foucault, speaking of the relation between power and knowledge, asks

if, concerning a science like theoretical physics or organic chemistry, one poses the problem of its relations with the political and economic structures of society, isn't one posing an excessively complicated question? . . . But on the other hand, if one takes a form of knowledge (*savoir*) like psychiatry, won't the question be much easier to resolve[?] . . . Couldn't the interweaving of effects of power and knowledge be grasped with greater certainty in the case of a science as "dubious" as psychiatry? (Foucault 1980b, 109)

I will return to the ambiguity of this passage; here it serves to underscore Foucault's focus on the human sciences and the relative irrelevance of the hard sciences to his treatment of truth.

The trouble with all of this is, of course, the tacit-realist use. The truths of the hard or "nondubious" sciences impose themselves when Foucault talks about truths that are to be discovered, or truths that are not constructs, or a reality that does not come out of someone's head. Searle offers a compelling argument that bears on how truths about the physical world determine his own conception of truth and should determine Foucault's. Incidentally, note how this argument supports my claim, made in Chapter 2 and alluded to earlier, that Searle's relational conception of truth follows from his realism.

In an e-mail to me in which Searle rejects my attribution to him of the traditional correspondence theory (Prado 2003b), Searle writes, "I will conclude with a philosophical point that I don't know that I have ever made in print but it certainly bears on this discussion." He then offers the following argument. Note, though, that Searle's references to "correspondence" and the "correspondence theory" in the argument should be understood as described in Chapter 2, namely, with correspondence as trivially true and an extension of disquotation:

I think once you accept external realism, you are forced to the correspondence theory. Here is why: Go through these steps.
1. External realism. There exists a reality totally independent of us.
2. As the world turned out, in that reality there are lots of objects and these objects have features.

3. We have evolved a language which among other things contains noun phrases for referring to objects and predicate expressions for ascribing features to objects.
4. Statements made that refer to objects and describe features of objects will be true if and only if the objects referred to will have the features ascribed.
5. 4 above states the essential features of the correspondence theory. You can make it more complex and generalize it, but that is the basic idea. I do not see how anybody who grants 1 can avoid 4. (personal correspondence)

Certainly it does seem that if the mind- and language-independent existence of objects is granted, and a sentence ascribes a feature to such an object, and the sentence is true, it must be true in virtue of the object referred to having the feature attributed to it, regardless of what discursive conditions the sentence may also satisfy.

Foucault's tacit-realist use of truth seems to involve reference to independent objects and their features, since surely if there are any truths "which are to be discovered and accepted," some must be ascriptions of features to independent objects (Foucault 1980b, 132). How, then, can Foucault separate truth and the world by making truth wholly discursive, or does he do so only in *some* cases? And if he does do so only in some cases, how are we to understand the boundaries on the constructivist nature of discursive truth? Notice, too, the danger here of saying that Foucault's tacit-realist use of truth is basic or fundamental, and the others supervene on it. That option immediately leads to the familiar but mistaken interpretation of Foucault as concerned only with ideologically or otherwise distorted truth.

The first thing to recall is that Foucault denies that truth is simple (Foucault 1989, 314). Foucault's treatment of truth discloses a degree of complexity regarding sentences being true that traditional philosophy denies, ignores, or obscures. The simplicity of truth is generally an article of disciplinary faith. Even Davidson, while insisting that *truth* is a complex interrelatedness of sentences, speakers, and dates, avers that talk of "fitting the facts, or of being true to the facts, adds nothing intelligible to the simple concept of *being* true" (Davidson 1985, 193–94; my emphasis).

However, for Foucault, a sentence's being true is never simple because a sentence's being true is not only an interrelatedness of sentences, speakers, and dates, it is also being current in a discourse, and being current in a discourse is a complex matter of being used repeatedly in a manner that satisfies multiple and diverse discursive conditions. This is why, as noted earlier, Foucault cannot accept disquotation as usually understood, but it is also why the tacit-realist use of truth poses a problem. In the case of

the tacit-realist use, truth is independent of the relevant discursive conditions to the extent that those conditions might be met or not met, and
the sentence still be true or false with respect to how things are in the
world.

We need to look more closely at just what Foucault acknowledges when
he employs the tacit-realist use or refers to truth that is not produced by
power. Sentences like "Water expands when it freezes" may not *interest*
Foucault, but he cannot ignore that those sentences being true is not just
a matter of their being current in a discourse.

Rorty is much cagier about his acknowledgment of objective reality.
Consideration of his acknowledgment, and of how he eludes Searle's
argument, casts light on Foucault's position. As with Foucault, many take
Rorty's pragmatism and rejection of correspondence as tantamount to
denial of the world. Rorty addresses charges of idealism or irrealism lev-
eled against himself and other (neo)pragmatists by claiming that the
pragmatist "differentiate[s] himself from the idealist" by agreeing "that
there is such a thing as brute physical resistance" (Rorty 1991c, 81). There
is brute resistance not only in that we are stopped by solid walls, but also in
that we cannot go about our business if our keys turn out not to be on the
table and the like. Our actions are obstructed when things are other than
as we believe and say they are, hence Rorty adds that pragmatists extend
"wholehearted acceptance to the brute, inhuman, causal stubbornness
of the physical world" (Rorty 1991c, 83).

Rorty is careful to speak of "brute physical resistance" and "causal
stubbornness" in acknowledging objective reality. There is no mention
here, as there is in Searle's various articulations of external realism, of
mind- and language-independent objects or features. What Rorty offers is
very like Locke's way of conveying an understanding of solidity by asking
that you hold something between your hands, "a Flint, or a Foot-ball,"
and then to try to bring your hands together (Locke 1975, 126). What
Rorty acknowledges is not a world of objects with their various features,
but *resistance.*

Rorty's care with respect to what he acknowledges is most evident
in the wording of his concession that despite the notion of sentences
"corresponding" to states of affairs being misconceived, we do have the
capacity to "pair off bits of the language with bits of what one takes the
world to be," as when we identify something and "we rap out routine
undeliberated reports like 'This is water,' 'That's red.'" Rorty admits that
our reports "do indeed pair little bits of language with little bits of the
world," though he has doubts about how far we can go in exercising this

capacity, noting that "[o]nce one gets to negative universal hypotheticals, and the like, such pairing will become messy and *ad hoc*," but allows that "perhaps it can be done" (Rorty 1982, 162).

The point of acknowledging the pairing-off capacity is to deal with the intuitively compelling idea that there are relations established between sentences and the world in the process of using language, an idea that is likely the source of, and perhaps all there is to, the notion of "correspondence." But we need to note that Rorty speaks of pairing sentences or bits of language "*with bits of what one takes the world to be.*" It is only given this more precise articulation of his point that Rorty speaks more loosely of pairing bits of language with bits of the world.

The importance of Rorty's phrasing is that it qualifies his reference to the mind- and language-independent world, and in this way circumvents what would be commitment to realism of the sort Searle thinks incompatible with rejection of some form of correspondism. And it is precisely in exercising care in this way that Rorty ducks Foucault's problem with the tacit-realist use. Rorty is unwilling to commit to realism because he dismisses the realism/irrealism issue as misconceived, as a remnant of Cartesianism. But Rorty's unwillingness to play the Cartesian epistemological game is not an agnostic stance vis-à-vis objective reality; brute reality is acknowledged, despite remaining "the ineffable cause of sense" (Rorty 1982, 15).

A common objection to Rorty's qualified references to reality, which also applies to Foucault, although for a different reason, is Rorty cannot refer to brute reality because he "give[s] up reference" in adopting pragmatism. The reasoning, according to Frank Farrell, is that Rorty's pragmatism entails that "our symbol sequences are meaningful only insofar as they help bring about habits of action that turn out to be useful," hence those "symbol sequences" cannot be about the world (Farrell 1995, 157). Whether Rorty talks about physical resistance, the ineffable cause of sense, or brute reality, then, he can only be endorsing useful "habits of action," not referring to anything extralinguistic. However, the conception of reference underlying this claim is question-begging against Rorty, for whom no "symbol sequences" reach out of language in the way the objection assumes words and sentences do. The objection that Rorty gives up reference, then, seems to come to no more than that Rorty denies what he intends to deny, namely, that words and sentences are true in virtue of "corresponding" to or "hooking up" with extralinguistic reality. Moreover, the objection ignores Rorty's careful avoidance of reference as a reaching out of language by acknowledging that we can and do "pair off bits of the language with bits of what one takes the world to be" (Rorty 1982, 162).

The way the reference-failure objection applies to Foucault has nothing to do with pragmatism and all to do with his relativization of truth to discourse. As Rorty supposedly gives up reference by making truth the utility of sentences, Foucault gives up reference by making truth internal to discourse. The real issue is, of course, not reference but truth. The source of the objection is that if truth is sentential utility or discursive currency, then there is no connection to the world's disposition.

Unfortunately, Foucault is not as circumspect as Rorty; his tacit-realist use of truth is not qualified as is Rorty's acknowledgment of brute reality. We can put the problem in the form of a dilemma: One horn of the dilemma is that power-produced truth supervenes on a more fundamental sort of truth that, in Searle's terms, has to do with ascription of features, including existence, to mind- and language-independent things and events. The positive aspect of this first horn casts Foucault as a realist and allows him to hold consistently that "[t]here are some games of truth in which truth is a construct and others when it is not" (Foucault 1988b, 17). The negative aspect of this horn is that the sort of truth attributable to ascriptions of features to mind- and language-independent things and events subordinates power-produced, discursive truth to "real" truth. The result is that despite his denials, Foucault is concerned only with distorted truth or what he calls ideological truth (Foucault 1980b, 118, see also 131–32).

The second horn of the dilemma is that power-produced truth is the only kind of truth there is. The positive aspect here is that Foucault is correct in denying his interests are limited to ideological truth. The negative side of this horn is that Foucault is inconsistent when he employs the tacit-realist use of truth or says that in some games of truth, truth is not a construct. This second horn also means that charges of linguistic idealism or irrealism against Foucault cannot be met by his acknowledgments of objective reality. Given the second horn, the truth of those acknowledgments is itself power-produced and wholly discursive, rather as the foregoing objection has it that Rortyan mention of brute reality can only be endorsement of a utile sentence.

In my view, the second horn of the dilemma is the less plausible of the two interpretive options, and this is borne out by how so many read Foucault not as inconsistent, but as focused on ideological truth. That is, many serious readers and critics assume that Foucault must differentiate between discursive and Searlean truths about the ascription of mind- and language-independent features to mind- and language-independent objects. They read Foucault's pronouncements about truth being power-produced and wholly discursive as about ideological truth. The question, then, is whether the dilemma can be circumvented. Can Foucault be interpreted as accommodating Searlean truths but right about not being concerned only with ideological truth? Differently put, can he mean it that the truth he considers is all there is, that it is not underlain by "real" truth? We need to consider more carefully just what Foucault denies regarding ideological truth.

Consider again a passage quoted earlier, where Foucault avers that "there are different truths and different ways of saying [the truth]" (Foucault 1989, 314). In Chapter 3, I used this passage to support my five-way differentiation of Foucault's uses of *true* and *truth*. This passage encapsulates the dilemma because it can be read two ways. On a permissive reading, "different" truths include both Searlean and discursive truths; on a stricter reading, "different" truths include only various types of discursive, power-produced truths.

The stricter reading disallows the tacit-realist use by making its use inconsistent. However, the more permissive reading seems at odds with Foucault's avowed reasons why he is not concerned only with ideological truth. He insists that ideology "always stands in . . . opposition to something else *which is supposed to count as* truth" (Foucault 1980b, 118; my emphasis). Foucault, then, is denying the distinction between power-produced truth, or what many take as ideological truth, and underlying truth. Recall, also, Foucault's ridiculing of critics who respond to his assertion of "a relation between truth and power" by thinking "'Ah good! Then it is not the truth'" (Foucault 1988b, 17). The object of the ridicule is the idea that power-produced truth is only what passes for true in a given cultural, social, or disciplinary context, and contrasts with underlying truth.

The danger Foucault faces if he allows the ideological/underlying truth distinction is that the distinction either precludes or seriously circumscribes genealogy. Given the distinction, genealogy's purpose would cease to be problematization of dominant "knowledges" and become discernment of the underlying truths that ideology distorts. If truth underlies them, the problematization of established histories, disciplines, and practices could not be conducted for its own sake, to enable us "not to think the same thing as before" (Foucault 1991b, 27). Genealogy would have to strive to discern whether those histories, disciplines, and practices distort or conform to underlying truth. Recall that ideology "always stands in . . . opposition to something else which is supposed to count as truth"; if there is such truth to be discerned, discernment of it must take precedence and genealogy must be rethought or abandoned as frivolous (Foucault 1980b, 118).

It is significant that Hoy and Habermas raise the question of how Foucault can present his genealogies as compelling. If they believed that Foucault is concerned only with ideological truth, they would not raise that question, because they would take it, as others do, that *Discipline and Punish* and *The History of Sexuality* are offered as discerning and relating the *correct* development of the penal system and the *correct* explication of sexual behavior. What prompts the question Habermas and Hoy ask is precisely that, though presented in a didactic manner, Foucault's genealogies of penality and sexuality are *not* offered as articulating the underlying truth of penality's history or sexuality's nature. They are offered as problematizing analyses of how the penal system evolved as a paradigm of social and individual control under the guise of the humanization of punishment, and how a constructed essence of human sexuality was deployed in an economy of knowledge.

It seems, then, that Foucault is concerned to show that power-produced truth is all there is. While there are different truths, it seems they are all cases of discursive currency. Foucault tells us, "'[t]ruth' is to be understood as a system of ordered procedures for the production, regulation, distribution, circulation and operation of statements" (Foucault 1980b, 133). This seems to leave no room for the tacit-realist use of truth, except as a series of inconsistent remarks.

What, then, about the truth of sentences like "Water expands when it freezes"? Surely *these* truths are not the products of power. However, the first thing to note is that while the sentence "Water expands when it freezes" is a truth about a feature of the extralinguistic world, the *content* of the sentence has varied over time. Such sentences, as articulated truths, are couched in discipline-determined terms and the language of a particular discourse. At one time, the sentence "Water expands when it freezes" was true in a theoretical context in which freezing was a loss of caloric fluid, and at another time the sentence came to be true in a theoretical context in which freezing is a loss of mean kinetic energy. There is, then, a bit more to the truth of sentences like this one about water. The question is whether that bit more is enough to get Foucault off the hook with respect to the tacit-realist use. The trouble is that whether we explain water's expansion on freezing in terms of loss of caloric fluid, reduced mean kinetic energy, or the doings of the gods, water *does* expand when it freezes, and the truth of the sentence "Water expands when it freezes" is in a crucial and irreducible way due to what happens in the mind- and language-independent world, regardless of what may be current in how that expansion is understood. It will not do, then, to claim that even sentences like "Water expands when it freezes" are true in virtue of wholly discursive factors.

Relevant here is the passage quoted earlier about the difficulty of mapping power relations if the focus is "a science like theoretical physics or organic chemistry" (Foucault 1980b, 109). As noted, that passage is ambiguous. On one understanding, Foucault is attributing the difficulty of mapping power's role in the production of the truths of the hard sciences to the sheer complexity of tracing determinants through theoretical and empirical levels. On another understanding, Foucault is drawing a hard distinction between discursive truths and Searlean truths about the features of independent objects.

Regarding Foucault's position, Dreyfus and Rabinow take a hard line, contending that it is clear that with respect to truth, "[w]hether we are analyzing propositions in physics or phrenology," concern is not with those propositions' relations to the world but rather with "their place within the discursive formation" (Dreyfus and Rabinow 1983, 117). Their question is whether Foucault's treatment of "every discipline as a discursive formation" can allow room "for the nondubious sciences (physics, biology, and so forth)" (Dreyfus and Rabinow 1983, 206).

In my view, this question is misconceived, because it fails to acknowledge the tacit-realist use of truth. I agree that for Foucault, whether we are analyzing propositions in physics or phrenology, the concern is not with how those propositions or sentences square with reality. However, while this is correct, it is incomplete. The reason is that not all sentences like "Water expands when it freezes" are disciplinary sentences or propositions that must be either internal to a "discursive formation" or require squaring with extralinguistic reality. Briefly put, some of those sentences are Rortyan "routine undeliberated reports" that do no more than "pair little bits of language with little bits of the world" (Rorty 1982, 162).

The most productive way to interpret Foucault is to take seriously his tacit-realist use of truth, and his remarks about truths that are not constructs of power, and not construe them as posing daunting questions about the hard sciences or dismiss them as inconsistencies. The daunting questions about the hard sciences are daunting only if one begins with the assumption that the pronouncements of the "nondubious sciences" must correspond to aspects of brute reality in the way Searle describes.

But, of course, that is precisely what Foucault denies and hence what is at issue. The remarks are not merely inconsistent, because in employing the tacit-realist use and saying what he does about some nonconstructed truths, Foucault is implicitly relying on the distinction that Rorty explicitly draws between *truth* and *factuality*.

What I am suggesting is that Foucault's tacit-realist use of truth, and his remarks about truths that are not discursive constructs, are on a philosophical par with Rorty's references to brute reality and brute physical resistance. Both Foucault and Rorty need to acknowledge the mind- and language-independent reality of the world, if only to rebut charges of linguistic idealism or other forms of irrealism. The trouble is that both need to make that acknowledgment without affirming realism and thereby granting the legitimacy of the realism/irrealism debate as a philosophical issue. Both see that debate as misconceived, as a lamentable legacy of Cartesian epistemology. Both of them need to refer to Searle's real world without embroiling themselves in what is, to them, a bogus issue. In this, Foucault and Rorty are very much at odds with Searle and Davidson, both of whom, albeit in different ways, think it important to *refute* irrealism.

Foucault and Rorty need to refer to the real world without jeopardizing their respective constructivist and pragmatic wholly linguistic accounts of truth. But they cannot allow acknowledgment of the objectivity of the world to commit them to correspondism as Searle believes affirmation of realism does, and as Farrell believes is necessary to enable successful reference to the world. Both need to acknowledge the real world without doing so in a manner that ties the truth of sentences to the world as the determiner and guarantor of truth. This is why the truth/factuality distinction is of crucial importance to Rorty, who draws it explicitly, and to Foucault, who fails to do so. The distinction enables acknowledgment of the factuality of the world without connecting that factuality to the truth of sentences. The distinction also enables Rorty, and by extension Foucault, to further acknowledge that we can and do establish a certain relation between sentences and the disposition of the world when we pair those sentences with things and events. The distinction allows Foucault to deal with the propositions of the hard sciences either as sentences that are true in virtue of their currency in theory-defined discursive contexts, or as sentences we pair with things and events; he need not inconsistently treat them as Searlean attributions that must have a "word-to-world" fit to be true.

As noted, Rorty's drawing of the distinction between truth and factuality is explicit. Recall his claim, discussed in Chapter 4, that pragmatic accounts of truth are "met by changing the subject from truth to factuality" (Rorty 1991c, 80). His contention is that critics shift the focus of discussion by distinguishing between sensory data and interpretation of the data, and arguing that a given sensory datum "is utterly real quite apart from the interpretation it receives" (Rorty 1991c, 81). The point is to focus on sensory data, in contrast to its interpretation, in order to reduce or dismiss the pragmatic account of truth as discursive utility, as about articulated interpretations of sensory data, and so, as with Foucault and ideological truth, not about "real" truth because not about the relation of the uninterpreted sensory data to what causes the data.

In Rorty's view, the reality of sensory data has to do not with truth, but with factuality. Key here is that, for Rorty, the reality of the sensory data is of the same order as the reality of the data's causes: both are instances of brute reality, so neither is an instance of truth and neither plays an epistemic role regarding truth. Factuality per se is not at issue; in discussion of truth, factuality is what "inquiry at the moment is leaving alone" (Rorty 1982, 15). To introduce factuality into a discussion of pragmatism and truth, then, is in fact to change the subject. And what is most important is that it is a change of subject that proceeds on the misconception that we can and actually must consider the juxtaposition of certain things and events in parts of the central nervous system, to certain things and events outside and sometimes inside the body, as a relationship in which the former *are true* of the latter to the extent that the former depict or replicate the latter.

However, my concern here is not with Rorty; it is with Foucault, and the point of reintroducing Rorty's claim regarding truth and factuality is that the distinction greatly clarifies Foucault's tacit-realist use of truth and occasional references to truths that are not constructs of power.

Foucault's rather offhand employment of the tacit-realist use is essentially the same as Rorty's occasional references to brute reality and brute physical resistance, and both are saved from inconsistency with their wholly linguistic or discursive conceptions of truth by the truth/factuality distinction. Despite their conceptions of truth, which give the disposition of the world no epistemic role in the determination and confirmation of truth, neither Rorty nor Foucault impugns the mind- and language-independent reality of the world. What so many find hard to understand, beginning with Searle, is that both think brute reality is separable from discussion of truth because that reality has no evidentiary role to play, no epistemic or justificatory function in consideration of truth.

Rorty's is the more careful and familiar treatment of the point. For him, factuality is not at issue in discussion of truth, and his position as to why it is not is compelling. A causal relation between sensory data and its causes, even if it involves some sort of structural isomorphism between the two, is not a matter of the sensory data *being true of* or even *being true to* the configuration of things and events that cause the sensory data. Sensory data are as much objectively real phenomena as are their causes. For example, a retinal image of a bust of Plato is something in the world, just as the bust of Plato is something in the world, and the retinal image is not true *of* the bust, anymore than the bust is true of Plato, despite *our* perception of likeness. The point is that no mere juxtaposition of two things or events constitutes an instance of an intentional relation, so no juxtaposition of a sensory datum and its cause can be a case of the former being true of the latter. Sensory data is not, in itself, intentional; no matter how accurately isomorphic or replicatory it may be deemed to be. A retinal image is not, in itself, the sort of thing that is true or false.

I close this section by observing that the distinction between truth and factuality can be described as rejection of what Davidson thinks is at the root of correspondism, namely, "the desire to include in the entity to which a true sentence corresponds . . . whatever it is the sentence says about [it]" (Davidson 1985, 49). The truth/factuality distinction separates true sentences from the things and events with which they may be paired. The distinction is a way of preventing the reading into things and events of what true sentences say about them. It is, in short, a way of thwarting efforts at equating truth, a linguistic or discursive status given some sentences, and the disposition of the things themselves. These efforts are little more than misguided attempts to guarantee human knowledge by not so much grounding it on, but rather *identifying* it with, what is external and forever indifferent to it.

Conclusion

In my view, the truth/factuality distinction saves Foucault's tacit-realist use of truth, and his remarks about truths that are not products of power, from inconsistency. Factuality plays no epistemic role regarding truth, so acknowledgment of it in the tacit-realist use does not jeopardize Foucault's other four uses of truth. In particular, acknowledgment of factuality does not undermine or seriously qualify Foucault's constructivism. Borrowing from Rorty, we can say that Foucault can pair sentences that are true, in virtue of their discursive currency, with states of affairs, and he can do so without thereby implying that those sentences are true *in virtue of* those states of affairs. Foucault's acknowledgment of factuality is not the sort of affirmation of realism that Searle thinks commits one to a relational conception of truth, that is, to some form of correspondism.

Searle and Foucault are both realists, but their understandings of realism differ. For Searle, acknowledgment of the independent existence of extralinguistic reality is fundamental, a condition of intelligibility; for Foucault, extralinguistic reality is an uninteresting given, something calling for mention only when challenged or denied by implication. These different understandings have extremely significant consequences for Searle's and Foucault's respective views on truth. Searle's conception of truth basically follows on his realism. Searle's realism is conceptually prior and fundamental to truth; it is also *practically* prior to truth, in that realism is not only a condition of intelligibility, it is a condition of our being able to think and talk about, and to move around in, the world. Against this, Foucault's conception of truth is basically of it as separate from mind- and language-independent states of affairs. For him, philosophical inquiry into truth can leave alone Rortyan brute physical resistance or Searle's "facts"; extralinguistic reality need be gestured toward only when the discursive nature of truth is misunderstood as having irrealist metaphysical implications.

The question we are left with regarding Foucault, and the question that Searle certainly would press, is whether acknowledgment of factuality is enough to assuage reservations that sentences like "Water expands when it freezes" really are true *of the world* rather than only being true in virtue of their currency and their regularly being paired, in Rorty's sense, with the relevant states of affairs. In other words, we are brought back to the question of the legitimacy of Foucault's separation of truth and the world.

Unfortunately, this question cannot be tackled directly without reaching a frustrating impasse because, as suggested earlier, there is simply not enough material to work with. Foucault disdained metaphysical debates and, like Rorty, thought that embroiling himself in them conceded far too much to traditional Cartesian epistemology. A more productive approach to the question is to say more about the place of the realist intentional stance in Foucault's account of the shaping of subjectivity. To provide a context for discussion of the realist intentional stance, I offer below what is, in my view, the most direct account Foucault offers of the separation of truth and discourse from the world, from the silent or "dumb existence of . . . reality" (Foucault 1972, 49).

The passages I have in mind, parts of which I quote earlier, occur in *The Archaeology of Knowledge*, where Foucault is explaining "discursive formations" – basically, theoretical disciplines – and how discursive formations are defined by the establishment of objects of study. The discussion runs from page 44 through page 49, but the parts most significant to our interests can be presented briefly. Foucault tells us that while "a history of the referent" – of what discourses are about, of what signs designate – "is no doubt possible," what he is concerned with doing

is not to neutralize discourse, to make it the sign of something else . . . What, in short we wish to do is to dispense with "things." . . . To substitute for . . . "things" anterior to discourse, the regular formation of objects that emerge only in discourse. . . . To define these *objects* . . . by relating them to the body of rules that enable them to form as objects of a discourse . . . I would like to show that discourse is not a slender surface of contact, or confrontation, between a reality and a language . . . I would like to show . . . that in analyzing discourses themselves, one sees the loosening of the embrace, apparently so tight, of words and things, and the emergence of a group of rules proper to discursive practice. These rules define not the dumb existence of a reality . . . but the ordering of objects. . . . Of course, discourses are composed of signs; but what they do is more than use these signs to designate things. . . . It is this "more" that we must reveal and describe.
(Foucault 1972, 48–49)

As stressed above, Foucault is setting aside extralinguistic reality, "referents," and concerning himself with discourse, with signs and how they operate according to rules that not only govern their status, manipulation, and referentiality, but also enable the emergence of new objects of study that are *constructed in discourse* but are dealt with as if *discerned in the world*: madness, abnormality, sexuality, and other essences and natures.

The passage just quoted, when taken with others quoted earlier, should leave no doubt that Foucault is not impugning the objectivity of mind- and language-independent reality. The trouble is that, like Rorty, Davidson, and Sellars, but decidedly unlike Searle, Foucault does not think that things and events themselves are what make sentences true and what guarantees their truth.

To proceed, I consider something that I have not seen discussed elsewhere, namely, the way in which Searle's account of how we are social beings, and Foucault's account of how we are shaped as subjects, share a crucial dependence on *habit formation*. Considering this shared dependence shifts the focus from brute reality to social reality regarding Foucault's separation of truth from states of affairs, but there is little more of a productive nature that can be said about his tacit realism with respect to the physical world. Against this, it is enlightening to see how the reliance on habit formation that Foucault shares with Searle presupposes the realist intentional stance.

The human aptitude for *habit* formation differs from what we share with most animals, which is the capacity for *conditioning.* Just like Pavlov's dog, we can be conditioned in various ways by things that happen to us or around us in a repeated manner. The underlying mechanics of Foucauldian disciplining of subjects is basically this sort of conditioning. However, habit formation seems to be peculiar to human beings to the extent that it can be and often is *self-*conditioning. That is, we are capable of disciplining ourselves to behave habitually. Anyone who has ever browsed a self-help section in a bookstore knows that reams have been written on how we can change our lives through self-directed habit formation.

Both Searle and Foucault give habit formation their own respective twists. Searle basically treats habit formation as the acquisition of Background capacities; Foucault treats habit formation as the internalization of norms. The key similarity is that, for both Searle and Foucault, habit formation is essentially *an aptitude to convert intentional activities to nonintentional capacities.*

Habit formation enables the acquisition of a very broad range of abilities through the gradual making of conscious and deliberate behavior into ingrained or "automatic" behavior. When a habit is intentionally developed, the intended and actual result is that one no longer engages in the relevant behavior consciously and deliberately, and even finds that again becoming conscious of the behavior actually interferes with performance. Learning to play tennis is an obvious example. At first, one is very aware of holding and swinging the racket in a certain way, but after a time, thinking about holding and swinging the racket becomes distracting and hinders play. Less obvious, but even more common, an example is learning to converse in different contexts and with different groups of interlocutors. We learn different "vocabularies," as Rorty would put it, or different "passing theories," as Davidson might say, in various situations. The most obvious example is how we learn the idiom of our workplace. Initially, we are very alive to how our co-workers use the workplace idiom, but, after a time, consciousness of employing the idiom becomes *self-*consciousness and both hampers our conversation and communicates artificiality or unease to our interlocutors.

Philosophical consideration of habit formation goes back at least to Plato's programmatic discussion of the training of the Guardians of the

Republic and to Aristotle's discussions of the crucial role of habituation in ethical training. In a remark Foucault could have written, Aristotle tells us that individuals "must keep on observing their regimen and accustoming themselves to it" (Aristotle 1976, 337). The aim is that the initially regimented behavior become habitual, and that habituated individuals then behave as they should without reflection or enforcement.

What is important in the present context about habit formation is not primarily that we have this capacity or how it works in detail, or even whether it is self-directed or otherwise, but rather the role of realism in its working at all. To better appreciate realism's role in habit formation, recall Searle's distinction between "deep" and "local" Background. The importance of the distinction is twofold. First, as is clear in Chapter 2 and elsewhere, the role of realism is fundamental to deep Background capacities: Searlean Background capacities presuppose independent reality. Second, as is also clear in Chapter 2 and elsewhere, the role of realism is equally presupposed by local Background capacities; everything to do with social reality and culture must "bottom out" in what is "not itself an institutional construction" (Searle 1995, 191). It appears, then, that realism's role in Foucauldian habit formation must be just as problematic as the tacit-realist use of truth itself. However, there is some clarity to be gained by considering that what is common to Searle's and Foucault's views is the role of realism with respect to *local* Background capacities, that is, with respect to all the nonintentional capacities we acquire as we are enculturated and shaped as subjects in being social beings.

As we saw in Chapter 2, Searle's Background is "a set of nonrepresentational mental capacities that enable all representing to take place" (Searle 1987, 143). Representing is essential to the "biologically fundamental capacities of the mind (or brain) to relate the organism to the world by way of such mental states as belief and desire, and especially through action and perception" (Searle 1987, vii). Background capacities, then, are what enable us "to cope with the world" (Searle 1999, 107).

Searle amplifies: "Right now I have the intention to go to a bookstore and buy some books... This complex intention presupposes an enormous metaphysical apparatus. Some of that apparatus is on the surface in the form of beliefs and desires." However, Searle adds that "underneath these conscious thoughts is a vast apparatus... too fundamental to be thought of as just more beliefs and desires. For example, I know how to walk and how to behave in bookstores" (Searle 1999, 108).

Knowing how to walk and unthinkingly taking it that the ground will support us are deep Background capacities; knowing how to behave in bookstores and how to read are local Background capacities. Again as we saw in Chapter 2, deep Background constituents are common to all human beings, whereas the particular constituents of local Background differ for members of various groups. These latter constituents are all the many culture-shaped elements that enable us to function as social entities in particular societies. It is these latter Background capacities that we acquire by initially engaging in activities in a conscious and deliberate way, and eventually engaging in those activities in a habitual and unreflective manner.

What is most important here about Searle's account of the Background is that both deep and local Background capacities require that agents take it that "*there is a way that things are* in the world that is independent of our representations of how they are." Moreover, this realist intentional stance is "not to be thought of as a theory." Rather, in being a Background presupposition, the taking of it that there are mind- and language-independent things that are as they are, is "something that is taken for granted by us when we perform many sorts of intentional actions" (Searle 1999, 39). For Searle, then, a realist intentional stance is an enabling condition for the exercise of Background capacities of both the deep and local sorts. If we want to think of the realist intentional stance itself as a Background capacity of the most fundamental sort, we can easily imagine it being acquired when as infants we learn the crucial and initially upsetting lesson that there is much that is not under our volitional control.

Since both deep and local Background capacities presuppose the realist intentional stance, *social* reality is no different in this respect from the physical reality we encounter, manipulate, and navigate in. As we saw in Chapter 2, Searle's concern regarding social reality is precisely to determine how there can be "an *objective* world of money, property, marriage, governments, elections . . . in a world that consists entirely of physical particles" (Searle 1995, xi; my emphasis). However, before applying this point about the realist intentional stance to Foucault, I need to make clear that in applying the point to Foucault, I am neither endorsing Searle's account of the Background nor retracting my earlier criticism of it. What is central here is *the realist intentional stance*, not the Background as such. Whatever account may be offered of them, there can be no question that we do have the sorts of capacities Searle consigns to "the Background." The basic question about his account is whether anything is gained in postulating "the Background," and there is *some* postulation in Searle's account; his description of the Background and his insistence on capitalizing the term preclude that reference to the Background is no more than a *façon de parler.*

With respect to Foucault, what I am contending is that he is as much a realist as is Searle with respect to mind- and language-independent reality. Foucault's realism emerges most clearly with respect to social reality when we consider the reliance on habit formation that he shares with Searle. Foucault has no interest in metaphysics and, as we have seen, raises the issue of realism only in rather casually dismissing it or in occasionally alluding to extralinguistic reality. Social reality, however, is another matter.

If subjectivity-shaping discipline is to be effective, individuals on whom practices are imposed must gradually internalize those practices in the sense that willful compliance must become habitual behavior. It is essential to Foucault's notion of discipline that disciplined subjects initially engage in intentional compliance with discipline-imposed activity, and that their intentional compliance gradually develops into nonintentional dispositions to behave in the way the discipline dictates.

How this works is clearest in Foucault's adoption and extension of the core idea exemplified in Jeremy Bentham's invention of the Panopticon, the ideal prison. The Panopticon is so constructed that inmates are always observable from a central tower by guards who are not themselves visible to the inmates. In this way, the design of the Panopticon ensures that the *possibility* of being observed at any moment forces continuous inmate compliance with disciplinary regulations. The Panopticon effectively shifts the burden of surveillance onto the inmates themselves. The inmates, because they *may* be being watched at any time, must assume that they *are* being watched all the time. They then, in effect, oversee themselves. Foucault's extension of the Panopticon's principle of self-surveillance is that conscious compliance gradually becomes habitual, and in becoming habitual inculcates *norms* in disciplined subjects, thus reshaping their subjectivity (Foucault 1979; Prado 2000, 53–84). It is crucial in Foucault's thought that disciplined subjects do not merely conform to regulations but internalize them. Disciplined subjects are not only controlled individuals; they are *changed.*

Foucauldian discipline and power relations *do not work* if disciplined subjects do not internalize practices imposed on them; they must come – and come to *want* – to self-condition themselves to conform to established norms. If discipline-imposed practices remain intentional, if they continue to be engaged in deliberately in order to avoid sanctions, those practices remain open to intentional variation. The moment surveillance is relaxed or absent, the practices may be changed or dropped. And not only is compliance jeopardized if it remains intentional, if compliance with discipline does remain intentional, the values, objectives, and self-images – the norms – that should be inculcated by the imposed practices will not be inculcated. Since subject will not engage in self-conditioning habit formation, their subjectivity will not be redefined in accordance with operant norms. Habit formation, then, is pivotal; without it, discipline would remain enforced compliance and power relations would remain only restrictive; power relations would not be productive, as Foucault insists they are.

My point should now be obvious. Self-conditioning habit formation by internalization of deliberate effort or, in Searle's terms, the acquisition of local Background capacities presupposes a realist intentional stance toward observed or imposed practices prompting initially deliberate compliant actions. Foucauldian disciplined habit formation is inconceivable unless subjects take it that there is *a way that things are* in their social environment. Moreover, those subjects not only take how things are in their social environment as independent of them, they take how things are as determining what and how they themselves *should* be. Inmates or sexual agents cannot see themselves as deviant or abnormal, and seek to comply with norms established by their society or their nature, unless they unquestioningly take their society and nature as wholly objective.

Foucauldian discipline and power relations, then, require individuals to take it, at the most fundamental level, that there is a way that things are. This is clearest in Foucault's treatment of the deployment of sexuality. It is precisely the point of his genealogy of sexuality to show how those subjected to the deployment of sexuality take social constructs – most notably human sexual nature – as objectively real. The deployment of sexuality is the disciplined dispersion of a discipline-manufactured sexuality, but it is a dispersion that is presented as discernment and dissemination of an objective human nature. Even those most importantly instrumental in the deployment of sexuality take themselves to be discerning and disseminating hard-won facts about objective reality. The exponents of learned disciplines, and those whom they teach and treat, all take themselves to be learning deep truths about their objective nature as human beings. None of this could occur without a realist intentional stance regarding both social constructs and "dumb" or impartially silent reality.

A possible response here is that what Foucault is doing is only showing that it is a mistake to take *anything* as objectively real. That is, some may reason that if it is wrong to take it that power-produced sexuality is one of

Searle's features of objective reality, it is because it is wrong to take it that there is anything other than the products of language. This response is recourse to the common understanding of Foucault as a linguistic idealist, and acknowledges the realist intentional stance as necessary for the effectiveness of discipline and power relations, but construes that stance as itself part of the mistake of taking constructs as objective realities. However, this response misses the point of what Foucault has in mind when he says that "in analyzing discourses themselves, one sees... the emergence of a group of rules... [that] define not the dumb existence of a reality... but the ordering of objects" (Foucault 1972, 49).

Foucault's concern is with the ordered objects that constitute our social reality. What genealogical analysis does, at the most basic level, is reveal *net additions* to dumb reality, as when an essential human sexual nature is supposedly unearthed by the very disciplinary activity and pronouncements that construct that nature. The point is not to reduce dumb reality to so many constructs, it is to expose how many constructs have been and continue to be "deployed" as constituents of that reality.

In our day-to-day lives, we do not distinguish between our social environment and dumb reality; we do so only when we philosophize. As Searle might insist, a five-dollar bill is not seen first as a physical object, and then as a component of the social institution of money; it just is a five-dollar bill. Whether explained in terms of collective intentionality or established individual practice, participation in social reality is not *inferential*, as we might put it. When we look at a five-dollar bill, we do not look at a physical piece of paper and consciously or unconsciously bestow the piece of paper with the status of legal tender. Dealing with money is a habitual action for all but the youngest of us who are being taught how to use money. Whether it is walking successfully or behaving as we should in a bookstore, the nonintentional capacities that enable our actions presuppose that we take it that there is a way things are quite independently of us.

Foucault's concern with deployed sexuality is not primarily that we take sexuality as real, it is that we take it as an essence that determines much of our thought and action. His genealogical aim has nothing to do with reducing reality to constructs, and little to do with simply showing constructs to be constructs. Foucault's genealogical aim is to reveal how certain constructs, in being deployed as discerned essences, generate norms that dictate how we think and live. He wants to show us that our thoughts and actions can be other than they are without violating "our nature."

If we can conclude that Foucault is as much a realist as Searle, albeit unwilling to debate the matter as a philosophical issue, what can we conclude about Foucault's unwillingness to tie truth to states of affairs in extralinguistic reality?

It is arguable that most philosophers in the twenty-first century accept that the general position to be taken on truth is a deflationary one. Few now attempt to expound substantive theories of truth such as the traditional correspondence one. Few feel it necessary to offer a theoretical explanation of the Tarskian point that to say "'Snow is white' is true" is just to say that snow is white. The problem is that this seems not to be enough for Searle, despite his endorsement of disquotation and his claim that correspondence is only trivially true. He needs to go further and maintain that, in the end, assertions about snow being white, disquoted or otherwise, are true in virtue of snow *being* white.

The reason for the further step is that, for Searle, realism is prior to truth and therefore how things are *must* be what determines truth, so whatever account we give of truth has to relate true sentences to how things are in the mind- and language-independent world. The further step is troublesome in that it demands a plausible account of just how sentences relate to "the facts" that not only do the sentences supposedly state, but which make those sentences true. The unresolved problem with the further step is, of course, making out the precise nature of what true sentences relate *to*. As Williams notes, there is simply no available account of "facts" that is "general enough" to identify the other *relatum* in the correspondence relation other than by "trivially reiterat[ing] the content of the sentences" (Williams 2002, 65).

Some will agree with Searle's remarks, quoted in Chapter 2, about what we did to *facere* to refer to the "nonlinguistic" correlates of sentences, and think that sufficient, but I find the account unconvincing. For one thing, it is not the case, as Searle claims, that most who consider the question of correspondence believe that "we have two entities . . . the statement over here and the fact over there" (Rorty and Searle 1999, 34–35). As noted in Chapter 2, this is too literal a view of what many take to be the relation of correspondence, and it does not succeed in avoiding the puzzle posed by facts or what true sentences supposedly correspond to. The real question has to do not with some simplistically conceived comparison, but with how we delineate bits of brute reality to be what true sentences correspond to in the correspondence relation, given that even the smallest bits of brute reality are underdetermined by any method we have of describing them. So long as Searle maintains that states of affairs are what make sentences true, and so ties true sentences to "facts," or what he calls "the nonlinguistic counterpart of true statements," Searle has a problem (Rorty and Searle 1999, 35).

For his part, Foucault offers us several ways of understanding how sentences are true. Two of those ways, the criterial and constructivist uses, are wholly discursive in that the truth of sentences is simply their currency in discourse. Two others, the perspectivist and experiential uses, are tangled with subjectivity in that they have as much to do with individuals' self-defining perspectives, beliefs, and attitudes as with discursive currency. A third way, the tacit-realist use, has to do mainly with acknowledgment of and allusion to the way that things are independently of mind and language. The tacit-realist use is Rortyan in that it sets aside brute or dumb reality, but it is also Searlean to the extent that it denies linguistic idealism and other forms of irrealism; it denies "that everything comes out of somebody's head" (Foucault 1988b, 17).

Neither my nor anyone else's efforts are going to achieve a reconciliation of Searle's and Foucault's views on truth, especially on the question of whether true sentences must relate to states of affairs. There are, however, important conclusions to draw from the comparison of their views. First, Searle's endorsement of disquotation, his efforts to present correspondence as trivially true, and his acknowledgment of the inescapability of perspective indicate that even as staunchly relational a conception of truth as his can no longer be correspondist in nature as correspondence is traditionally conceived. We have learned that truth is not a reality-mirroring relation between sentences and states of affairs that those sentences reproduce or depict. Wittgenstein's "picture theory" was perhaps the most sophisticated attempt to make out such a conception, and it is now only of historical interest.

Second, if we focus on Foucault's concern with the human sciences, such as psychiatry and economics, we better understand the source and nature of his pluralistic conception of truth. We see that disciplinary knowledge and power relations are inextricably entwined in the determination of the currency of sentences in learned and ordinary discourses. Once we give up on correspondence, we appreciate that the conditions sentences must meet to be current, to be true, in a discourse are quite complex and require more than mapping of relations between Davidson's sentences, speakers, and dates. In particular, we realize that every speaker carries complex historical baggage that shapes each sentence uttered on any given date, and that every listener carries complex historical baggage that shapes how each sentence is understood on any given date. Once we move even a little beyond Davidson's basic field-linguist scenario, and consider speakers as interlocutors, we realize that their background, beliefs, values, intentions, and previously uttered sentences all play a part in determining what they say and what they hear. Foucault's concern is to map those determining influences.

Third, when we sort out his uses of truth, we appreciate how what Foucault says about truth enhances Davidson's account, that is, by the way he fills out how relations among sentences, speakers, and dates presuppose a host of historical, social, and individual factors. These factors define speakers' perspectives and govern the relations that exist between them and the sentences they utter. We then see that Foucault's conception of truth does not imply linguistic idealism or some other form of irrealism.

Perhaps, in the end, the most fruitful conclusion to a comparison of two understandings of truth as conceptually and canonically opposed as Searle's and Foucault's is one that is clear enough with respect to Foucault, but less clear with respect to Searle. This is, that both reject the old philosophical hankering for a *theoretical* story about truth. Both seem to agree with Davidson that talk of correspondence to facts or the like adds nothing of explanatory value to our understanding of truth (Davidson 1985, 193–94). However, neither Searle nor Foucault wants to change the subject as Rorty would have us do (Rorty 1982, xliii). Both think it necessary to say a fair bit about truth. Searle wants to establish beyond epistemological quibbling that truth is just beliefs and sentences squaring with "the facts." Foucault wants to say how sentences come to be true, but without involving Searle's "facts."

The price Searle pays for his efforts is philosophers demanding a theoretical account of just how beliefs and sentences relate to "the facts" and a more satisfactory story about just what "facts" are. The price Foucault pays is philosophers and others taking his separation of truth from the world as an irrealist ontological move rather than as a concentration on the mechanics of discourse involved in privileging some sentences over others.

Nonetheless, despite their difficulties, both Searle and Foucault are trying to move beyond the sort of theorizing about truth's "nature" that has proven so unproductive; both are doing something very like what Quine tried to do with epistemology and Davidson more or less succeeded in doing with truth. Searle and Foucault are trying to "naturalize" truth, though in quite opposed ways. Foucault is trying to say how truth works *in discourse* but without theorizing about how true sentences relate to extralinguistic states of affairs. Searle is trying to say how true beliefs and sentences work *in our coping with how things are* but without theorizing about some "relation of correspondence" to the objective world.

However, in his attempts to demystify correspondence, to cast it as trivially true, Searle asserts realism as a philosophical precept. In this, he is thinking like Davidson, who, "unlike the pragmatist, does not present himself as repudiating the skeptic's question, but as *answering* it" (Rorty 1991c, 136 my emphasis). Unlike Davidson, however, Searle also insists that it is objectively real states of affairs that make beliefs and sentences true. Nor does he see this as problematic; he seems to think that if the point about true beliefs and sentences relating to "the facts" is made clearly enough, the triviality of correspondence will be evident, that it will be *seen* that "the facts" are what make beliefs and sentences true, and that the desire for a theoretical account of the relation will evaporate. Unfortunately, so long as facts remain nonlinguistic counterparts of true statements, truth remains relational and Searle remains answerable for a cogent theoretical account of just how beliefs and sentences relate to bits or the whole of extralinguistic reality. Searle's problem of relating truth to the world, though, looks innocuous in comparison to Foucault's problem, namely, how his separation of truth and the world makes him vulnerable, if not to irrealism as I have tried to show, then to inconsistency.

At this point, Rorty's pragmatic change of subject might look attractive as a way out of what looks like an impasse, but its attractiveness at this juncture is precisely what makes that change too convenient: more evasion than resolution. The pragmatic option seems even less viable when the issue between Searle and Foucault is as apparent as it now is. We cannot simply opt for truth being sentences' utility, because surely Searle is right that the truth of beliefs and sentences involves how things are in the world; Foucault approaches granting the point in employing his tacit-realist use of truth. But surely Foucault is also right that the truth of sentences is currency in perspective-determined and historically shaped discourse, and has little or nothing to do with the disposition of dumb reality; Searle approaches granting the point in acknowledging the inescapability of perspective.

What seems to emerge, then, is that the truth about truth must lie somewhere between the extremes marked by Searle's and Foucault's positions. Most simply put, it seems that some true beliefs and sentences are true in virtue of the disposition of the world, and some true sentences are true in virtue of their status in a discourse. Putting the point in this way brings out something that has been implicit all along, which is that regarding Searle's position, *beliefs* are true in their own right, as in the case of believing but not articulating that one's keys are on the table and finding them there, while regarding Foucault's position, beliefs must be rendered as *sentences* to be true. This sheds a bit more light on Foucault's tacit-realist use of truth, in that the bulk of what we believe but do not articulate is realist in nature in that it is about our physical and social surroundings. In this, Foucault and Searle are of a mind: our representation of the world, our "belief map" of our environment, is wholly realist.

Once the threat of linguistic idealism is removed from Foucault's position on truth, it becomes evident that his opposition to Searle has to do not with extralinguistic reality per se, but with dumb reality's epistemic role regarding confirmation or justification of sentences as true. Once this is seen, it looks as if the impasse between them has mainly to do with Searle being wrong about making extralinguistic reality's role decisive and fundamental, if only because despite his deflation of correspondence, he has no cogent account of how we relate all true beliefs and sentences to "the facts." For his part, Foucault contributes to the impasse by being wrong about relegating dumb reality's role to asides and allusions, if only because despite his tacit-realist use of truth, and however he may want to ignore unspoken beliefs about the disposition of the world, he has no cogent account of how sentences like "Water expands when it freezes" are true.

In general, what a contrastive comparison of Searle and Foucault on truth shows us is that, as Gadamer once said in conversation about philosophy, "There is much to be said." We need to say how neither Searle nor Foucault can be wholly right; we need to say there is a difference between how unarticulated beliefs and articulated sentences are both true. We also need to say how truth does, after all, seem to come in two flavors, "hard" and "soft," how some truths have to do with relations to states of affairs and some with discursive currency. We need to say how there are truths about physical reality and truths about social reality in the broadest sense. In particular, the contrastive comparison of Searle and Foucault shows us that we cannot hope to get all of these things said clearly and correctly if we listen to and read only philosophers working our favored side of the canonical and priority divides.

Works Cited

I reiterate my thanks to John Searle and Wallace Matson for their e-mails, some of which I quote in the text and have noted as "personal correspondence."

Allen, Barry. 1993. *Truth in Philosophy*. Cambridge, Mass.: Harvard University Press.
  2003. "Another New Nietzsche." *History and Theory* 42 (October): 363–77.
  2004. *Knowledge and Civilization*. Boulder, Colo., and New York: Westview Press.
Arac, Jonathan, ed. 1991. *After Foucault*. New Brunswick, N.J.: Rutgers University Press.
Aristotle. 1941. *Metaphysics*. In *The Basic Works of Aristotle*, ed. R. McKeon, 1011b. New York: Random House.
  1976. *Aristotle: Ethics (The Nicomachean Ethics)*. London: Penguin Classics.
Armstrong, D. M. 1968. *A Materialist Theory of the Mind*. London: Routledge and Kegan Paul.
Audi, Robert, ed. 1996. *The Cambridge Dictionary of Philosophy*. Cambridge: Cambridge University Press.
Austin, John L. 1962. *How to Do Things with Words*. Oxford: Clarendon Press.
Babich, Babette E. 2003. "On the Analytic-Continental Divide in Philosophy: Nietzsche's Lying Truth, Heidegger's Speaking Language, and Philosophy." In Prado 2003a, 63–103.
Baruchello, Giorgio. 2001. "Reading Ian Hacking's 'The Social Construction of What?'" *Symposium* 5 (1): 103–14.
Bernauer, James W., and David Rasmussen, eds. 1988. *The Final Foucault*. Cambridge, Mass.: MIT Press.
Borradori, Giovanna. 1994. *The American Philosopher*. Chicago: University of Chicago Press.
Bullock, Alan, Oliver Stallybrass, and Stephen Trombley. 1986. *The Fontana Dictionary of Modern Thought*. 2nd ed. London: Fontana.
Chisholm, Rodrick M. 1957. *Perceiving: A Philosophical Study*. Ithaca, N.Y.: Cornell University Press.

Critchley, Simon. 2001. *Continental Philosophy: A Very Short Introduction*. Oxford: Oxford University Press.

Dancy, Jonathan, and Ernest Sosa. 1993. *A Companion to Epistemology*. Oxford: Basil Blackwell.

Davidson, Arnold. 1986. "Archaeology, Genealogy, Ethics." In Hoy 1986, 221–33.

Davidson, Donald. 1973/1974. "On the Very Idea of a Conceptual Scheme." *Proceedings and Addresses of the American Philosophical Association*, 47: 5–20.

———. 1985. *Inquiries into Truth and Interpretation*. Oxford: Clarendon Press.

———. 1986a. "A Coherence Theory of Truth and Knowledge." In *Truth and Interpretation: Perspectives on the Philosophy of Donald Davidson*, ed. Ernest LePore, 309–19. Oxford: Basil Blackwell.

———. 1986b. "A Nice Derangement of Epitaphs." In *Truth and Interpretation: Perspectives on the Philosophy of Donald Davidson*, ed. Ernest LePore, 433–46. Oxford: Basil Blackwell.

Dawkins, Richard. 1976. *The Selfish Gene*. Oxford: Oxford University Press.

Deleuze, Gilles. 1993. *The Fold: Leibniz and the Baroque*. Minneapolis: University of Minnesota Press.

Dennett, Daniel. 1991. *Consciousness Explained*. Boston: Little, Brown.

Derrida, Jacques. 1976. *Of Grammatology*. Trans. G. C. Spivak. Baltimore: Johns Hopkins University Press.

Dreyfus, Hubert, and Paul Rabinow. 1983. *Michel Foucault: Beyond Structuralism and Hermeneutics*. 2nd ed., with an afterword by Michel Foucault. Chicago: University of Chicago Press.

Eribon, Didier. 1991. *Michel Foucault*. Trans. Betsy Wing. Cambridge, Mass.: Harvard University Press.

Farrell, Frank B. 1995. "Rorty and Antirealism." In *Rorty and Pragmatism: The Philosopher Responds to His Critics*, ed. Herman J. Saatkamp, Jr., 154–88. Nashville, Tenn., and London: Vanderbilt University Press.

Feyerabend, Paul. 1978. *Against Method*. New York: Verso.

Fink-Eitel, Hinrich. 1992. *Foucault: An Introduction*. Trans. Edward Dixon. Philadelphia, Pa.: Penn bridge Books.

Fotion, Nick. 2000. *Searle*. Princeton: Princeton University Press.

Foucault, Michel. 1965. *Madness and Civilization: A History of Insanity in the Age of Reason*. Trans. Richard Howard. New York: Random House.

———. 1971. "Nietzsche, Genealogy, History." In Rabinow 1984, 76–100.

———. 1972. *The Archaeology of Knowledge* (including *The Discourse on Language*). Trans. A. M. Sheridan-Smith. New York: Harper and Row.

———. 1973. *The Order of Things*. New York: Vintage.

———. 1979. *Discipline and Punish: An Archaeology of the Human Sciences*. Trans. Alan Sheridan. New York: Pantheon.

———. 1980a. *The History of Sexuality, Volume 1*. Trans. Robert Hurley. New York: Vintage.

———. 1980b. *Power/Knowledge: Selected Interviews and Other Writings*. Ed. Colin Gordon. New York: Pantheon.

———. 1983. "The Subject and Power." Afterword to Dreyfus and Rabinow 1983, 208–26.

———. 1986. *The Use of Pleasure*. Trans. Robert Hurley. New York: Vintage.

1988a. "Critical Theory/Intellectual History." In Kritzman 1988, 17–46.

1988b. "The Ethics of Care for the Self as a Practice of Freedom." In Bernauer and Rasmussen, 1–20.

1989. *Foucault Live*. Ed. Sylvère Lotringer and trans. John Johnston. New York: Semiotext(e).

1991a. "Questions of Method: An Interview with Michel Foucault." In *The Foucault Effect: Studies in Governmentality. With Two Lectures by and an Interview with Michel Foucault*, ed. Graham Burchell, Colin Gordon, and Peter Miller. Chicago: University of Chicago Press.

1991b. *Remarks on Marx: Conversations with Duccio Trombadori*. Trans. James Goldstein and James Cascaito. New York: Semiotext(e).

2001. *Fearless Speech*. Los Angeles: Semiotext(e).

Guttenplan, Samuel, ed. 1996. *A Companion to the Philosophy of Mind*. Oxford: Blackwell Publishing.

Gutting, Gary, ed. 1994. *The Cambridge Companion to Foucault*. Cambridge and New York: Cambridge University Press.

Habermas, Jürgen. 1987. *The Philosophical Discourse of Modernity: Twelve Lectures*. Trans. Frederick Lawrence. Cambridge, Mass.: MIT Press.

Hacking, Ian. 1981. "The Archaeology of Foucault." *The New York Review of Books*. Reprinted in Hoy 1986, 27–40.

Hekman, Susan. 1990. *Gender and Knowledge: Elements of a Postmodern Feminism*. Boston: Northeastern University Press.

Honderich, Ted, ed. 1995. *The Oxford Companion to Philosophy*. New York: Oxford University Press.

Hoy, David Couzens, ed. 1986. *Foucault: A Critical Reader*. Oxford: Basil Blackwell.

Krausz, Michael. 1989. *Relativism: Interpretation and Confrontation*. Notre Dame, Ind.: Notre Dame University Press.

Kritzman, Lawrence D., ed. 1988. *Michel Foucault: Politics, Philosophy, Culture: Interviews and Other Writings 1977–1984*. New York and London: Routledge.

Kuhn, Thomas. 1970. *The Structure of Scientific Revolutions*. Chicago: University of Chicago Press.

Lacey, A. R. 1990. *A Dictionary of Philosophy*. London: Routledge.

Lackey, Michael. Forthcoming. Review of Prado 2003a in *The Journal of Speculative Philosophy*.

Lawson, Hilary. 1985. *Reflexivity: The Postmodern Predicament*. London: Hutchinson.

Locke, John. 1975. *Essay Concerning Human Understanding*. Ed. Peter N. Nidditch. Oxford: Oxford University Press.

Macey, David. 1993. *The Lives of Michel Foucault*. London: Hutchinson.

Machado, Roberto. 1992. "Archaeology and Epistemology." In *Michel Foucault: Philosopher*, ed. Timothy Armstrong, 3–19. New York: Routledge.

MacIntyre, Alisdair. 1977. "Epistemological Crises, Dramatic Narrative and the Philosophy of Science." *The Monist* 60 (4): 453–72.

Marian, David. 2002. "The Correspondence Theory of Truth." In *The Stanford Encyclopedia of Philosophy*, ed. Edward N. Zalta. http://plato.stanford.edu/archives/sum2002/entries/truth-correspondence.

Matson, Wallace I. 2000. *A New History of Philosophy, Volume Two: From Descartes to Searle*. 2nd ed. New York: Harcourt Brace.

May, Todd. 1993. *Between Genealogy and Epistemology: Psychology, Politics, and Knowledge in the Thought of Michel Foucault*. University Park, Pa.: Pennsylvania State University Press.

Miller, James. 1993. *The Passion of Michel Foucault*. New York: Simon and Schuster.

Munteanu, Vasile. 1998. Review of C. G. Prado 1995 in *International Studies in Philosophy* 30 (2): 153–54.

Nagel, Thomas. 1997. *The Last Word*. New York: Oxford University Press.

Nehamas, Alexander. 1985. *Nietzsche: Life as Literature*. Cambridge, Mass.: Harvard University Press.

Nietzsche, Friedrich Wilhelm. 1968. *The Will to Power*. Ed. Walter Kaufman and trans. Kaufman and R. J. Hollingdale. New York: Vintage Books.

Nola, Robert. 1994. "Post-Modernism, A French Cultural Chernobyl: Foucault on Power/Knowledge." *Inquiry* 37 (1): 3–43.

Oxford Dictionary of Quotations. 1980. 3rd ed. Oxford: Oxford University Press.

Oxford English Dictionary. 1971. Compact ed., complete text reproduced micrographically. Oxford: Oxford University Press.

Pearce, Frank, and Anthony Woodiwiss. 2001. "Reading Foucault as a Realist." In *After Postmodernism: An Introduction to Critical Realism*, ed. José López and Garry Potter, 51–62. London: Athelone Press.

Prado, C. G. 1995. *Starting with Foucault: An Introduction to Genealogy*. Boulder, Colo., and San Francisco: Westview Press.

——— 2000. *Starting with Foucault: An Introduction to Genealogy*. 2nd ed. Boulder, Colo., and San Francisco: Westview Press.

——— ed. 2003a. *A House Divided: Comparing Analytic and Continental Philosophers*. Amherst, N.Y.: Humanity Press.

——— 2003b. "Correspondence, Construction, and Realism." In Prado 2003a.

Putnam, Hilary. 1987. *The Many Faces of Realism*. LaSalle, Ill.: Open Court.

Rabinow, Paul, ed. 1984. *The Foucault Reader*. New York: Pantheon Books.

——— 1997. *Michel Foucault: Ethics, Subjectivity and Truth; Essential Works of Foucault, 1954–1984*. Vol. 1. New York: The New Press.

Rorty, Richard. 1979a. *Philosophy and the Mirror of Nature*. Princeton: Princeton University Press.

——— 1979b. "Transcendental Argument, Self-Reference, and Pragmatism." In *Transcendental Arguments and Science*, ed. Peter Bieri, Rolf Horstman, and Lorenz Kreuger, 77–103. Dordrecht: Reidel.

——— 1982. *The Consequences of Pragmatism*. Minneapolis: University of Minnesota Press.

——— 1986. "Foucault and Epistemology." In Hoy 1986, 41–49.

——— 1989. *Contingency, Irony, and Solidarity*. Cambridge: Cambridge University Press.

——— 1991a. *Essays on Heidegger and Others: Philosophical Papers, Volume 2*. New York: Cambridge University Press.

——— 1991b. "Feminism and Pragmatism." *Radical Philosophy* 59 (Autumn 1991): 3–12.

——— 1991c. *Objectivity, Relativism, and Truth: Philosophical Papers, Volume 1*. New York: Cambridge University Press.

Rorty, Richard, and C. G. Prado. 2003. "A Conversation with Richard Rorty." *Symposium* 7 (2): 227–31.

Rorty, Richard, and John Searle. 1999. "Rorty v. Searle, At Last: A Debate." *Logos* 2 (3): 20–67.

Routledge. 2000. *The Concise Routledge Encyclopedia of Philosophy.* London and New York: Routledge.

Russell, Bertrand. 1945. *A History of Western Philosophy.* New York: Simon and Schuster.

Ryan, Alan. 1993. "Foucault's Life and Hard Times." *The New York Review of Books* 40 (7): 12–17.

Searle, John R. 1964. "How to Derive 'Ought' from 'Is.'" *The Philosophical Review* 73 (January): 43–58.

    1969. *Speech Acts.* Cambridge: Cambridge University Press.

    1979. *Expression and Meaning.* Cambridge: Cambridge University Press.

    1980. "*Las Meninas* and the Paradoxes of Pictorial Representation." *Critical Inquiry* 6 (3).

    1983. "The World Turned Upside Down." *The New York Review of Books* 30 (16): 74–79.

    1987 (1983). *Intentionality: An Essay in the Philosophy of Mind.* Cambridge: Cambridge University Press.

    1992. *The Rediscovery of the Mind.* Cambridge, Mass.: MIT Press.

    1995. *The Construction of Social Reality.* New York: Free Press.

    1999. *Mind, Language and Society.* London: Phoenix.

Sellars, Wilfrid. 1968. *Science and Metaphysics.* New York: Humanities Press.

Strawson, P. F. 1963. *Individuals: An Essay in Descriptive Metaphysics.* Garden City, N.Y.: Anchor Books, Doubleday and Company.

Sycara, Katia. 1998. "Multi-Agent Systems." www.aaai.org/AITopics/html/multi.html.

Webster's New Twentieth Century Dictionary Unabridged. 1979. 2nd ed. New York: Simon and Schuster.

Williams, Bernard. 1998. "The End of Explanation?" Review of T. Nagel 1997 in *The New York Review of Books* 45 (18): 40–44.

    2002. *Truth and Truthfulness: An Essay in Genealogy.* Princeton and Oxford: Princeton University Press.

Wisdom, John. 1955. "Gods." In *Logic and Language* (1st series), ed. Antony Flew, 187–206. Oxford: Basil Blackwell.

Zalta, Edward N., ed. 2002. *The Stanford Encyclopedia of Philosophy.* Fall 2002. http://plato.stanford.edu/archives/fall2002/entries/truth.

Index